Pink Tides, Right Turns in Latin America

This book presents case studies around issues of national development, right wing populism and use of social media, left wing authoritarianism and popular uprisings as well as reflections on short and long term political and economic cycles in Latin America in the past 10 years.

Scholars, government and civil society practitioners have long recognized both the democratic and development deficit in Latin American countries, as well as their potential. The path towards a consolidated democratic state and civil society, as well as socio-economic collective well-being, has been far from linear and this edited collection provides theoretical clarity on the social, political and economic dynamics driving these changes such as historical cycles in the commodities market, the emergence of new social movements, the rise and pitfalls of populism, the influence of corporate media and the erosion of democratic institutions. The chapters in this volume approach the topic of Latin American Right and Left forces by attempting to determine whether a new and potentially long-term political cycle is unfolding in the region. To this end, the chapters focus on a perspective that compares the emergence of the new Right with the successes and limitations of the previous 20 years of Pink Tide governance.

This volume will be of great use to students and researchers interested in Latin American studies, comparative politics as well as political leadership. The chapters in this book were originally published as a special issue of *Globalizations*.

Charmain Levy is Full Professor at the Université de Outaouais (UQO) in the Department of Social Sciences. She specialises in Latin America, particularly Brazil; social movements; feminist, urban and development studies. Her current research projects focus on feminist urban commons in Montevideo, and urban feminist politics and initiatives in Latin America.

Manuel Larrabure is Assistant Professor in the Department of International Relations at Bucknell University. His current research, combining theoretical and methodological insights from political economy, social movement studies and critical pedagogy, focuses on the crisis of the "pink tide" and the rise of the new right in Latin America.

Rethinking Globalizations

Edited by **Barry K. Gills**, *University of Helsinki, Finland* and **Kevin Gray**, *University of Sussex, UK.*

This series is designed to break new ground in the literature on globalization and its academic and popular understanding. Rather than perpetuating or simply reacting to the economic understanding of globalization, this series seeks to capture the term and broaden its meaning to encompass a wide range of issues and disciplines and convey a sense of alternative possibilities for the future.

The Reconfiguration of Twenty-first Century Latin American Regionalism
Actors, Processes, Contradictions and Prospects
Edited by Rowan Lubbock and Ernesto Vivares

Capitalism, Coronavirus and War
A Geopolitical Economy
Radhika Desai

The Rise of Green Extractivism
Extractivism, Rural Livelihoods and Accumulation in a Climate-Smart World
Natacha Bruna

Globalization, Urbanization, and Civil Society
A Non-Western Critique
Bagoes Wiryomartono

Capital Redefined
A Commonist Value Theory for Liberating Life
S. A. Hamed Hosseini and Barry K. Gills

From 'Carbon Democracy' to 'Climate Democracy'?
James Goodman and Tom Morton

Pink Tides, Right Turns in Latin America
Charmain Levy and Manuel Larrabure

The Far-Right in World Politics
Alexander Anievas and Richard Saull

For more information about this series, please visit:
https://www.routledge.com/Rethinking-Globalizations/book-series/RG

Pink Tides, Right Turns in Latin America

Edited by
Charmain Levy and Manuel Larrabure

LONDON AND NEW YORK

First published 2025
by Routledge
4 Park Square, Milton Park, Abingdon, Oxon OX14 4RN

and by Routledge
605 Third Avenue, New York, NY 10158

Routledge is an imprint of the Taylor & Francis Group, an informa business

© 2025 Taylor & Francis

All rights reserved. No part of this book may be reprinted or reproduced or utilised in any form or by any electronic, mechanical, or other means, now known or hereafter invented, including photocopying and recording, or in any information storage or retrieval system, without permission in writing from the publishers.

Trademark notice: Product or corporate names may be trademarks or registered trademarks, and are used only for identification and explanation without intent to infringe.

British Library Cataloguing in Publication Data
A catalogue record for this book is available from the British Library

ISBN13: 978-1-032-75075-0 (hbk)
ISBN13: 978-1-032-75076-7 (pbk)
ISBN13: 978-1-003-47227-8 (ebk)

DOI: 10.4324/9781003472278

Typeset in Minion Pro
by Newgen Publishing UK

Publisher's Note
The publisher accepts responsibility for any inconsistencies that may have arisen during the conversion of this book from journal articles to book chapters, namely the inclusion of journal terminology.

Disclaimer
Every effort has been made to contact copyright holders for their permission to reprint material in this book. The publishers would be grateful to hear from any copyright holder who is not here acknowledged and will undertake to rectify any errors or omissions in future editions of this book.

Contents

Citation Information vi
Notes on Contributors viii

Introduction: Pink Tides, right turns in Latin America 1
Charmain Levy and Manuel Larrabure

1 Broadened embedded autonomy and Latin America's Pink Tide: towards the neo-developmental state 19
Patrick Clark and Antulio Rosales

2 What are they doing *right*? Tweeting right-wing intersectionality in Latin America 37
Paulo Ravecca, Marcela Schenck, Bruno Fonseca and Diego Forteza

3 Is Jair Bolsonaro a classic populist? 59
João Feres Júnior, Fernanda Cavassana and Juliana Gagliardi

4 Neo-structuralist bargain and authoritarianism in Nicaragua 75
Miguel González

5 The gendered political economy of Chile's rebellious discontent: lessons from forty-five years of neoliberal governance 92
Verónica Schild

6 Roundtable: the Latin American state, Pink Tide, and future challenges 113
Manuel Larrabure, Charmain Levy, Maxwell A. Cameron, Joe Foweraker, Lena Lavinas and Susan Jane Spronk

Index 129

Citation Information

The chapters in this book were originally published in *Globalizations*, volume 20, issue 1 (2023). When citing this material, please use the original page numbering for each article, as follows:

Introduction
Pink Tides, Right Turns in Latin America
Charmain Levy and Manuel Larrabure
Globalizations, volume 20, issue 1 (2023), pp. 1–19

Chapter 1
Broadened embedded autonomy and Latin America's Pink Tide: towards the neo-developmental state
Patrick Clark and Antulio Rosales
Globalizations, volume 20, issue 1 (2023), pp. 20–37

Chapter 2
What are they doing right? Tweeting right-wing intersectionality in Latin America
Paulo Ravecca, Marcela Schenck, Bruno Fonseca and Diego Forteza
Globalizations, volume 20, issue 1 (2023), pp. 38–59

Chapter 3
Is Jair Bolsonaro a classic populist?
João Feres Júnior, Fernanda Cavassana and Juliana Gagliardi
Globalizations, volume 20, issue 1 (2023), pp. 60–75

Chapter 4
Neo-structuralist bargain and authoritarianism in Nicaragua
Miguel González
Globalizations, volume 20, issue 1 (2023), pp. 76–93

Chapter 5
The gendered political economy of Chile's rebellious discontent: lessons from forty-five years of neoliberal governance
Verónica Schild
Globalizations, volume 20, issue 1 (2023), pp. 94–114

Chapter 6
Roundtable: the Latin American state, Pink Tide, and future challenges
Manuel Larrabure, Charmain Levy, Maxwell A. Cameron, Joe Foweraker, Lena Lavinas and Susan Jane Spronk
Globalizations, volume 20, issue 1 (2023), pp. 115–131

For any permission-related enquiries please visit:
www.tandfonline.com/page/help/permissions

Notes on Contributors

Maxwell A. Cameron is Professor in the Department of Political Science at the University of British Columbia. He specialises in comparative politics, democracy and ethics. His publications include *Democracy and Authoritarianism in Peru* (St. Martin's, 1994), *The Peruvian Labyrinth* (Penn State University Press, 1997), *Latin America's Left Turns* (Lynne Rienner, 2010), *Democracia en la Region Andina* (Lima: IEP, 2010), *New Institutions for Participatory Democracy in Latin America* (Palgrave, 2012), *The Making of NAFTA* (Cornell, 2000), *Strong Constitutions* (Oxford University Press, 2013), *Political Institutions and Practical Wisdom* (Oxford University Press, 2018) and over 50 peer-reviewed articles. Cameron has taught at Carleton University, Yale University and the Colegio de Mexico. Between 2011 and 2019 he served as the Director of the Centre for the Study of Democratic Institutions. In 2013 Cameron won a UBC Killam Teaching Prize and in 2020 he became the Canadian Association of Latin American and Caribbean Studies' Distinguished Fellow.

Fernanda Cavassana is Postdoctoral Research Fellow (Capes Brasil/INCT – Institute of Democracy and Democratization of Communication) at the Institute of Social and Political Studies (IESP) of UERJ, where she is a researcher at the Laboratory of Studies on Media and Public Sphere (Lemep). She has a bachelor's degree in social communication (State University of Londrina – UEL), master's in communication and PhD in political science (Federal University of Paraná – UFPR).

Patrick Clark completed a PhD in political economy from Carleton University in 2019 and is currently a sessional assistant professor in the Business and Society programme in the department of social science at York University in Toronto, Canada.

João Feres Júnior is Associate Professor of political science at the Institute of Social and Political Studies (IESP) of State University of Rio de Janeiro (UERJ), FAPERJ CNE scholar, CNPq productivity scholar, coordinator of the Laboratory of Studies on Media and Public Sphere (Lemep) and of the news media watchdog website "Manchetometro" (www.manchetometro.com.br), and coordinator of the Observatory of the Brazilian Legislative (OLB).

Bruno Fonseca works at the Department of Research and Educational Statistics of the National Administration of Public Education, Uruguay. He is a statistics analyst specialised on education and demographic policies.

Diego Forteza works at the National Institute of Educational Evaluation, Uruguay. He is a data scientist specialised on education and health policies.

Joe Foweraker has published extensively on democracy and democratic government in Latin America, focussing first on social mobilisation and citizenship rights, and subsequently on comparative democratic performance and democracy's discontents. His recent work *Polity: Demystifying Democracy in Latin America & Beyond* (Lynne Rienner Publishers, 2018), constructs a novel framework for analysing the democratic regimes of Latin America in the context of specific patterns of state formation that support the survival and expansion of oligarchic powers and prerogatives in the region, while his latest book on *Oligarchy in the Americas* (Palgrave Macmillan, 2021) compares modes of oligarchic rule in Latin America and the United States and reveals a close resemblance between them that challenges claim to US exceptionalism and the superiority of its democracy. He demonstrates that the populist insurgencies of recent decades – whether of the "left" or the "right" – can best be explained by the recurrent tensions between oligarchic rule and democratic appeals to popular sovereignty.

Juliana Gagliardi is Executive Coordinator of the Laboratory of Media and Democracy (Lamide/UFF) and Postdoctoral Researcher at Universidade Federal Fluminense (Fluminense Federal University, UFF). She has bachelor's degrees in history (Rio de Janeiro State University – UERJ), social communication and journalism (Federal University of Rio de Janeiro – UFRJ), and a master's and PhD in communication (UFF).

Miguel González is Assistant Professor in the International Development Studies programme at York University, Toronto, Canada. In recent years Miguel has taught both in the undergraduate and graduate programmes in International Development at York University. His current research relates to indigenous self-governance and territorial autonomous regimes in Latin America and the governance of small-scale fisheries in the Global South, with a particular geographical concentration in the Nicaraguan Caribbean Coast. Miguel is a researcher associated with the Centre for Research on Latin America and the Caribbean (CERLAC) at York University. His current research involves the comparative study of multi-ethnic and indigenous governance regimes in the Americas, which resulted in the publication of a volume on Indigenous autonomy in the Americas (*Indigenous Territorial Autonomy and Self-Government in the Diverse Americas*, co-edited with Ritsuko Funaki, Araceli Burguete Cal y Mayor, José Marimán, and Pablo Ortiz-T.)

Manuel Larrabure is Assistant Professor at the Department of International Relations at Bucknell University. He holds a PhD in political science from York University and carried out his post-doctoral studies at the University of California, Santa Cruz. Professor Larrabure does research in political economy, globalisation and social movements. His research is on post-capitalism and social movements in twenty-first-century Latin America. His work has been published in a number of international journals, including *Latin American Perspectives*, *Historical Materialism* and the *Canadian Journal of Development Studies*.

Lena Lavinas is a Professor of Welfare Economics at the Institute of Economics at the Federal University of Rio de Janeiro. Most of her research focuses on how welfare regimes adjust to changes in contemporary capitalism, especially under the aegis of financialisation. She is member of the International Advisory Board of Development and Change (2018–2023), among others. She was a member of the School of Social Science at the Institute for Advanced Study at Princeton in 2019–2020 and a 2016–2017 fellow at the Wissenschaftskolleg zu Berlin. Her recent publications include the following: "The Collateralization of Social Policy by Financial Markets in the Global South" (*The Routledge International Handbook of Financialization*, edited by Mader, Mertens and

Van der Zwan, Routledge, 2020); *The Takeover of Social Policy by Financialization: The Brazilian Paradox* (Palgrave Macmillan, 2017) and *A Moment of Equality for Latin America? Challenges for Redistribution*, along with Barbara Fritz (Ashgate, 2015).

Charmain Levy is a professor of social sciences at the Université du Québec en Outaouais since 2005 where she teaches international development studies. Her research specialises in the fields of international development studies, feminist studies, political sociology and Latin American studies on which she has published several articles and book chapters. She is a member of the Research team on Inclusion and Governance in Latin America (ÉRIGAL) and the Quebec Feminist Studies and Research Network (Réqef). Her most recent publication is the volume *Twenty-first Century Feminismos: Women's Movements across Latin America and the Caribbean* (co-edited with Simone Bohn).

Paulo Ravecca works at the Department of Political Science at the Universidad de la República, Uruguay. His research focus includes epistemology and the history of political science; the intersections between critical theories (queer, neo-marxist, postcolonial and poststructural approaches); political economy and international relations; and gender and sexuality. He is the current editor of the *Journal of Narrative Politics* and the author of *The Politics of Political Science: Re-Writing Latin American Experiences* (Routledge, 2019).

Antulio Rosales completed a PhD in global governance in 2017 from the Balsillie School of International Affairs, University of Waterloo. He is currently an assistant professor in political science at the University of New Brunswick in Fredericton, Canada.

Marcela Schenck works at the Institute of Health Psychology at the Universidad de la República, Uruguay. Her research focus includes gender, sexual and gender diversity, and public policy. Marcela has published in English, Spanish and Portuguese on issues related to her research interests.

Verónica Schild, born in Chile, is Professor Emeritus of Political Science at the University of Western Ontario, in London, Ontario, Canada. She has written extensively on feminism and the women's movement in Chile and Latin America, on market citizenship, and on the neoliberalisation of Latin American states.

Susan Jane Spronk teaches at the School of International Development and Global Studies at the University of Ottawa. Her research focuses on the impact of neoliberalism on the transformation of the state, social policy and the rise of anti-privatisation movements in Latin America and South Africa. She is also a research associate with the Municipal Services Project, an international research project that focuses on policy alternatives in municipal service delivery in Africa, Asia and Latin America (www.municipalservicesproject.org). Her articles have appeared in *Studies in Political Economy*, *Water Alternatives*, *Latin American Perspectives*, *International Labor and Working-Class History*, amongst others. Her most recent book in English and Spanish is *Public Water and Covid-19: Dark Clouds and Silver Linings* (with David A. McDonald and Daniel Chavez).

Introduction: Pink Tides, right turns in Latin America

Charmain Levy and Manuel Larrabure

ABSTRACT
This special issue emerged from the seminar of the same name in which took place at the Université du Québec en Outaouais in Gatineau, Quebec in June 2019. It focused on two interrelated political and economic dynamics currently taking place in Latin America. First, the decline of the wave of Left and Centre-Left governments that emerged in the region in the early 2000s, known as the Pink Tide. Second is the recent emergence of the region's new right-wing political and social movements, which picked up in intensity and influence around 2015.

Scholars, government and civil society practitioners have recognized both longstanding democratic and development deficits, as well as the potential of Latin American countries to improve the breadth and depth of their democracies and work toward the well-being and inclusion of large swaths of marginalized populations. The path towards a consolidated democratic state and civil society, as well as socio-economic collective well-being, has been far from linear. Almost all Latin American countries have experienced extended periods of authoritarian rule and political, social and economic exclusion of historic minorities while the state has traditionally served the interests of the elites and Western capital. Comprehending the complexity of the region's developmental trajectory requires multiple theories, case studies and a variety of methodologies that cover several social science disciplines (e.g. political science, geography, development studies) and perspectives. It is for this reason that this special edition brings together scholars from different disciplines, schools of thought and backgrounds, whose combined research and expertise are essential for advancing knowledge on Latin American politics and development.

In addition to understanding the various empirical changes taking place in the region, the goal of this special edition is to provide theoretical clarity on the social, political and economic dynamics driving these changes. Recent work attempting to theorize the changes in the region points to a number of causal factors, including historical cycles in the commodities market (Ocampo, 2017), the emergence of new social movements (Larrabure, 2016), the rise and pitfalls of populism (Webber, 2016), the influence of corporate media (Artz, 2017), and the weakening of democratic institutions (Cameron, 2018). In light of the most recent studies, the articles will address these questions: Can we say that these explanations are still valid? If not, what theoretical and methodological tools do we need to better explain this crucial moment in the region's developmental trajectory?

To address these questions, we believe it is important to pay particular attention to some of the most recent developments in the region. Certain scholars began debating the end of a political cycle of progressive governments (Gudynas, 2015) five years ago. Since then, taking into consideration the soft coup in Brazil in 2016, the election of Macri in Argentina, the election of Bolsonaro in Brazil, the coup in Bolivia and the election of more right-wing governments in Chile and Uruguay, there is a definite shift in governments. Somewhere between these two poles, we find the 2018 presidential victory of Andrés Manuel López Obrador (AMLO) in Mexico who was elected on a progressive platform, but who quickly adopted a more conservative and authoritarian tone. Subsequently, AMLO's inconsistent discourse and policies have produced feelings of frustration and deception among social movements and activists. Another example of a Pink Tide government turning into an outright neoliberal repressive government is the case of Ecuador (Ponce et al., 2020). In addition, the Left in Argentina and Bolivia have made a quick come back electoral turn around. The case of Venezuela is particularly volatile, featuring repeated US-backed coup attempts against the Maduro government, notably through its support of Juan Guaidó (Guardiola-Rivera, 2019), and most recently through a surreal failed maritime invasion known as Operation Gideon (Pressly, 2020).

Beyond the formal political arena, both traditional and new types of contention are visible in politically underrepresented social sectors. In addition, new generations of social and political activists are questioning the old guard. This divide become explicit in the 2013 Brazilian protests when both Pink Tide and Right-wing governments struggled to understand the claims and nature of the different movements protesting as well as how to respond to them. In many Latin American countries, beyond the political polarization is a strengthening of the civil society Right and a fragmentation of the Left (Fernandes, 2017).

In order to understand these historical shifts in Latin America, we must combine multiple levels of analysis and a plurality of explanatory factors (Tomini, 2018, p. 156). Chiasson-LeBel and Larrabure (2019) offer a relational perspective focusing on interactions between governments and social forces to the Right and to the Left. With the intention of analysing these developments, this special edition is organized around three axes, each corresponding to key themes not only in the field of Latin American Studies but also in the social sciences more broadly. These are (1) political economy and development; (2) democratic consolidation and regressions; and (3) social movements and social justice. This introduction explores the structural conditions of the end of Pink Tide cycle and the beginning of the right turn tendency; issues around democracy and governance; right-wing agency; Leftist and progressive renewal.

Structuring conditions

This theme aims to shed light on the political-economic model of the Pink Tide, often referred to as neo-structuralism or neo-developmentalism (Hilal, 2018; Leiva, 2006, 2008). Of particular interest is one of the economic pillars of this model, namely the aggressive implementation of export policies tied to the natural resources sector, otherwise known as extractivism. This took place within the reconfiguration of the global economic division of labour with the ascent of China and other emerging markets and the collaboration among the 'BRICS'. We will highlight the cases of countries that have been particularly dependent on extraction in recent decades, including Venezuela, Ecuador and Bolivia. In addition, we will analyse the impact of the recent downturn in commodity prices, often highlighted as the key causal factor behind recent sharpened social conflict and crisis.

It merits to ask to what extent have Pink Tide governments represented continuity with neoliberal and path-dependent macro-economic policies. To what extent have they broken with them?

Most analysts agree that there was more continuity than rupture in terms of giving neoliberalism a new lease on life. Both the social and political Left engaged in a balancing act between implementing social transformation and defending against attacks from the right. Several progressive governments were anti-neoliberal in rhetoric and social democratic and even social liberal in practice. They saw the state as the driver of the economy and practised redistributionist policies to reduce poverty. However, they remained integrated into the global economy relying on extractivist rents to sustain their domestic policies (Munck & Sankey, 2020). In other words, as Svampa (2013) argues, we can think of the 'progressive cycle' in Latin American politics as a partial shift from finance-driven accumulation, the 'Washington consensus', to accumulation driven by the exploitation of land, what she calls the 'commodities consensus'. On the economic front, the high levels of growth and trade achieved have been the result of an overwhelming reliance on the export of primary goods, and have come alongside a decline in industrial production.

The turn towards an extractivist model and reliance on primary commodities formed the economic foundation of Pink Tide governments (Pickup, 2019, p. 24). The inability of progressive governments to overcome the patterns and structures that hold back economic development demonstrates dependency in its multiple forms as well as rentier capitalism (Ellner, 2019). Indeed, the overwhelming reliance on the export of primary goods during the peak of the 'commodities boom' came alongside a decline in industrial production (Bárcena, 2010; Katz, 2015). These governments reacted in the context of the global economy by implementing pragmatic strategies to win over or neutralize members of the private sector and traditional elites (Webber, 2017, p. 69) in order to ensure governability. To a greater or lesser extent, these governments continued to expand nonrenewable natural resources and agricultural exports to OEDC countries with China becoming the number one export market to most of the Latin American countries. In addition, this break with the traditional economy trading relation with the USA was coherent with the Left's desire to end American imperialism in the region and represents continuity with Latin America's place in the international division of labour as a provider of cheap primary resources to Western countries.

Many Latin American economies experienced an important rate of growth during the first 15 years of the twenty-first century thanks to these policies. Ironically, this has also been accompanied by a decline in industrial sectors and a concentration of low skill and low paying jobs in the service sector:

> Rather than an 'ebbing of the pink tide', the multifaceted contemporary Latin American crisis is better understood as an outcome of never resolved deep social contradictions that emerge from the super-exploitation of labour and the consequent unequal exchange vis-à-vis central capitalist countries. (Antunes de Oliveira, 2019, p. 1146)

These governments continued to implement a market-oriented, export-led growth model (Riggirozzi & Tussie, 2012). The neo-developmentalist policy was implemented in the context of a global expansion of capital that drove the economic sectors of agribusiness, energy, mining and public works. These governments justified the need for economic growth driven by these sectors in order to create and expand social programmes and reduce poverty.

The Pink Tide governments were influenced both directly and indirectly by the post-Washington Consensus, which in the wake of the 2009 financial crisis advocated the need to bring the state back into the development process in the form of new social policy-oriented towards poverty reduction and a more inclusive form of development (Birdsall & Francis, 2011). Using a more interventionist strategy, Pink Tide governments attempted to chip away at structural historic overlapping racial, ethnic and socio-economic inequities through important changes in the constitution (Venezuela, Bolivia, Ecuador) and through public policies (Argentina, Brazil, Mexico, Uruguay, Chile) (Democracy in Latin America, 2011).[1] They all recognized and focused on the role of the state in regulating the economy, increasing political participation and distributing economic benefits (Macdonald & Ruckert, 2009). The bulk of these programmes consisted of cash transfer programmes and specific health, education and housing-related programmes. Although they did reduce poverty, it was in a way that did not expand universal social and health services.[2] In addition, in countries like Brazil, the reduction of poverty was a direct result of job creation and the expansion of formal employment thanks to economic growth and greater state intervention for distributive and redistributive purposes (Pickup, 2019, p. 27).

As mentioned above, most of these initiatives include cash transfer programmes, raising the minimum wage, improving access to basic needs (higher education, water, electricity). In contrast, in Uruguay, the FA government enacted a set of labour laws, including a broad-based labour law for private-sector workers and another for the public sector that institutionalized tripartite negotiations in the country (Carneiro et al., 2020). Although a significant mass of jobs was created, most of them were low skill ones. Most of them were occupied mainly by women, young people, and people of colour, further accentuating the distorted logic that had long been endemic in the labour market: low wages among people who traditionally have been more discriminated against in the market (Antunes et al., 2018, p. 95; Braga, 2015; Braga et al., 2019).

Cash transfer programmes and increases in the minimum wage led to a greater monetization of the most vulnerable social groups and their incorporation into the market through consumption, although without changing the structural heterogeneity characteristic of the labour market (Barbosa, 2020). These advances in poverty reduction did not reduce existing socio-economic and racial inequalities. When commodity prices decreased and growth stagnated, so did low and intermediate skill jobs. What followed was a return to poverty for the working and precariat classes. There was no plan B or extended effort into diversifying the economy or reducing its reliance on the global economy. Even in the case of Venezuela, which featured a conscious albeit insufficient attempt by Chavismo to break out of poverty and inequality through innovative experiments in cooperative labour and grassroots democracy, the legacies of oil dependence proved impossible to overcome (Larrabure, 2019a).

The macro-economic choices of Pink Tide governments influenced their political policies and programmes. As Gaudichaud (2021) points out, extractivism is a political regime that fosters authoritarianism, encourages corruption, generates tensions with social and indigenous movements, devastates territories and fragments the popular classes. During the Pink Tide governments, the structural power of transnational capital was consolidated in Latin America. The loss of hegemony of the former revealed contradictions with any kind of real popular political agenda breaking with colonialist structures (Barbosa, 2020). Most Pink Tide governments' strategic choice of reliance on an export-led model was also based on short-term gains around the electoral cycles allowing them to re-elect themselves during the economic boom years. For example, the PT did not take measures to combat the pillars of capitalism in Brazil, such as the concentration of rural poverty, and the concentration of profits in the hands of the bourgeoisie (Antunes et al., 2018, p. 88).

Finally, while the existing literature has argued that sustained democracy is a strong predictor of poverty alleviation, in neo-patrimonial contexts poverty reduction is also less likely to occur (Giraudy et al., 2020, p. 89) in the long term. State economic intervention benefited certain countries in getting through the 2008 global economic crisis unscathed, but it also lead to political interference, gross public oversight and abuses of power. In several countries, electoral and economic alliances were built on corruption and kickbacks as the Car Wash scandal has demonstrated in many countries. One of the outcomes was the fracturing of the governments' political support (Pickup, 2019, p. 40) on both the Left and the Right. As we will see in the following section, their political alliances were also built on short-term goals of governability.

Democratic deficits, governability and hegemony

It is important to recall that the progressive cycle of the pink tide was preceded by an unprecedented wave of social movements throughout the region. This wave of movements largely departed from the more traditional forms of resistance associated with the Import Substitution Industrialization (ISI) period, namely unions and guerilla groups. The new movements of the 1980s and 1990s featured diverse and often heterogeneous groups experimenting with more direct, communitarian and local forms of democratic participation (Harris, 2003; Kay, 2008; Petras & Veltmeyer, 2001; Stahler-Sholk et al., 2014; Vanden, 2003). It is from this wave of resistance that Pink Tide governments were elected to office. However, the relationship between the pink tide and social movements was never stable, expressing partial alliances between the two sides and the political left's need for broader coalition building. The result was a rather vague and fluid anti-neoliberal stance by the Pink Tide.

While recognizing the diversity of the Pink Tide governments, we can roughly divide them up into two groups: those that built political alliances with the Centre-right designed to avoid discord and achieve governability and those who have confronted traditional national elites and imperialism to various degrees of intensity. The latter has been reluctant to negotiate agreements with or grant significant concessions to their adversaries (Ellner, 2013). It should be noted that both strategies sooner or later led to class and political polarization.

The social democratic strategy that attempts to minimize confrontation and achieve harmonious change contrasts with the complex dynamic of radical policies followed by resistance from hegemonic forces and sharp political polarization in a democratic setting that characterizes the twenty-first-century radical left in power (Ellner, 2013). Politically, the governments' strategies disorganized the working classes and social movements, as they depended on class conciliation measures and the repression of independent struggles (Loureiro, 2018; Loureiro & Saad-Filho, 2018). As a result, the social Left in many countries were then incapable of mounting (extra-institutional) pressure after years of either demobilizing or immobilizing social movements.

All Pink Tide governments prioritize short-term macro-economic goals (growth) over social ones, which ultimately depend on the success of the first goals. In order to achieve both goals, alliances are forged with traditional economic and political elites in the form of participation in important government positions (ministries, agencies, etc.), kickbacks and specific economic policies in certain sectors (construction, natural resources, moral issues, law and order, infrastructure) benefiting big business. The general idea behind these alliances is that they could guarantee governability and the implementation of social policies that reduce poverty, increase the well-being and garner support of the poorest and middle classes. This in turn would guarantee a minimum of political stability for at least one political cycle.

In Brazil, Singer (2020) describes how the imminent risk of a radicalization of politics in favour of a popular agenda gave rise to what he calls 'Lulism,' a conservative pact in the spirit of conciliation and compromise, and political alliances in favour of transnational capital. Braga (2016) sees it as the regulation of class conflict configured in terms of the 'passive consent' of the working class in accepting benefits and the 'active consent' of the union bureaucracy and popular organizations in participating in certain state activities and instances. Oliveira et al. (2010) describe it as a pact between the forces of capital and the forces of labour that avoided possible tensions related to the interests of financial and transnational capital and therefore an 'inside-out hegemony'.

This 'tightrope' model continues to inspire governments including that of AMLO who on the one hand, demonstrated adherence to principles in order to lend credibility to his commitment to the fight against corruption. On the other hand, through flexibility and pragmatism, he demonstrates that his government's relationship with the private sector could be a win-win situation (Ellner, 2020). The risks of this strategy include the alienation of social movements and betrayal of the economic elites.

Another distinction between Pink Tide governments concerns the relations they have forged with their social movement base. Certain governments have maintained cordial relations that can be defined as conflictive cooperation while others have taken on a more confrontational 'you are either with us or against us' stance leading to violent opposition and at times violent government repression. According to Carneiro et al. (2020), the makeup of coalitions of social and political actors in power can partially explain not only state withdrawal from the economy but also the new forms of intervention in the same period following the rise of structural reforms.

In the first case of neocorporativism, social movements are immobilized or demobilized. These relations between governments and social movements built historically through contradictory political strategies became a pattern as a reaction of the leftist governments confronted pressure to preserve the backing of broad sectors of the electorate with the support of coalitions representing diverse ideological positions (Carneiro et al., 2020). Conflict is contained or channelled through formal and informal negotiations and structures between the leaders of social movements and government and party officials (Levy, 2012). Through this process, social movements rely on both mobilization of their members at strategic times and sites and on their ability to access decision-makers to whom they are tied through party linkages. Social movements can privately but rarely openly disagree with allied governments. When their political allies need them, social movements come out to support them with the idea that ('it could be worse') a bent or compromised ally in government is better than a right-wing repressive government. This relation can help them advance in certain material claims but also constrain their larger missions (social transformation, change in concentration of wealth, economic oppression, exclusion, marginalization) possibly limiting their autonomy. This autonomy involves the terms on which the movement-state relationship is negotiated and raises the issue of co-optation (Munck & Sankey, 2020).

Some Pink Tide governments could be classified under the neocorporativist strategy in their first terms and these same governments shifted to a more confrontational strategy with parts of their social movement base. For example, during this initial period of the MAS, movement incorporation had three dimensions: (1) co-optation from above, (2) the creation of parallel social organizations by the government, and (3) the propensity of social organizations to be co-opted. The central demands of social movements of the previous period 2000–2005 were incorporated into the government's project, consolidating the position of the MAS government and stripping movements of their most powerful collective mobilizing frames (McNelly, 2020). From 2011 on, social movements were positioned either as supporters of the MAS and beneficiaries of their policies or as oppositional movements to be (violently) repressed with no right to government or any other funds (McNelly, 2020). Conflicts intensified in 2016 when social movements accelerated their independent organization detached from the Morales government which led to direct action (blockades, marches, occupations, strikes) against him (de Carvalho, 2020). Nevertheless, it is important to recognize that this kind of conflict is also rooted in contradictions within social movements themselves. In the case of Bolivia, featuring demands for the unlimited cultivation of the coca leaf, expressing both indigenous democratic and spiritual values, and a dependence by these same communities on the international and illegal cocaine trade, which the MAS has very little control over (Grisaffi, 2019).

In the case of social movements which break with Pink Tide governments (Ecuador, Nicaragua, El Salvador), there is often severe and violent repression. In Ecuador, President Correa (2007–2017) clashed with the collectivist orientation of the indigenous and labour movements. He created civil society organizations and marginalized those who did not support his government (Becker, 2013). He worked with the small and not very representative Federación Ecuatoriana de Indios rather than with the much more solid Confederación de Nacionalidades Indígenas del Ecuador (Confederation of Indigenous Nationalities of Ecuador – CONAIE). This strategy was, in fact, successful in splitting the indigenous political party Pachakutik, several of whose leading members joined his seemingly unstoppable 'populist" political machine. For those who maintained an autonomous political stance and resisted his environmental destruction, Correa implemented a policy of ruthless criminalization of protest. Eventually, many of his supporters – not least prominent environmentalists – split from his movement because of what they saw as extractivist policies that contradicted his much-vaunted support for buen vivir/sumak kawsay (living well) (McNelly, 2020).

In Nicaragua in 2007, the Sandinista government led by Daniel Ortega was elected without a majority. Like other Pink Tide governments, he allied his government with the private business sector and the Catholic Church hierarchy, but went further to introduce and sustain 'crony capitalism' (Thaler, 2017). Thanks to Alianza Bolivariana para los Pueblos de Nuestra América (ALBA), the Ortega Administration was able to co-opt both the traditional and economic elites and the most impoverished sectors of the country. Cooptation of the elites was possible because Ortega had maintained the economic production and commercialization model promoted since 1990 and boosted it with privileged access to the Venezuelan market (Martí i Puig & Serra, 2020). It implemented new initiatives, which have benefitted the poor majority, such as the zero-hunger programme that began which improved nutrition and food security for beneficiaries and their families. However, this government created partisan Citizens' Power Councils (CPCs) headed by Ortega's wife, Rosario Murillo, that acted as parallel local governments and controlled the distribution of public goods and services. Ortega has coopted former opponents while delegitimizing and repressing his government's critics (Thaler, 2017, Gonzalez, in press). In April 2018, following the government announcement of reforms to the social security system, students and a wider public of protesters took to the streets. They clashed with pro-government supporters and police who responded with heavy-handed repression.

Not only did these governments invite protest from the socially disenfranchised, but they also drew a backlash from political and conservative forces who saw this as threatening their status and power. In Brazil, the crisis of Dilma's administration should be understood as the end of a cycle of a government model developed and put in place through a 'skillful policy of polyclassist compromise' (Antunes et al., 2018, p. 100). There were also no measures to combat the media monopoly, which played an important role in eroding the PT's image.

The tail end of the progressive cycle and agency from the right

Certain scholars such as Petras and Veltmeyer (2015) principally attribute the end of the golden age of progressive governments and their setbacks to imperialism and US foreign policy. Others such as

Gaudichaud (2021) point to internal contradictions and dead ends: loss of links with the popular movements, bureaucratization or the emergence of new castes, authoritarianism, and unbridled neo-extractivism. A 'left' that wanted to change power has been caught by the verticality of the state machine, by state capitalism too, which has sucked in part of the living forces that came out of social movements. From this perspective, the Left succumbed to its own weaknesses and shortsightedness, unable to look into the mirror. In this context, the emerging Right took advantage of these weaknesses as well as the economic downturn – despite their own shortcoming principally around a lack of charismatic leadership.

The Latin American right turn appears as a response to a demand from the Left for more social equity, economic development and distribution and political representation and inclusion. When this demand is perceived as a threat by the elites, this combination leads to a concentration of power, the entrenchment and even suspension of rule of law (Tomini, 2018, p. 158). Other issues at play include the concentration of executive power, the fragmentation of the party system, and the fragmentation of civil society.

In the last part, we have already indicated certain actors, characteristics and origins of the new Right and the politics of de-democratization. This axis will identify and analyse the key aspects of the new Right, including its actors, origins and central political and economic programmes. Of particular interest will be new policies, discourses, and state initiatives that threaten the democratic fabric of the region, such as clientelism (Hilgers, 2008), authoritarianism, and media manipulation (Herrmann, 2017). In addition to the empirical concerns outlined, these articles will approach the topic of this axis by attempting to determine whether a new and potentially long-term political cycle is unfolding in the region. To this end, the articles will focus on a perspective that compares the emergence of the new Right with the successes and limitations of the previous 20 years of Pink Tide governance.

The most nondemocratic regimes we observe in the region have tended to become Mafia-riven, corrupt, and violent political systems that fall apart under the weight of internal tensions and civil society resistance (Cameron, 2018, p. 17). Enabling contexts for political crises are structural ones such as economic inequality and historical racial and ethnic inequalities and exclusion to power. Conjunctural contexts include the crisis in economic development, a break or change in political coalitions and alliances (either on the left or the right) and increasing authoritarian and violent behaviours from ruling parties and their supporters. This can lead to massive protest that becomes a litmus test for governments. A deeply divided society may be a contextual factor favouring social conflicts, political instability thus weakening democracy (Tomini, 2018, p. 16). In these situations, elections are insufficient for democratic bona fides, but they play a very important role in undemocratic regimes. Heightened social conflict thus highlights that authoritarian practices and institutions can be introduced in democratic contexts (Cameron, 2018, p. 16).

The ascension to power of the Right and Extreme right in countries such as Brazil, Chile, Argentina (Macri), Uruguay and Boliva (in this case temporarily thwarted by the return of the MAS to government) demonstrates the strengthening of political and economic liberal forces. In some cases, this is a more traditional economic right. In others, such as Brazil, it is a non-traditional coalition involving sectors of the military, agro-business and Evangelical and Pentecostal political actors. The turn to the right in Latin America reveals the loss of hegemony and political leadership of the progressive left, which in fact is following the trend of the left around the world. The return of right-wing movements also took place via the electoral route: Maurício Macri in Argentina, Sebastián Piñera in Chile, Iván Duque in Colombia, Luis Alberto Lacalle Pou in Uruguay and Jair Bolsonaro in Brazil (Barbosa, 2020).

This complexity of democratic governance in recent years became perhaps best expressed in the case of Bolivia. In early 2020, then President Evo Morales was ousted from power in what became the latest example of a 'soft coup' in the region. Many mainstream commentators quickly cheered these events on the grounds of democracy, arguing that in pursuing a fourth consecutive presidential term, Morales had breached the classic liberal democratic principle of transfer of power. However, this interpretation of events is highly problematic, raising an important question, namely why should the standards of liberal democracy be applied to an individual (Morales), and a party (the MAS), that at least to some degree articulate a completely different interpretation of democracy, one rooted in indigenous traditions? Indeed, from the perspective of indigenous communitarian democracy and the values of Buen Vivir, the liberal concept of transfer of power is an unwelcome abstraction legitimizing a coup d'état. This scepticism of liberal principles is sharpened given that the OAS report (2019) claiming electoral irregularities, which played such a decisive role in legitimizing the coup, proved to be largely baseless, as a subsequent MIT study detailed (Williams, 2020).

In the case of Brazil, Goldstein emphasizes that the biggest threat to Brazilian democracy is not Bolsonaro itself, but the 'elitist, corrupt, and restricted democratic system, which by deceiving society has created the conditions for the emergence from within of the agents of its own destruction' (2019, p. 258). Elites play a role through their strategic decisions, which are often dictated by their pre-existing beliefs and commitment or opposition to democracy (Tomini, 2018, p. 18). In Latin America, historical elites' relation to democracy has been limited to their instrumentalization of the state and democracy in order to keep their hegemony and maintain stability and control over the population. They have always been reticent to the political, economic and social participation of increasing numbers of citizens that do not belong to their own social, economic and racial group. Their idea of democracy is bounded to social harmony where everyone knows their place in the hierarchy and stays in it.

That said, religious political actors such as Evangelical and Pentecostal politicians and elected officials played an important role in the ascension of Conservative governments providing them with an ideological and moral discourse capable of attracting popular support. Their values are patriarchal and homophobic and embrace intolerance and exclusion of difference. They reflect an imaginary Brazil of hierarchical social harmony where everyone knows their place and keeps it. In addition, the political Right orchestrated and invigorated its discourse with the Lava-Jato Operation (Car Wash Operation), PT President Rousseff's removal and impeachment in 2016, the deepening of the economic crisis and the arrest of former President Lula in 2018.

It is also important to note the means by which the Right increased its influence and power in politics and society. The Right conquered the digital world by proliferating websites, social network communities and, above all, the generation of digital influencers or YouTubers. This interface with the digital world contributed to the reconfiguration of the Right and the creation of organizations in many different ideological hues (Negri et al., 2019), especially ultra-liberal, libertarian, racist and patriarchal. In the dispute over hegemony, the Brazilian Right has clearly made important gains in advancing its conservative agenda and influencing collective values and beliefs. An important part of their offensive was portraying the Left and modern social democratic society in general as morally corrupt. Bolsonaro was capable of resignifying the Left and associating it to the negative conception of ideology. This way, he characterized the Right as ideology in its positive or neutral sense (Negri et al., 2019).

Finally, Latin American right-wing governments have been quick to erode democratic institutions and practices in a slash and burn manner. Contrary to Pink Tide governments, they do not play by the formal and informal rules of the game. Some insight or condone violence and abuses of power with a law of the strongest discourse. Participative democratic institutions that have taken decades to build have been destroyed. Many of these governments use a contradictory anti-systemic discourse while depending on alliances with traditional political and economic elites, many of which have decided to play along while hoping to reverse the electoral tide in the next elections. What is certain is that pressure from the Left is needed in order to make the population aware of the dangers involving more right-wing governments.

The dynamics, advances, and legacies of social movements and the Pink Tide, particularly in the areas of decolonialization, poverty reduction, equality and inclusion

As some analysts (Munck & Sankey, 2020) point out, certain Latin American social movements (labour unions, peasant movements) are currently on the defensive, struggling to survive, while other movements such as the feminist movement in Argentina, Uruguay, Chile (Bohn & Levy, 2021), the student movement in Chile (Larraburre, 2019b; Schild, in press), and the indigenous movement in Ecuador in 2019 (Ponce et al., 2020) are winning historical struggles. To understand these situations, there is a need to analyse both the internal intricacies and external conditions of social movements as well as their relationship to the state.

This axis looks at the complex and at times conflictual relationship between social movements and Pink Tide governments, and their evolution in the last 20 years. Its articles will analyse different aspects of the relationship between state and civil society actors (Levy, 2012) and the lessons learned from recent years. While it is generally understood that part of the success of the Pink Tide stems from the support it received from popular classes, including historically oppressed and marginalized sectors of society (women, indigenous groups, afro-descendent communities and low-income populations), it is now clear that this support is no longer as stable (or perhaps that it never really was) and that this has negatively impacted once vibrant civil societies.

Within this context, new social movements have emerged that have called into question the Pink Tide's commitment to social justice and progressive governance (Alvarez et al., 2017). Protest becomes 'a default mode of voice' for engaged citizens, exemplified by Argentina (Moseley, 2018). 'The brown wave of peripheral fascism in the region shall remind us that the only way to preserve democracy in Latin America is through its radicalization' (Antunes de Oliveira, 2019, p. 1160). We cannot understate the importance of the political activism of the peasant movements of the 1990s that led to widespread disenchantment and the rejection of the neoliberal policy agenda. Indigenous movements, particularly in the Andean region, continue to challenge extractivist development projects managed by both Left and Right-wing governments (Svampa, 2011, 2015; Kowalczyk, 2013; Zibechi, 2015).

Latin America is also experiencing a new wave of women's movements in countries such as Argentina, Uruguay, Mexico and Chile that are driving other national women's movements in the hemisphere (Bohn & Levy, 2021). Driven by both the #metoo movement that first emerged in the United States, as well as more long-standing region-specific grievances, new generations of women and feminists across Latin America have taken to the streets in demand of the legal access to abortion, as well as new laws that protect them against sexual harassment and violence (Boesten, 2018). The recent Chilean case is particularly notable, in which students organized mobilizations under the banner of #EducaciónNoSexista (non-sexist education), a demand that has now become central in this country's political debates. Indeed, gender equality more broadly became a centrepiece of the historic constitutional reform process taking place in the country, which features a citizens' constitutional convention composed equally of men and women.

The organizational fragmentation suffered by unionism during the liberalization period since the early 1990s determined its possibilities for resurgence as a progressive party came to power (Carneiro et al., 2020). Deindustrialization, loss of unionized jobs and growth of labour informality played into the weakening of unions in political society and their influence on progressive governments (Lazar, 2017). The subsequent neoliberal reforms during the past 30 years have weakened and divided labour unions ultimately undermining the capacity of traditional Leftist parties to meet certain popular demands (Chiasson-LeBel & Larrabure 2019). As Carneiro et al. (2020) demonstrate, the fragmentation of union federations is another important variable in analysing the influence of labour unions on progressive government policy.

In Bolivia, the radical opening created by the social movements of the revolutionary cycle closed with the ostensible implementation of their central demands, the nationalization of gas and the refoundation of the country through a popular constituent assembly. Through this process, social movements were redirected toward the state as a pressure point for change by the MAS via CONALCAM. This marked the transformation of offensive social movements with radical transformative horizons beyond the state to defensive movements protecting the social movement demands incorporated through technocratic means during the first years of the MAS government (McNelly, 2020). Movement claims ceased to determine government policy, and a growing number of conflicts emerged in reaction to government policy, in concert with a waning movements influence on government policy (McNelly, 2020).

In Brazil, the renewal of the Left can be traced to massive demonstrations in June 2013, which began with student protests against bus fares' raises promoted in multiple cities. Police repression of these protests led to an outpouring of indignation and multiple successive demonstrations during the month which depicted the latent ideological polarization in Brazil. The content of the June mobilizations remains highly contested, some arguing that they revealed a lack of direction and organization (Saad-Filho, 2013), while others arguing that they revealed new albeit incipient forms of representation that attempted to articulate a new left politics, something the PT simply did not understand, and in turn opened new spaces for the right to manoeuvre in (Larrabure, 2016, 2019b).

Some argue that Pink Tide advances in poverty reduction, higher levels of education and increased access to information have made certain segments of middle and lower classes increasingly aware of the situation of economic and political precariousness in which they find themselves and of the injustices that situation implies (Fuentes-Nieva & Feroci, 2017). Socio-economic disparities are no longer perceived as naturally occurring or teleological, but as the unacceptable consequences of structural injustice and neoliberal states. These inequalities become sources of indignation, unrest and mobilization aimed at change (PNUD-PAPEP, 2012) as seen in the case of Chile.

The strength of civil society organizations to influence public opinion, create a counter-narrative to that of the powerful and make political decision-makers accountable is an important factor. They share common features such as the generational and social class factor (youths, university students, and the urban better-off class play a key role in most of the mobilizations), the role of social media and the use of ICTs, the gap between institutional politics and the citizenry, and the weakening of classic social movements' convening and mobilization power (Fuentes-Nieva & Feroci, 2017). The case of Chile perhaps best exemplifies the interplay of these factors. The historic process of constitutional reform the country is currently embarked upon is the product of a long process that began with high school student mobilizations in 2006. The 'penguin revolution', as this movement was called, transformed into the public education movement in 2011, and ultimately culminated in the youth revolts for free transit in 2019. This process featured a complete re-articulation of the progressive political landscape in the country and broke through what had become a decades long withering of democratic institutions largely under the watch of the centre-left. Indeed, the constitutional reform process currently underway aims to eliminate the Pinochet era neoliberal constitution, and its outcome is therefore likely to have significant repercussions not only in Chile but also for progressive movements throughout the region.

Highlights of contributions to this special edition

In the first article of this issue, Clark and Rosales build on Evans' concept of 'embedded autonomy' (1995), applying the concept to Venezuelan, Ecuadorian and Bolivian governments' different degrees of state capacity in order to assess the outcomes and prospects of (neo)-developmental statecraft in the Pink Tide period. The Brazilian case under the Worker's Party governments is used as an ideal type, possessing a strong political base and ties to domestic capital. The authors ask to what extent has embedded autonomy been attempted and how developmentalism has fared comparatively as well as how the political strategies of these governments and their unique national circumstances shaped their attempts at neo-developmental statecraft. Using a comparative methodology, they argue that state capability is dependent on certain kinds of state-society relations that can either enhance or limit the emergence of neo-developmentalism as embedded autonomy. The authors go beyond a traditional understanding of embedded autonomy leading to private enterprise government collaboration to put forth a much broader concept that leads to a range of projects for social and economic transformation across state and society. They demonstrate that the potential for embedded autonomy, based on co-production across state and society, depends on actors in society in the private economy that can be mobilized and embedded in the neo-developmental efforts of governments.

The second article by Ravecca, Schenck, Fonseca and Forteza analyses the capacity of current Latin American conservative voices to persuade and inspire the masses through their aggressive public discourse on the Left, feminism, and the social diversity agenda. They demonstrate how the right wing that includes evangelical pastors, Catholic opinion leaders and activists as well as young social media influencers, both mirror and reverse 'intersectionality', a political narrative they call 'right-wing intersectionality' (RWI). RWI meshes the old cold-war rhetoric against Marxism (Ravecca, 2015; Scirica, 2014) with the current conservative backlash around feminism and LGBTQ+ scholarship and activism using social media to amplify and legitimate their extreme views. By analysing the discourse of young social media influencers and nontraditional activists and politicians, the authors situate RWI within right-wing politics in Latin America and expand on the centrality of the notion of gender ideology in its script. The authors identify a metadiscourse where RWI defends inequality and oppression by claiming that they do not exist and that the social justice activists are the ones destroying social harmony. Using a mixed-methods approach, the authors creatively demonstrate how the narrative of RWI plays out by identifying the presence of, and correlation between, theoretically significant terms as well as the emotions attached to them. Through an aggregated analysis and more detailed focus on three activists, they conclude that RWI is both theoretically and politically significant as well as a salient way in which the right currently produces political identities.

In the article 'Mapping democratic Threats', Balan analyses the democratic threats facing Latin American democracies in the context of Pink Tides and Right turns. He describes what it is about democracy that may be threatened, and details the mechanisms that may be producing these threats. He then discusses the impact of polarization and populism and how they play into the threats to democracy. Then the analysis moves to seven cases (Argentina, Bolivia, Brazil, Chile, Ecuador, Venezuela, and Uruguay) of Left Turn governments, six of which (all except for Venezuela) were followed by some type of turn rightwards, using the framework proposed. The conclusion highlights how the perceived threats to democracy related to concentration of power in the Left Turn were only realized in the outlier case of Venezuela, with alternation through elections in most other cases. Another important finding is that Brazil is the right turn case where the current threats to democracy are the strongest, both in terms of concentration of power as well as in terms of restrictions and threats on liberal rights.

In the fourth article, Feres and Gagliardi take on how the concept of populism has been understood and employed by classical and modern social scientists. They then deductively use the analysis of the Brazilian case to illuminate and test the key conclusions around theoretical debates on populism. They begin with a description of classic examples of Brazilian populism and how it was analysed by Brazilian social scientists and identifying three different schools of thought (liberal, modernist, and Marxist). They observe that all of these schools of thought shared the elitist view that the masses were utterly irrational and easily captured by ideological discourses that clouded their understanding of their own self-interest or class position. They ask if the concept of populism usually employed to study the Left help us further our understanding of Bolsonaro's role and meaning in present-day Brazilian politics. To answer this question, the authors employ a discourse analysis of 2018 presidential electoral video recordings of interviews, documents containing his platform, and videos produced by his campaign team and made available on his official YouTube page. They demonstrate how, while campaigning, Bolsonaro showed two different personas. The first is typically populist: informal, amateurish and buffoonish, used at events, rallies, and public speeches. The other is the 'good guy' and victim who wants to unify the Brazilian people, denying the accusation that he is a bigot or hate monger.

A key aspect of Bolsonaro's discourse corresponds with classical definitions of populism in his constant deployment of an extreme dichotomous rhetoric that opposes 'us' to 'them' and points to an anti-systemic stance. Drastically sidelining debates on policy, Bolsonaro's campaign was organized around two banners: a radical defence of conservative family values and a rabid anti-corruption discourse. Reinforcing arguments made in the Ravecca et al. article, the authors point out how in the 2018 election social media appeared as a viable and strong means of unfiltered communication, amplifying his populist message in an echo chamber. Bolsonaro managed to fashion himself as a champion of the new alt-right, whose different groups were almost exclusively built on social media. They arrive at the conclusion that Bolsonaro displays many characteristics that authors have ascribed to populism, most of them linked to his politics of authenticity, but the lack of a central place for 'the people' in his discourse does suggest the contrary. Finally, the authors highlight how the new means of communication that are refashioning the political landscape of today's world must be taken into account in order to fully understand today's populism in Brazil.

In González's article on the relation between social movements and the successive Ortega governments in Nicaragua. This country's Pink Tide emerges in a different historical context than most Latin American countries in that it suffered successive dictatorships propped up by American intervention that were overthrown by force. What followed was a long and violent civil war between the Sandinistas and the American backed Contras. In 2007, Daniel Ortega was democratically elected, and has since been re-elected and remains president. The author analyses how the mobilization of peasant, indigenous and afro-descendant organizations against Ortega's neo-developmentalist strategies is an indication of the political limits of a 'neostructuralist bargain'. This article demonstrates that even though the Ortega governments succeeded in reversing the social impact of two decades of liberal and conservative governments that preceded his administration, they have created and sustained an authoritarian clientelist network with civil society organizations as well as political rivals in order to pursue neoliberalist economic policies. The author points to Campesino activism which has largely been formed out of a re-peasantry process and has repoliticized neo-developmentalism, by presenting claims around peasant economies and social inclusion and opposing agribusiness and large transport infrastructure projects prioritized by FSLN governments.

The author highlights specific cases, such as the conflict between afro-indigenous and peasant activists on the Caribbean Coast and the FSLN administration, which prioritized development projects linked to the Chinese capital. These movements emerged as a reaction to the Ortega administration's unwillingness to support the claims to land and autonomy of these communities via dubious judicial and electoral practices. This government position eventually made these movements stronger as they articulated a vision of local, and livelihood-based development against the extractive, plantation-based model promoted by the government. Creole activism has also denounced the discriminatory and racialized nature of the process of development promoted by the Ortega governments. The author argues that these struggles and their contention against FSLN neo-developmentalist policies must be understood within the context of this government's alliances with international capital.

The article by Schild offers a detailed description and a historical-structural and cultural analysis of protest and government repression since 2018 in Chile. She uses a political economy frame to fully understand the social consequences of a development path fundamentally based on economic liberalism, incorporating a gender-sensitive analysis through which neoliberalism is explored as a cultural form in its own right, as the logic or rationality of state restructuring and government policy. In doing so, she shows how a strictly political economy lens is incomplete in grasping the scope of socio-economic transformations in the country. Most importantly, her work shows the importance of understanding neoliberalism not merely as an economic phenomenon, but also as a political form of government with far-reaching implications for the reorganization of social and political life.

The second dimension of the analysis presented by the author is the generalized social exhaustion with the relentless subordination of society and individuals to the laws of the capitalist market, which in the Chilean case explains the generalized crisis of political and institutional legitimacy that has challenged the country's position as a paradigmatic case of evolving, crisis-prone entrenched neoliberalism. Crucial to this exhaustion is the 1980 Constitution, a document whose political origins and intent has been largely ignored in critical political economy analyses. This article provides a detailed analysis of the socio-economic consequences of this dictatorship-era Constitution which not only enshrined the privatizations and deregulations associated with the first phase of neoliberal restructuring but set the political and institutional bases for the successful implementation of those reforms associated with the neo-developmentalist project.

In light of the findings presented in this issue, we can articulate three conclusions about the moment the region currently finds itself in, and potential paths forward. First, we cannot blame the current crisis on the failures of an outdated left dogmatically committed to statism, the argument of mainstream political science and economics, grounded in what, as Shivakumar (2005) outlines, is an almost inexorable law that drives any attempt by the state to intervene in market forces toward populism and predatory rent-seeking. This argument must be rejected for the simple reason that in the cases where market-friendly right-wing governments have risen to power (notably Chile and Brazil) that result has been not a return to governability and at least a semblance of social cohesion, but rather the deepening of political and economic instability. Given this, it is clear that the current crisis has roots that are deeper than what formal political contestation is able to cope with.

Our second conclusion is that there currently does not exist any kind of political project capable of organizing sufficient social forces that can guarantee even a semblance of stability. In other words, there is a political vacuum at work. The neoliberal project of equating human freedom with free markets and minimal government has become as suspect as appeals to 'the people' by presidential strongmen articulating a vision of progress via state action. From this stems our third and final conclusion, namely that the current crisis is not likely to go away anytime soon. Indeed, we are likely entering an extended period of uncertainty, characterized by damage control and crisis management, irrespective of who is in power. From this perspective, the case of Chile stands out as perhaps capable of providing early clues of how this crisis may eventually find some kind of resolution. If the country is able to rewrite its Pinochet-era constitution, the first in the world to formalize neoliberalism as a form of rule, it may prove to be the first step out of the region's current impasse.

Notes

1. ECLAC (2014) data indicate that between 2005 and 2011 there was a reduction of extreme poverty from 10.7% to 6.1% and of poverty from 36.4% to 20.9%.
2. This trend is partially due to the decentralisation of the state that took place during the 1990s where social and health services are often ambiguously shared among different levels of the state.

Disclosure statement

No potential conflict of interest was reported by the author(s).

Funding

This work was supported by the Social Sciences and Humanities Research Council of Canada.

References

Alvarez, S. E., Rubin, J. W., Thayer, M., Baiocchi, G., & Laó-Montes, A. (2017). *Beyond civil society: Activism, participation, and protest in Latin America* (pp. xvi + 386 pages). Duke University Press.

Antunes, R., Santana, M. A., & Praun, L. (2018). Chronicle of a defeat foretold: The PT administrations from compromise to the coup. *Latin American Perspectives*, *46*(1), 85–104. https://doi.org/10.1177/0094582X18807210

Antunes de Oliveira, F. (2019). The rise of the Latin American far-right explained: Dependency theory meets uneven and combined development. *Globalizations*, *16*(7), 1145–1164. https://doi.org/10.1080/14747731.2019.1567977

Artz, L. (2017). *The Pink Tide: Media access and political power in Latin America*. Rowman & Littlefield International.

Barbosa, L. P. (2020). Challenges facing Latin American peasant movements under progressive governments and new right-wing parties: The case of Brazil. *Latin American Perspectives*, *47*(5), 94–112. https://doi.org/10.1177/0094582X20946408

Bárcena, A. (2010). Structural constraints on development in Latin America and the Caribbean: A post-crisis reflection. *Cepal Review*, *100*, 7–27. https://www.cepal.org/en/articles/2010-structural-constraints-development-latin-america-and-caribbean-post-crisis-reflection

Becker, M. (2013). The stormy relations between Rafael Correa and the social movements in Ecuador. *Latin American Perspectives*, *40*(3), 43–62. https://doi.org/10.1177/0094582X13479305

Birdsall, N., & Francis, F. (2011). *The post-Washington consensus: Development after the crisis* (Working Paper 244). https://www.cgdev.org/publication/post-washington-consensus-development-after-crisis-working-paper-244

Boesten, J. (2018). Between fatigue and silence: The challenges of conducting research on sexual violence in conflict. *Social Politics: International Studies in Gender, State & Society*, *25*(4), 568–588.

Bohn, S., & Levy, C. Eds. (2021). *Twenty-first-century feminismos women's movements in Latin America and the Caribbean*. McGill Queens.

Braga, R. (2015). Contornos do pós-lulismo. *Cult*, no. 206 (October), 46–49.

Braga, R. (2016). On standing's a precariat charter: Confronting the precaritisation of labour in Brazil and Portugal. *Global Labour Journal* 7(2)(Special Issue), 148–159.

Braga, R., & Barbosa dos Santos, F. L. (2019). The political economy of Lulism and its aftermath. *Latin American Perspectives*, *47*(1), 169–186. https://doi.org/10.1177/0094582X19887806

Cameron, M. A. (2018). Making sense of competitive authoritarianism: Lessons from the Andes. *Latin American Politics and Society*, *60*(2), 1–22. https://doi.org/10.1017/lap.2018.3

Carneiro, F., Fuentes, G., & Midaglia, C. (2020). Old friends in new times: Progressive parties and union movements in the southern cone. *Latin American Perspectives*, *47*(4), 112–130. https://doi.org/10.1177/0094582X20924368

Chiasson-LeBel, T., & Larrabure, M. (2019). Latin America's changing balance of class forces. *European Review of Latin American and Caribbean Studies/Revista Europea de Estudios Latinoamericanos y del Caribe*, (108), 87–107.

de Carvalho, S. (2020). The end of the oppression of indigenous peoples under capitalism? Bolivia under the Morales government. *Latin American Perspectives*, *47*(4), 58–75. https://doi.org/10.1177/0094582X20920271

Democracy in Latin America. (2011). *Democracy in Latin America political change in comparative perspective* (2nd ed). Oxford University Press.

ECLAC (Economic Commission for Latin America and the Caribbean). 2014. Exports of primary products as percentage of total exports. *CEPALSTAT Databases*, December 11. http://interwp.cepal.org/sisgen/ConsultaIntegrada.asp?IdAplicacion=6&idTema=119&idIndicador=1910&idioma=i

Ellner, S. (2013). Latin America's radical left in power: Complexities and challenges in the twenty-first century. *Latin American Perspectives*, *40*(3), 5–25.

Ellner, S. (2019). Different perspectives on twenty-first-century Latin America. *Latin American Perspectives*, *46*(1), 282–284. https://doi.org/10.1177/0094582X18808772

Ellner, S. (2020). Introduction: Salient characteristics of Mexico's neoliberal turn and Andrés Manuel López Obrador's critique. *Latin American Perspectives*, *47*(6), 4–19. https://doi.org/10.1177/0094582X20953102

Fernandes, S. (2017). Crisis of praxis: Depoliticization and leftist fragmentation in Brazil. https://doi.org/10.22215/etd/2017-11812

Fuentes-Nieva, R., & Feroci, G. N. (2017). The evolving role and influence and growing strength of social movements in Latin America and the Caribbean. In *Alternative pathways to sustainable development: Lessons from Latin America*, International Development Policy Series No.9 (pp. 323–338). Graduate Institute Publications, Brill-Nijhoff.

Gaudichaud, F. (2021). *Amérique latine: nouvelle période, nouvelles luttes*. CADTM. https://www.cadtm.org/Amerique-latine-nouvelle-periode-nouvelles-luttes-Entretien-avec-Franck

Giraudy, A., Hartlyn, J., Dunn, C., & Carty, E. (2020). The impact of neopatrimonialism on poverty in contemporary Latin America. *Latin American Politics and Society*, *62*(1), 73–96. https://doi.org/10.1017/lap.2019.46

Goldstein, A. A. (2019). The new far-right in Brazil and the construction of a right-wing order. *Latin American Perspectives*, *46*(4), 245–262.

Gonzalez, M. (in press). Solo El Pueblo Salva Al Pueblo': Indigenous, afro-descendant and campesino activisms in post-revolutionary Nicaragua. *Globalizations*.

Grisaffi, T. (2019). *Coca yes, cocaine no: How Bolivia's coca growers reshaped democracy*. Duke University Press.

Guardiola-Rivera, O. (2019). What has happened in Venezuela is a coup. Trump's denial is dangerous. https://www.theguardian.com/commentisfree/2019/jan/28/venezuela-coup-trump-juan-guaido

Gudynas, E. (2015, October 7). La identidad del progresismo, su agotamiento y los relanzamientos de las izquierdas. *América Latina en Movimiento*. http://www.alainet.org/es/articulo/172855

Harris, R. L. (2003). Popular resistance to globalization and neoliberalism in Latin America. *Journal of Developing Societies*, *19*(2–3), 365–426. https://doi.org/10.1177/0169796X0301900209

Herrmann, J. D. (2017). Media and subnational democracy: The case of Bahia, Brazil. *Democratization 24*, 81–99.

Hilal, G. (2018). From neoliberalism to neo-developmentalism? The Political Economy of Post-crisis Argentina (2002–2015). *New Political Economy*, *23*(1), 66–87. https://doi.org/10.1080/13563467.2017.1330877

Hilgers, T. (2008). Causes and consequences of political clientelism: Mexico's PRD in comparative perspective. *Latin American Politics and Society*, *50*(4), 123–153.

Katz, C. (2015). Dualities of Latin America. *Latin American Perspectives*, *42*(4), 10–42. https://doi.org/10.1177/0094582X15574714

Kay, C. (2008). Reflections on Latin American rural studies in the neoliberal globalization period: A new rurality? *Development and Change*, *39*(6), 915–943. https://doi.org/10.1111/j.1467-7660.2008.00518.x

Kowalczyk, A. M. (2013). Indigenous peoples and modernity: Mapuche mobilizations. *Perspectives, Latin American*, *40*, 121–135.

Larrabure, M. (2016). The struggle for the new commons in the Brazilian free transit movement. *Studies in Political Economy*, *97*(2), 175–194.

Larrabure, M. (2019a). Post-capitalist development in Latin America's left turn: Beyond Peronism and the Magical State. *New Political Economy*, *24*(5), 587–604.

Larrabure, M. (2019b). Chile's democratic road to authoritarianism. *European Review of Latin American and Caribbean Studies/Revista Europea de Estudios Latinoamericanos y del Caribe*, (108), 221–243.

Lazar, S. (2017). *Where are the unions? Workers and social movements in Latin America, the Middle East and Europe* (pp. 296). Zed Books.

Leiva, F. I. (2006). Neoliberal and neostructuralist perspectives on labour flexibility, poverty and inequality: A critical appraisal. *New Political Economy*, *11*(3), 337–359. https://doi.org/10.1080/13563460600840175

Leiva, F. I. (2008). *Latin American neostructuralism*. University of Minnesota Press.

Levy, C. (2012). Social movements and political parties in Brazil: Expanding democracy, the 'struggle for the possible' and the reproduction of power structures. *Globalizations*, *9*(6), 783–798. https://doi.org/10.1080/14747731.2012.739340

Loureiro, P. M. (2018). Reformism, class conciliation and the Pink Tide: Material gains and their limits. In M. Ystanes & I. Strønen (Eds.), *The social life of economic inequalities in contemporary Latin America. Approaches to social inequality and difference*. Palgrave Macmillan. https://doi.org/10.1007/978-3-319-61536-3_2

Loureiro, P. M., & Saad-Filho, A. (2018). The limits of pragmatism: The rise and fall of the Brazilian workers' party (2002–2016). *Latin American Perspectives*, *46*(1), 66–84. https://doi.org/10.1177/0094582X18805093

Macdonald, L., & Ruckert, A. (2009). Post-neoliberalism in the Americas: An introduction. In L. Macdonald & A. Ruckert (Eds.), *Post-neoliberalism in the Americas* (pp. 1–20). Palgrave Macmillan.

Martí i Puig, S., & Serra, M. (2020). Nicaragua: De-democratization and regime crisis. *Latin American Politics and Society*, *62*(2), 117–136. https://doi.org/10.1017/lap.2019.64

McNelly, A. (2020). The incorporation of social organizations under the MAS in Bolivia. *Latin American Perspectives*, *47*(4), 76–95. https://doi.org/10.1177/0094582X20918556

Moseley, M. W. (2018). *Protest state: The rise of everyday contention in Latin America* (pp. xvi + 241). Oxford University Press.

Munck, R., & Sankey, K. (2020). Introduction: Social movements in Latin America, part 2. *Latin American Perspectives*, *47*(5), 4–8. https://doi.org/10.1177/0094582X20944392

Negri, C., Igreja, R. L., & Pinto, S. R. (2019). 'It happened in Brazil too': The radical right's capture of networks of hope. *Cahiers des Amériques latines*, *92*(92), 17–38. https://doi.org/10.4000/cal.9877

OAS. (2019). https://www.oas.org/documents/eng/press/Preliminary-Report-EOM-Bolivia-23-10-19.pdf

Ocampo, J. A. (2017). Commodity-led development in Latin America. In G. Carbonnier, H. Campodónico, & S. T. Vázquez (Eds.), *Alternative pathways to sustainable development: Lessons from Latin America* (pp. 51–76). Brill. http://www.jstor.org/stable/10.1163/j.ctt1w76w3t.11

Oliveira, F., Braga, R., & Rizek, C. (Org.). (2010). *Hegemonia às avessas*. Boitempo.

Petras, J., & Veltmeyer, H. (2001). Are Latin American peasant movements still a force for change? Some new paradigms revisited. *The Journal of Peasant Studies*, *28*(2), 83–118. https://doi.org/10.1080/03066150108438767

Petras, J., & Veltmeyer, H. (2015, November 2). *Power and resistance*. Brill. doi: https://doi.org/10.1163/9789004307421

Pickup, M. (2019). The political economy of the new left. *Latin American Perspectives*, *46*(1), 23–45. https://doi.org/10.1177/0094582X18803878

Ponce, K., Vasquez, A., Vivanco, P., & Munck, R. (2020). The October 2019 indigenous and citizens' uprising in Ecuador. *Latin American Perspectives*, *47*(5), 9–19. https://doi.org/10.1177/0094582X20931113

Pressly. (2020). https://www.bbc.com/news/stories-53557235

Proyecto de Análisis Político y Escenarios Prospectivos (PNUD-PAPEP). (2012). *La Protesta Social en América Latina*. Siglo vientiuno editores.

Ravecca, P. (2015). Our discipline and its politics. Authoritarian political science: Chile 1979–1989. *Revista de Ciencia Política*, *35*(1), 145–178.

Riggirozzi, P., & Tussie, D. (2012). The rise of post-hegemonic regionalism in Latin-America. In P. Riggirozzi & D. Tussie (Eds.), *The rise of post-hegemonic regionalism – the case of Latin America* (pp. 1–16). Springer.

Saad-Filho, A. (2013). Mass protests under 'left neoliberalism': Brazil, June-July 2013. *Critical Sociology*, *39*(5), 657–669. doi:10.1177/0896920513501906

Schild, V. (in press). The political economy of rebellious discontent: Lessons from forty-five years of market rule in Chile. *Globalizations*.

Scirica, E. (2014). Comunistas y anticomunistas: redes políticas y culturales en Argentina y Chile durante la guerra fría (circa 1960). *Anuario del Instituto de Historia Argentina*, *14*. http://www.memoria.fahce.unlp.edu.ar/art_revistas/pr.6728/pr.6728.pdf

Singer, A. (2020). The failure of Dilma Rousseff's developmentalist experiment: A class analysis. *Latin American Perspectives*, *47*(1), 152–168. https://doi.org/10.1177/0094582X19877187

Shivakumar, S. (2005). *The constitution of development: Crafting capabilities for self-governance*. Springer.

Stahler-Sholk, R., Harry, V., & Becker, M. (2014). Introduction: New directions in Latin American social movements. In R. Stahler-Sholk, H. E. Vanden, & M. Becker (Eds.), *Rethinking Latin American social movements: Radical action from below* (pp. 1–18). Blue Ridge Summit.

Svampa, M. (2013). Consenso de 'commodities' y lenguajes de valoración en América Latina. *Nueva Sociedad*, *244*, 30–46. www.nuso.org

Svampa, M. (2011). Modelo de Desarrollo y cuestión ambiental en América Latina: categorías y escenarios en disputa [The development model and environmental question in Latin America : Categories and scenes in dispute]. In F. Wanderley (Ed.), *El desarrollo en cuestión. Reflexiones desde América Latina*. CIDES, OXFAM y Plural.

Svampa, M. (2015). Commodities consensus: Neoextractivism and enclosure of the commons in Latin America. *South Atlantic Quarterly*, *114*(1), 65–82. https://doi.org/10.1215/00382876-2831290

Thaler, K. M. (2017). Nicaragua: A return to caudillismo. *Journal of Democracy*, *28*(2), 157–169. https://doi.org/10.1353/jod.2017.0032

Tomini, L. (2018). *When democracies collapse. Assessing transitions to non-democratic regimes in the contemporary world*. Routledge.

Vanden, H. E. (2003). Globalization in a time of neoliberalism: Politicized social movements and the Latin American response. *Journal of Developing Societies*, *19*(2–3), 308–333. https://doi.org/10.1177/0169796X0301900207

Webber, J. (2017). *The last day of oppression and the first day of the same: The politics and economics of the new Latin American left*. Pluto Press.

Williams, C. (2020). https://jackrw.mit.edu/sites/default/files/documents/Bolivia_report-short.pdf

Zibechi, R. 2015. Se acelera el fin del ciclo progresista. *La Jornada*, October 30. http://www.jornada.unam.mx/2015/10/30/opinion/021a1pol

Broadened embedded autonomy and Latin America's Pink Tide: towards the neo-developmental state

Patrick Clark and Antulio Rosales

ABSTRACT
A central issue in the scholarly literature on the Latin American Pink Tide is the renewal of state-led development, or neo-developmentalism, and dependence on primary resources or the so-called resource curse. In this article, we consider the question of neo-developmentalism during the Pink Tide and state capacity, analyzing whether the three 'radical' Pink Tide governments in Ecuador, Venezuela, and Bolivia were able to achieve their respective neo-developmental political objectives. We employ a comparative approach building on the theory of 'broadened embedded autonomy' as conceptualized by Peter Evans. We argue that while reliance on resource extraction posed a challenge for the construction of state capacity for Pink Tide governments, national-level differences help explain why some governments were relatively more successful than others at inducing neo-developmentalism. A comparative approach focused on the politics of state-society thus provides a promising analytical framework for interpreting variations across cases.

Introduction

Left-leaning governments, dubbed early on as the Pink Tide phenomenon, were elected to power across Latin America in the first decade of the twenty-first century. The hallmarks of 'post-neoliberal' or Pink Tide politics included the expansion of social rights and increased public spending, greater regulation of markets and the construction of a type of state capable of overseeing the construction of a 'neo-developmental' model of political economy (Grugel & Riggirozzi, 2012; Levitsky & Roberts, 2011; Macdonald & Ruckert, 2009). The scholarly literature on the Pink Tide has assessed specific topics and issues, for example, agriculture and food politics (Vergara-Camus & Kay, 2017), oil and mining policies (Haslam & Heidrich, 2016; Perreault & Valdivia, 2010), health care and social protection (Riggirozzi, 2020). Moreover, contributions to the literature have advanced different theoretical approaches and questions, from renewed debates around dependency theory to colonial legacies in contemporary epistemologies (Antunes de Oliveira, 2019; Escobar, 2010). In terms of conceptualizing a Pink Tide model of political economy, for Saad-Filho, Latin American neo-developmentalism sought to build 'a new system of accumulation drawing upon strong linkages between the state and the private sector and between investment and consumption' (2020, p. 14), in short, a shift towards a demand-driven growth model as opposed to the supply-side economics of the previous period of economic liberalization in the region.

The first two decades of the twenty-first century coincided with a commodity boom in global markets. Many Pink Tide governments managed to use the increased income of the commodity boom to reduce economic inequality, namely through increased social and public investment, in an important break with other historical periods of commodity boom in the region (see Sánchez-Ancochea, 2021). However, a central question is how economic reliance or 'dependence' on primary commodity extraction in many Pink Tide countries undermined other political objectives of these governments, in particular the diversification of economies associated with neo-developmentalism. During the Pink Tide, primary commodity production in the region intensified generally to the detriment of secondary and tertiary sectors (with typically higher value-added). In Spanish, this process has been referred to as the *reprimarización* of Latin American economies and reflects a return to the classic dilemma posed by dependency theory (Cardoso & Faletto, 1979; Frank, 1969) and the structuralist school of Raúl Prebisch (1950). In this sense, the classic problem of dependency in the region, discussed in the contemporary literature as 'neo-extractivism' has not changed substantially since these earlier debates as ' ... most Latin American countries remain specialized in primary goods production and have generally been unable to move into sectors with high value-added, long- term demand expansion and sustained productivity growth' (Sánchez-Ancochea, 2009, p. 63). The importance of natural resource rents for many Pink Tide governments was then at odds with other neo-developmental objectives such as economic diversification or environmental protection, in that the growth model and increased social and public spending largely depended on deepening 'neo-extractivism' (North & Grinspun, 2016).

In contrast to the decades preceding the Pink Tide, many of these governments came to play a more central political role in striking new deals with foreign capital to access a more significant share of the rent pie or the revenues that extractive industries generate. This occurred through deepening ties in the global market of commodities, often with firms from non-traditional powers, such as China and India (Veltmeyer, 2013). In the literature, neo-extractivism is described as replicating the traditional dynamics of the region's dependent integration into the global economy through primary resource extraction (Mezzadra & Neilson, 2017) but exacerbated by the 'resource nationalism' of the Pink Tide governments and greater importance of resource rents as a source of public revenue (Haslam & Heidrich, 2016). The general thrust of the literature on neo-extractivism then overlaps with some of the predictions of 'resource curse' theory which has long linked dependence on revenues derived from underground rents with lack of economic diversification, authoritarian politics, and political corruption (Karl, 1997; Ross, 2015).

The question we are concerned with in this paper is the conflict between 'neo-extractivism' and 'neo-developmentalism' in the Pink Tide and whether, and why, some governments were relatively more successful at advancing neo-developmental objectives than others. As Peter Evans' work and contribution to the dependency theory debates of the 1970s argued with respect to industrial development in Brazil, economic dependency does not necessarily foreclose the possibility of national 'dependent development' (1979). We outline a conceptual framework which we apply through comparative analysis of Venezuela, Bolivia, and Ecuador, to identify variables that could help explain differences across the three cases and be analyzed through more in-depth studies in the future. Our analytical framework builds on Peter Evans' 'comparative institutional approach' (1995), in which he introduced the concept of 'embedded autonomy' as a theory of the dynamics behind successful 'developmental' statecraft.[1] Following Evans' proposal to broaden embedded autonomy, the argument we develop is that state capacity is undergirded by ties across state and society that either enhance or limit the emergence of what Evans has referred to as 'broadened embedded autonomy' (1995, p. 246). We build on this 'broadened' approach to embedded autonomy to consider not only the ties between state and private industries, as in Evans' original work, but to other social actors such as organized social and popular movements which with which ties also needed to be built to achieve the objectives of the Pink Tide governments around social and economic transformation.

In comparing the three cases, we argue that Venezuela is the closest of the three to Evans's typology of a 'predatory state' (1995), a scenario in which the power of the governing elites lacks constraining forces both institutionally (in state institutions) and within society, despite the strong opposition of different groups, including most business sectors, to the government. The slide into predation occurred despite the attempt by the government to create semi-autonomous institutions of 'popular power' from below which could potentially have served to check predation and were conceptualized as inductors of a socialist economic development that would diversify the economy away from oil by promoting the development of agriculture and other sectors. We argue that the scale of oil rents in Venezuela compared to the other cases undermined the depth and durability of 'popular power' and that the creation of these alternative institutions, which were dependent on the transfer of rents, led to the collapse in state capacity in Venezuela under Maduro. By contrast, we argue that Bolivia under the MAS government is an 'intermediate case' (Evans, 1995) which comes the closest of the three to approximating some elements of the neo-developmental state. Here, we highlight the greater degree of autonomy of the political base of the MAS party from the Morales governments and state resources and the ability of the government to broker alliances with both popular organizations and business groups which helped the government achieve some of its neo-developmental objectives. Finally, we argue that Ecuador under the Correa government is also an 'intermediate case' since the autonomy of state institutions improved in the Correa period. However, compared to Bolivia, the more top-down political style of the Correa government curtailed the potential for 'shared projects' (Evans, 1995, p. 42) with either popular social organizations or business or economic sectors more than in the Bolivian case.

Latin American (neo)-developmentalism and 'broadened' embedded autonomy: a theoretical framework

The literature of the 'developmental state' originated in the context of East Asia through studies of the processes of industrialization that countries in the region had undergone (Evans, 1995; Johnson, 1982; Woo-Cumings, 1999). However, different types of infant industry[2] protections and broader economic nationalist policies have a more extended history than just in East Asia. Such policies been implemented throughout European history and in the United States (see Caldentey, 2009; Helleiner, 2021). Most countries in the world implemented at least some of these policies during the 'golden age' of Keynesian economics and the international order characterized as 'embedded liberalism' (Ruggie, 1982), which afforded national states more significant policy space. In Latin America, the ideas and policies associated with the developmental state have their origins in Import Substitution Industrialization (ISI). The structuralist school of Raúl Prebisch and his work at the Economic Commission for Latin America (ECLAC) was a key source of theorization for the implementation of ISI. Prebisch's notion of 'declining terms of trade' (1950) posited that Latin American states would have to implement infant industry protection policies to stimulate domestic industrialization and transcend primary commodity dependence to overcome the negative consequences of trade inequalities. Put into practice throughout the first half of the twentieth century until the 1980s, the structuralist paradigm also involved extending social welfare policies. It brought with it the emergence of working-class and labour union movements linked to 'corporatist' (Collier & Collier, 1991) forms of class and interest mediation between labour, capital, state, and society, though these corporatist relations varied considerably across the region and never emerged in some countries.

In the context of economic globalization beginning in the 1980s, the set of policies associated with infant industry and national ISI became more untenable in most regions of the world but especially in the Global South with the shift towards economic liberalization and globalization. In this new context, the development of manufacturing and other heavy industries was no longer viable for many countries due to trade and economic liberalization. Evans (2010) has argued that the 'twenty-first-century developmental state' had to shift to being a 'capability enhancing state' focused on investments in health and education to enhance the capabilities of citizens and develop human talent or 'human capital' rather than one focused on stimulating industrial development. This suggestion builds on the prospect raised by Evans at the end of *Embedded Autonomy* that future research on the concept could focus on its 'broadening' (1995, p. 17) to consider the embedded autonomy between states and other groups in society, for example, social movements. More recently, Evans and Patrick Heller described the task of neo-developmental states as ' ... co-constructing shared coherent goals whose concrete implementation can then be co-produced [across state and society] ... ' (2015, p. 693). The rationale is that this approach will more effectively promote the development of secondary and tertiary economic sectors beyond traditional heavy industries, depending on a country's particular endowments and comparative advantages, while also helping to achieve other objectives like research and innovation or environmental protection (Evans, 2010).

The differences between Evans' original conception of the developmental state and the neo-developmental state have been captured well by work on the 'developmental network state' (Negoita & Block, 2012), 'mutual empowerment' across state and society (Wang, 1999), the 'co-construction and co-production' of public policies (Vaillancourt, 2009), perspectives which coincide with theorization of the state's role in development in the Pink Tide as well (see Grugel & Riggirozzi, 2012). In our framework, we propose joining this idea of broadened embedded autonomy with the state capacity of governments to exercise both 'positive' and 'negative' power and the relations between these two forms of political power (Hochstetler, 2021). As Hochstetler has argued in her recent work on energy transitions and climate change, 'state capacity' can be understood in two ways, in the 'positive' sense of the ' ... ability to plan and execute policy that provides public goods' and in the 'negative' sense of ' ... the ability to confront powerful societal interests' (2021, p. 32). Along similar lines, Cameron has proposed a conceptualization of state power, conceptualizing positive power as one that ' ... mobilizes the society's resources for collective purposes' and negative power as ' ... the power to dissolve, to obstruct, to discourage, to exclude, to undo and not do things' (in Larrabure et al., 2021, p. 5). Here, we extend their conceptualizations to consider how positive and negative power map onto embedded autonomy, contending that negative power maps onto autonomy and positive power onto embeddedness. Autonomy speaks to the power and capacity of government agencies to confront powerful groups or vested interests and embeddedness to the ability of the state/government to orchestrate forms of coordination with different groups in society or economic/industrial sectors to achieve development policy objectives. Another theory which works as a metaphor for these two interrelated tasks in political rule is the distinction between 'state building' and 'governance' (Yu & He, 2011).

The potential for neo-developmentalism as embedded autonomy depends on how actors in society or the private economy can be mobilized and embedded in states' developmental efforts (positive power) but also state autonomy and the capacity of a given state to exercise negative power through autonomous state institutions that to prevent, or at least curtail, capture and predation. In terms of a country case within the Pink Tide approximating the neo-developmentalist typology, though while likely still best classified as an 'intermediate case', the relative success of the Worker's Party (PT) governments in Brazil comes closest to this vision of broadened embedded autonomy. Studies of issues ranging from environmental protection and conservation (Hochstetler & Keck, 2007), industrial development (Massi & Singh, 2018), HIV/ AIDS policy (Rich, 2020), rural development (Kröger, 2011) and rural education (Tarlau, 2013) have pointed to overlapping ties across state and society in successful policy implementation and development initiatives. This diversity of tasks and interventions in a variety of policy areas speaks to the more diverse forms of embedded autonomy associated with a 'capability enhancing' (Evans, 2010) or (neo)-developmental state.

National-level politics and state-society relations help account for differences in state capacity, and it is these differences in state capacity that help account for whether the resource curse tendency is mitigated or instead has explanatory power (see Kurtz, 2009). From this starting point, in this article, we consider whether the 'resource curse' hypothesis as 'neo-extractivism' ultimately undermined neo-developmentalism in each of the cases and what variables either contributed to or mitigated this tendency? Central to the problem of moving away from primary resource production is the question of state capacity and the ability of these governments to establish embedded autonomy, not only to promote industrial development and economic diversification, but to achieve other objectives associated with neo-developmentalism, including social development and transformation, research and innovation, rural development, and environmental sustainability amongst others.

On a methodological note, we want to clarify that by employing the three ideal types proposed by Evans, we are not suggesting that they explain everything about each case. 'Ideal types', such as those proposed and used in this paper are '… *tools*, and not the end point of the analysis' (Swedberg, 2018, p. 183). The objective of using ideal types in comparative and empirical research is '… not to determine to which (singular) of a number of theoretical types they should each be allocated, but to determine which (plural) of these forms are to be found within them, in roughly what proportions, and with what change over time' (Crouch, 2005, p. 440). In this sense, the *Lavo Jato* scandal in Brazil under the PT certainly demonstrates that while Brazil under the PT might be somewhat closer to a neo-developmental state it is still a predatory state in other respects. At the same time, while Venezuela under Maduro might best be explained by predation, there may also be instances of positive power and embeddedness when pressure from more autonomous power blocs could exert pressure on the government and drive more developmental outcomes (see Felicien et al., 2020). The comparative analysis in this study is exploratory and we portend to identify conclusive causal links to explain differences across the cases. Instead, our objective is to identify variables that could be analyzed more in-depth in future studies which we discuss in the conclusions. Our analysis draws mainly on a review of the secondary literature on the Pink Tide period in each country. We also build on a decade's worth of primary research in Venezuela and Ecuador on the left turn conducted as part of different individual research projects (on energy and natural resource policy and rural development and agriculture). Our analysis focuses on state-society relations across different sectors, including agriculture and natural resource sectors but we consider other differences including the governing political parties in each case and draw on examples and evidence beyond these as well.

Venezuela

Venezuela is the outlier case of the Pink Tide and the case that most approximates Evans' ideal type of a 'predatory state' (1995), especially after the death of Hugo Chávez and the ascent of Nicolás

Maduro to power. Recurrent problems characterized Venezuela's past attempts at state-led development in the twentieth century. However, the situation in similar periods of low oil prices was less dramatic than the current collapse of the rentier economic model (Buxton, 2020). The lack of effective state institutions has contributed to the spiral towards an increasingly predatory state characterized by 'defensive authoritarian rentierism' (Bull & Rosales, 2020, p. 113). Broader international forces, and especially international sanctions, exacerbate these domestic trends. Venezuela's recent crisis and domestic disputes are shaped by global politics, such as the increasing influence of China and Russia and the attempts by the United States to reclaim its control over the region (Mijares, 2017).

The uncoordinated international sanctions against Venezuelan officials, its oil sector and treasury have served to strengthen the power of the Maduro government, which has used the sanctions as a unifying banner for the levers of power in the economy and military (Bull & Rosales, 2020). At the same time, the opposition has remained divided and lacked coordination capacity in response to different levels of government repression (Jiménez, 2021). In contrast with the concept of the predatory state proposed originally by Evans (1995), which was based on the case of Zaire, that country had broad international support. In contrast, the Venezuelan government faced strong opposition from Northern powers while it has managed to leverage foreign aid from other states like China and Russia (Mijares, 2017; Rosales, 2018). Despite the differences in international dynamics, the Venezuelan political elite has faced few constraining forces domestically in exercising negative power and the deepening of predation through resource rents ultimately undermined the very nature of the petro-state (Virgüez & Mijares, 2020).

To understand the current situation in Venezuela it is important to go back to the period when Hugo Chávez was initially elected in 1998. Chávez won the Presidency riding a wave of political dissatisfaction with the traditional party system and opposition to market reforms associated with structural adjustment. From the outset, the new government faced more opposition than either the Correa or Morales governments did. Perhaps the most important of these was the state oil company Petróleos de Venezuela (PDVSA), which the government managed to transform by replacing the top-management after the devastating 2002–2003 strike. Chavismo was a radical break with historical social and political forces in the country and while Correa and Morales have also used the language of revolution to describe their projects the term is much more apt in describing what occurred in Venezuela after the election of Chávez. The momentum of Chavismo was one of anti-system politics of the multitude rather than one based in an organized social movement (López Maya, 2003). In the sense of expanding the public sphere and citizenship, the Chavez period had elements of a democratizing social force (Spanakos, 2011). However, the importance of oil rents rather than taxation in Venezuelan politics and governance, what Coronil has called the 'magical state' (1997), allowed the government the political and economic autonomy and ability to pursue its agenda without having to negotiate with opposition groups or develop positive power in ways that could have led to the success of neo-developmental strategies.

Out of all the countries in Latin America that were impacted by the commodities boom in the region, Venezuela represents the most radical restructuring of resource policy and economic policies in general. When Chávez was elected, PDVSA was an arms-length company, in broader corporate terms, a capable corporation with technical capacity, albeit distant from societal demands and even at odds with state guidelines despite being state-owned. A cornerstone of the Bolivarian Revolution was that the oil industry had to be subordinated to the command of the government and revolutionary process. To achieve this objective, the government carried out purges in PDVSA and appointed loyal managers in the company regardless of their technical knowledge of the oil industry. Direct political control of PDVSA translated into a critical source of financing for the state to carry out social policies and wealth redistribution (Urbaneja, 2013). Direct political control over the oil industry gave the government political autonomy to exercise negative power with regards to the political opposition and economic elites opposed to the government far beyond anything either the Correa or Morales governments had as a tool of political rule.

PDVSA's activities expanded beyond oil extraction, and the government used it to bypass bureaucratic state structures or private actors accused of parasitically extracting the nation's wealth via foreign currency allocation (Rosales, 2018). After the 2003 takeover of PDVSA, high oil prices and foreign investment allowed the company to recover relatively quickly from a devastating strike, while the government managed to extract rents via taxes, royalties, and extraordinary social investment from the company. The commodity boom allowed the crafting of an ambitious foreign policy through oil diplomacy that attempted a form of counter-hegemonic globalization. Despite these changes, the oil industry remained vulnerable and highly dependent on incoming foreign capital and the projects of international solidarity were not sustained once the oil price declined, except for continued supply of the Cuban market.

Prior to the restructuring of PDVSA, Chavismo had been ambiguous regarding its political programme and the model of development it sought to induce, but in 2005, the government came out with the project of building twenty-first socialism through 'protagonistic and participatory democracy', 'popular power' and 'endogenous socialist development'. While the popular organization associated with Chavista *poder popular* had roots in popular social organization that preceded the election of Chávez (Fernandes, 2010; Velasco, 2015), the expansion of the social organization from below mushroomed significantly after the government gained control over PDVSA. The state encouraged the creation of new popular associations under the auspices of 'popular power' and the establishment of grassroots institutions like the communal councils through state funding. These forms of organization served, in theory, to develop forms of embeddedness or positive power necessary to achieve the government's political goals considering the opposition of other groups in society, like most business sectors, to its political project and promote neo-developmental objectives including economic diversification and the implementation of social policies.

Scholars of the Bolivarian Revolution have conceived of the transition to socialism and socialist development in Venezuela in gradualist terms, a process akin to developing embedded autonomy between grassroots organization from below (communal councils, co-operatives, etc.) and revolutionary state institutions. Considering the Bolivarian development model through the lens of Evans' theories, it would involve coordinated state actions both in 'husbandry' and 'handmaidening' of new socialist enterprises and forms of relatively autonomous social organization like communal councils and communes as a model of alternative socialist development (1995). This strategy for building socialism has been described as 'radiating out', a process through which these socialist enterprises, co-operatives, and communes ' ... Compete with and overtake capitalist production/relations ... [by] ... raising productivity in the state and communal sector above that of the private sector' (Yaffe, 2015, p. 30). It could be characterized as a form of 'anti-capitalist co-construction' (Vaillancourt, 2009, p. 294), which in theory, avoided the pitfalls of the centralization of power and command associated with the 'actually existing socialism' of the twentieth century. However, such a strategy assumes state agencies with relative autonomy so as not to succumb to capture as well as technical capacity and also a' ... *a non-instrumental relationship*, between the state and the social economy ... stakeholders from the social economy retain a degree of *autonomy* in relation to the state' (Vaillancourt, 2009, p. 295). In the end, most of these new state institutions did not develop a Weberian autonomy nor were grassroots social organizations able to exercise sufficient autonomy to partner in the implementation of state development programmes or hold government mismanagement to account.

The attempt of the Bolivarian Revolution to exercise positive power by husbanding the development of grassroots institutions of popular power failed in consolidating an alternative socio-political order. Although popular organizations were conceptualized as autonomous, and there was significant heterogeneity amongst them, they were ultimately dependent on government funds as well for services like credit, training, access to inputs and technology to foster socialist development. Studies have concluded that efforts to spark greater agricultural or industrial production were undermined by the more short-run pressures of oil dependence and the overvalued currency, which countered efforts to increase domestic production and failed to satisfy social need in strategic areas such as the agro-food sector which is still dominated by imports paid by petro-dollars (Larrabure, 2018; Purcell, 2017). In sum, new grassroots institutions served largely to undermine rather than strengthen state capacity and as a mechanism to redistribute rents rather than husband economic development or to hold the political leadership accountable due to their dependence on state rents.

The collapse of state capacity in Venezuela has finally included the oil industry itself, wherein the country cannot extract oil and distribute rents from it, not least influenced by foreign power disputes. Despite the unprecedented funds invested by the government in different kinds of development projects and programmes, state capacity declined rather than was strengthened during the Bolivarian Revolution. The predominance of predation, exacerbated by the chronic conflict with the political opposition and business sectors, international sanctions, and the inability of the popular power organization to root out predation meant that the government hindered rather than enhanced the state capability necessary to achieve its own neo-developmental objectives around diversifying the economy through social organization from below.

Bolivia

The victory of the *Movimiento al Socialismo* (MAS) party with the election of Evo Morales to the Presidency in 2005, like Venezuela and, later Ecuador, has been widely described as arising in the wake of mass mobilizations in the country against economic liberalization and restructuring during the 1980s–2000s (Silva, 2009). The MAS was a party constituted by linkages to popular social movements forged in this period and even further back (Anria, 2013; McKay, 2018). As a leader of lowland coca-producing peasant union, Morales had a long trajectory in the mechanics of popular organization and political negotiation. When MAS was elected in 2005, it was an established party with mechanisms for deliberative decision-making within the party structure, beginning with the *Pacto de Unidad* or Unity Pact that existed between 2004 and 2006 and after the constituent assembly *the Coordinadora Nacional por el Cambio* (CONALCAM) (Farthing, 2020, pp. 203–204). Though these mechanisms have been characterized as top-down in practice, the nature of having different constituent groups, (like rural and labour unions) not directly dependent on state rents allowed for at least some degree of deliberation over the government's policy agenda. These relationships also helped the government exercise positive power through pre-existing social organizations rather than ones largely created by the government as in Venezuela.

Bolivia's post or anti-capitalist aspirations played a role in shaping the government's discourse and its political project. However, the manifestation of many of these transformative ideas, as in Ecuador and later in Venezuela, turned out to be nearly the opposite, particularly regarding environmental issues. For example, the rural and agricultural development policies of the government often ended up being contradictory with the government's earlier stated goals of 'food sovereignty' as the promotion of 'agro-ecological agriculture' (Cockburn, 2014). The state made larger investments in programmes targeted at smallholder peasants and built partnerships with these organizations and this model of partnership between the MAS government and peasant organizations has been referred to as a model of 'neo-collectivism' based on state collaboration with farmer's organizations but for the most using conventional agricultural techniques (Córdoba & Jansen, 2014). While access to land and productive resources increased under the MAS government, the state took on a central role in promoting conventional agricultural production as mono-cropping or 'agrarian extractivism' in contrast to some of its original proposals for agro-ecological production (McKay, 2017).

Regardless of the criticisms that have been made of the social or environmental impacts of this 'agrarian extractivism', compared to Venezuela, the Bolivian case is positively developmentalist in terms of the capacity of the MAS government to exercise positive power through joint projects both with domestic agribusiness and with smallholder organizations (Córdoba & Jansen, 2014). Compared with the Venezuelan efforts to promote agricultural development through initiatives associated with popular power, the Bolivian model appears to have been relatively successful at promoting coordination between government programmes, domestic agri-business firms and popular rural organizations even if this did not reflect the focus of the government's policies original intent of enhancing food sovereignty through agro-ecological production methods.

The importance of the agricultural sector in relation to hydrocarbons, natural gas in the Bolivian case, is another factor that contributes to the potential enhancement of state capacity with other social sectors. Natural gas in Bolivia remains largely dependent on foreign capital, despite the attempts of the state to increase its participation revenue share (Kohl & Farthing, 2012). While popular organizations that have supported the MAS certainly benefited from the increased spending of the government (derived in great part from increased resource rents) many of these organizations were already established and independent in contrast with popular power in Venezuela. In Bolivia, the lesser importance of rents compared with Venezuela meant that the government had to pay more attention to other sectors and constituencies to foster growth and maintain stability. In Venezuela, the agricultural sector was smaller than in either Bolivia and Ecuador and rural social organization did not have the same density prior to the election of Chávez as these organizations were often created by the state and therefore dependent on transfers from the state derived from oil rents.

Another explanation for the differences between the MAS in Bolivia and the PSUV in Venezuela is the process of political decentralization that took place in Bolivia in 1990s. Studies of these processes have argued that decentralization served in the creation the MAS party by building capacity at the sub-national level (Faguet, 2012; Postero, 2006). However, the crucial difference is that in Bolivia these social movements had a longer history and an independent material base as unions of peasant farmers or unionized workers in the mining or industrial sectors. In Venezuela, most of the movements associated with popular power were created by the state during the Bolivarian Revolution and did not have a material base independent from rentier dynamics (Chiasson-LeBel, 2016). In short, the political base of the MAS did not depend as directly on the state through the direct distribution of resource rents which were channelled through broader public investments like infrastructure, education, health, etc. The 'political settlement' with renegotiated royalties on natural resources as well as with different economic elites proved relatively durable (Díaz-Cuéllar, 2017; Humphreys Bebbington & Huber, 2017) and improvements in state capacity and autonomy have been emphasized in recent studies on Bolivia (Wolff, 2016).

After the high watermark of the conflict with the Santa Cruz elite between 2006 and 2009, the MAS government pursued a pact of non-aggression with some of the main business organizations in Santa Cruz, isolating the most extreme and racist elements in the lowland political autonomy movements (Wolff, 2016). This strategy isolated the more radical interests as the party gained a near hegemony in the political system. Most importantly, it allowed for the exercise negative power in improving the relative autonomy of state institutions while also improving the ability of government agencies to exercise positive power as well. While some have argued that the Morales and Correa governments betrayed their original radical proposals, in both cases the lower levels political polarization allowed these governments to implement their respective 'post-neoliberal' or 'neo-developmental' goals such as investments in infrastructure, rural development programmes and increased public and social investment channelled through processes of building, or rebuilding, state institutions rather than through the creation of alternative institutions as in Venezuela. These bargains allowed for a high-growth economic models in each case that sustained, at least for some time, the political legitimacy of these governments.

The overthrow of the MAS government after the 2019 power suggests that the political settlement with the economic and political opposition to the project of the MAS was perhaps less stable than some suggested. Yet, the opposition to the ousting of Morales and the resounding victory of Luis Arce as the MAS candidate in October 2020 demonstrates the degree of popular political legitimacy of the MAS as a political force in the fabric of Bolivian society. More so, it crystalized alternance within the MAS movement, demonstrating a potential strengthening of democracy more broadly. This is an important contrast with Ecuador, as the shallower roots of AP as a political movement allowed Lenin Moreno to shift to the right with comparatively less opposition, as well as the subsequent triumph of conservative banker Guillermo Lasso over the Correista candidate Andrés Arauz in the 2021 elections.

Ecuador

The rise of Rafael Correa and the *AP political movement* has a different origin from Chavismo in Venezuela and the MAS in Bolivia. This origin story is a factor that helps explain some of the particularities of post-neoliberalism in Ecuador: state autonomy and the capacity of the state to exercise negative power improved in important ways but a lack of embeddedness with different groups in society limited the prospects for neo-developmentalism through the exercise of positive power. In both Venezuela and Bolivia, the turn towards post-neoliberalism occurred in the context of a longer cycle of popular social mobilization with upstart but comparatively more established insurgent political movements and parties. By contrast, Correa emerged as a political outsider without a party in the 2006 elections, creating AP to run for the Presidency with the discourse of a Citizen's Revolution that sought to invest in and strengthen the state. Correa was elected on an anti-neoliberal platform in the context of a political vacuum after a decade of political instability and contentious politics (Silva, 2009) by building on the anti-neoliberal discourse of the social movements of the 1990s and 2000s, led by the *Confederación de Nacionalidades Indígenas del Ecuador* (CONAIE) and other movements (Collins, 2014). At the outset, AP was made up of a mix of social movement leaders, political figures from different left-wing parties, social and environmental movements, and middle-class technocrats (Clark & García, 2019, p. 235).

Early on, AP established short-term alliances with the CONAIE but after the ratification of the 2008 constitution, there was a rift with the CONAIE and some other sectors, especially environmentalists that had initially supported Correa. In contrast to Bolivia, while social movements had some representation and participation in AP through individual leaders, there was no equivalent to the *Pacto de Unidad* that could mediate relations between the government and social organizations in Ecuador (Farthing, 2020, p. 203). However, high approval ratings, and strong support amongst the middle classes, allowed Correa to govern unbeholden to the social movements that had arguably framed the anti-neoliberal discourse in the pursuit of strengthening the state. The government pursued its state building project as a means of 'de-corporatizing' state-society relations, attempting to strengthen the autonomy of the state from private interests, be they business or social movements (Ramírez, 2016). This strategy has been described as 'technocratic populism' (De la Torre, 2013), of 'state building' (Sánchez & Polga-Hecimovich, 2019), a project of 're-incorporation' and turn away from neoliberalism with record public investment and the expansion of social programmes (Silva, 2017).

The Correa government was able to expand the state's role in the economy considerably through higher revenues from renegotiated oil contracts, taking advantage of higher oil prices while exerting increasing control over the industry (Rosales, 2020). The government used tariffs to stimulate import substitution and promote exports in certain sectors like agriculture and natural resources and invested heavily in infrastructure, including an ambitious network of roads and hydroelectric dams to transform the country's energy matrix (Purcell et al., 2017). The goal was to reduce subsidies and promote a transition to a low-carbon energy mix. This was done through foreign financing and increasing oil rents. Much like in the case of Venezuela, the Ecuadorian strategy required foreign investment and loans to finance large projects aimed at inducing domestic economic growth. Ecuador managed to set out industrial policies that sparked growth. Yet, due to the structural condition of a dollarized economy, these policies were dependent on foreign loans and increasing oil rent intake, which questioned their long-term sustainability. In this context, the country did not overcome oil and foreign investor dependence but unlike Venezuela, it kept production afloat even at times of external shocks and succeeded in completing many large-scale infrastructure projects. Ecuador's policies of investment and industrial promotion allowed a departure from the previous neoliberal period and led to record public investment and in particular the construction of public infrastructure and investments in health, education, social services, and the expansion of the public sector in general.

The Correa government took a largely pragmatic approach regarding the domestic business sectors but also demonstrated greater relative autonomy from domestic capital through more effective regulations and higher taxes than previous governments. In short, it demonstrated some ability to discipline capital through the exercise of negative power (Chiasson-LeBel, 2016; Wolff, 2016). The dollarized nature of the Ecuadorian economy meant that the government had no effective monetary policy, exerting constraints on the government's fiscal capacity. Paradoxically, the dollarization of the economy provided the wealthy with some relative security in the face of economic fluctuations. In addition to the state-led growth strategy implemented, the government attempted to stimulate the social economy enterprises as part of its own political model of '*socialismo del buen vivir*' (Vega Ugalde, 2016). In the case of both domestic business capital (Andrade, 2015) and government efforts to induce the expansion of the popular and social economy sector, Ecuador was less successful than Bolivia in exercising the kind of positive power associated with embeddedness due to a lack of effective political settlements as in the Bolivian case. While in agriculture the government's policies did not reflect a widespread focus on 'food sovereignty' as agro-ecological agriculture prevalent in AP's original platform and the 2008 constitution, state re-investment in agriculture, as in Bolivia, was in general a midwife for the expansion of conventional agriculture and the incorporation of smallholders into the value chains of domestic agribusiness firms (Clark, 2017). On this front, the government also appears to have been moderately successful at facilitating partnerships with certain industrial sectors and local organizations but largely failing at exercising positive power with organized social movements, for example with the CONAIE.

In contrast to Venezuela, and to a lesser extent Bolivia, peasant, or urban popular movements, did not participate directly as protagonists through deliberative political mechanisms within the state. On the contrary, the government sought to 'de-corporatize' the state (Ramírez, 2016), reflecting, as Bowen has put it, a dilemma of 'autonomy and accountability' in processes of state building (2015, p. 100). Ecuador had historically weaker state institutions as well as weaker and more fragmented corporatist institutions and political parties than both Bolivia and Venezuela and this allowed Correa more latitude to engage in state building in a quicksilver manner. Both Bolivia and Ecuador had gone further down the road of constructing the kind of more decentralized state due to the adjustment policies in the 1980s and 1990s for example. In this sense, out of the three cases, Ecuador reflects the political 'recentralization' that has been associated with the post-neoliberal turn (Eaton, 2014). There is no doubt that for the neo-development objectives of Citizen's Revolution to be successful, more effective, and autonomous state institutions were a necessary precondition. However, the focus of the government on 'state building' came at the expense of 'governance' (Yu & He, 2011) or what Pablo Andrade and Esteban Nicholls (2017) have similarly described as the gap between the establishment of state 'authority' and 'capacity' in the Correa period. Overall, the state building drive of the government aimed at establishing the autonomy of state institutions generated what has been called a 'bureaucratic centralism' (Fontaine & Fuentes, 2011) that undermined the establishment of informal networks that could have provided state institutions with ' ... sources of intelligence and channels of implementation that enhance the competence of the state' (Evans, 1995, p. 248) undermining the prospects for successful neo-developmentalism.

Conclusions

The success or failure of political ideas, when translated into policies and programmes, is determined, perhaps more than anything else, by state capacity. The enduring value of Evans' concept of embedded autonomy is the methodological point that ' ... state-society ties are inextricably linked to state capacity ... ' (Evans & Heller, 2015, p. 692). It is by studying the specific character of these linkages that we can understand what either undergirds or blocks the construction of state capacity and makes states developmental, intermediate, or predatory. Drawing on this interpretive framework, in this study we argued that Ecuador and Bolivia can be classified as intermediate cases and Venezuela as a predatory state. This underscores the truism that 'politics matters' in development (Leftwich, 2005), something which the burgeoning literature on the importance of 'political settlements' (Di John & Putzel, 2009) in development is once again bringing to the fore in recent theoretical debates on development.

The importance of politics in 'broadening' embedded autonomy was foreshadowed by Evans in the concluding chapter of *Embedded Autonomy*, in which he posited that the theory could 'broadened' out to consider the relationship between the state and other social groups beyond industrialists. Evans highlights the role of political parties, social movements and trade unions as determining factors in cases of broadened embedded autonomy including the cases of social democratic governance in Austria and democratic communist governance Kerala in India (1995, p. 246). The variables we identified in this preliminary comparative analysis are all political in a broad sense, including differences the political party systems prior to the election of the Pink

Tide governments, the strength of various opposition groups, the relative size of natural resource extraction as an overall share in the economy, the relative strength of social organizations and the different legacies of corporatist institutions which traditionally mediated cross-class and other sectoral settlements. What our preliminary comparative analysis suggests, drawing on this interpretive framework, is that the different approaches to the politics of statecraft helps to explain the different outcomes in each case. Future research, building on this framework, in each country could delve more deeply into understanding the role of political parties and the relations between these parties and social movements as well as business and industrial sectors as an explanatory variable in understanding why embedded autonomy emerged between specific state agencies and business/ economic sectors or social movements/ civil society organizations, or why not.

Despite the rhetoric of the three 'radical' Pink Tide governments about revolution, with the partial exception of Venezuela, these governments were for the most part best categorized as reformist. Only Venezuela had the kind of power, political autonomy, and economic resources (based on rents) to bring about any kind of post-capitalist transformation. However, in the end the model of popular power was largely a chimera of political change driven by the rentierism of the 'magical state' (Coronil, 1997) which failed to consolidate a stable and functional alternative political and economic order. As Evans states, the original comparative research out of which the concept of embedded autonomy was theorized was based on studies of ' ... capitalist societies in which neither investment nor production can be implemented without the cooperation of private actors ... Just as in reality markets work only if they are "embedded" in other forms of social relations, it seems likely that states must be "embedded" in order to be effective' (1995, p. 41). In this sense, the opposition of different groups that might have had the capacity to help the Bolivarian government achieve its different development objectives meant that its only option was to attempt to develop this capacity itself through institutions like PDVSA and amongst its core political supporters, strategy which was a monumental challenge and ultimately, largely a failure. In Bolivia and Ecuador by contrast, the focus of the Morales and Correa governments on state building and strengthening, or rebuilding, public services and infrastructure mitigated the social and political polarization of the Venezuelan case and allowed for more pragmatic relations with business sectors as well as a greater level of autonomy of popular and social movements making them less beholden to these governments.

Finally, while the Venezuelan case demonstrates the enormous challenge of developing embedded autonomy and forms of positive power in contexts of extreme political polarization and economic volatility, it also highlights the inverse relationship between the success of developmental states in accomplishing their objectives and their political staying power. Evans made this point in the conclusions of *Embedded Autonomy*, emphasizing that successful developmental states can become their own 'gravediggers', for example as infant industrialists turn against developmental policies, stating that South Korea was ' ... more susceptible to the gravedigger problem than Zaire as a stagnant predator' (Evans, 1995, p. 229). As the Venezuelan case demonstrates, predatory political rule is proving more durable than the source of rents it seeks to plunder as the decaying infrastructure in the oil sector that has led to drops in production and economic stagnation. In contrast, in both Ecuador and Bolivia, the economic growth resulting from the greater relative success of neo-developmental policies appears to have led some voters to shift their political loyalties to vote against Pink Tide incumbents in 2017, 2019 and 2021 elections respectively, perhaps an example of the 'gravedigger' (1995, p. 41) phenomenon posited by Evans. Here more in-depth analysis is necessary to parse the victory of the leftist successor

Luis Arce in the 2020 elections in Bolivia compared with the defeat of leftist successor Andres Arauz in 2021. Future research would be particularly valuable to consider these divergent outcomes, however, our preliminary analysis points to a potential causal link between the relatively more embedded nature of the MAS party in Bolivian society relative to the shallower roots of Citizen's Revolution movement as a factor contributing to the greater relative success of neo-developmentalism in Bolivia than in Ecuador.

Notes

1. In his comparative work on the developmental state, Evans identified South Korea as the case that most conformed to embedded autonomy which describes, on the one hand, a competent Weberian state as 'autonomy' joined with 'embeddedness' as non-clientelist linkages with actors in the private economy and society to enhance and support the development of industries or economic sectors. Evans (1995) developed the argument about developmental states as being characterized by embedded autonomy in relation to another ideal type, a 'predatory state', but argued that most states actual states were 'intermediate' cases between these two ideal types.
2. Infant industry is a nebulous description that includes a range of measures put in place by governments including subsidies to businesses, seed capital or funding for start-ups, protectionist policies like tariffs, public funding for research and development and programmes aimed at building the capacity of businesses. In *Embedded Autonomy*, Evans (1995, p. 13) describes two traditional roles that states play, referring to the legal and norm and demiurge roles that governments play in the development of economic activities or sectors: 'midwifery', which involves governments actions to fund start-ups or encourage the creation of new economic sectors or activities and 'husbandry' which involves supporting existing firms and industries at different points in the growth and expansion process. We recognize the gendered implications of these terms and we employ them without necessarily giving credence to the one-dimensional male-female partnership that they imply.

Disclosure statement

No potential conflict of interest was reported by the author(s).

ORCID

Patrick Clark http://orcid.org/0000-0002-6556-913X

References

Andrade, P. (2015). *Politica de industrialización selectiva y nuevo modelo de desarrollo*. Corporación Editorial Nacional/Universidad Andina Simón Bolívar.

Andrade, P., & Nicholls, E. (2017). La relación entre capacidad y autoridad en el estado: La construcción de un estado 'excepcionalista' en Ecuador. *Revista Europea de Estudios Latinoamericanos y del Caribe, 103*(103), 1–24. https://doi.org/10.18352/erlacs.10154

Anria, S. (2013). Social movements, party organization, and populism: Insights from the Bolivian MAS. *Latin American Politics and Society, 55*(3), 19–46. https://doi.org/10.1111/j.1548-2456.2013.00201.x

Antunes de Oliveira, F. (2019). The rise of the Latin American far-right explained: Dependency theory meets uneven and combined development. *Globalizations, 16*(7), 1145–1164. https://doi.org/10.1080/14747731.2019.1567977

Bowen, J. D. (2015). Rethinking democratic governance: State-building, autonomy, and accountability in Correa's Ecuador. *Journal of Politics in Latin America*, 7(1), 83–110. https://doi.org/10.1177/1866802X1500700103

Bull, B., & Rosales, A. (2020). Into the shadows: Sanctions, rentierism, and economic informalization in Venezuela. *European Review of Latin American and Caribbean Studies*, 109(109), 107–133. https://doi.org/10.32992/erlacs.10556

Buxton, J. (2020). Continuity and change in Venezuela's Bolivarian revolution. *Third World Quarterly*, 41(8), 1371–1387. https://doi.org/10.1080/01436597.2019.1653179

Caldentey, E. (2009). The concept and evolution of the developmental state. *International Journal of Political Economy*, 37(3), 27–53. https://doi.org/10.2753/IJP0891-1916370302

Cardoso, F. H., & Faletto, E. (1979). *Dependency and development in Latin America*. University of California Press.

Chiasson-LeBel, T. (2016). Neo-extractivism in Venezuela and Ecuador: A weapon of class conflict. *The Extractive Industries and Society*, 3(4), 888–901. https://doi.org/10.1016/j.exis.2016.10.006

Clark, P. (2017). Neo-Developmentalism and a 'Vía campesina' for rural development: Un-reconciled projects in Ecuador's Citizen's revolution. *Journal of Agrarian Change*, 17(2), 348–364. https://doi.org/10.1111/joac.12203

Clark, P., & García, J. (2019). Left populism, state building, class compromise and social conflict in Ecuador's Citizen's revolution. *Latin American Perspectives*, 46(1), 230–246. https://doi.org/10.1177/0094582X18807723

Cockburn, J. (2014). Bolivia's food sovereignty & agrobiodiversity: Undermining the local to strengthen the state? *Theory in Action*, 7(4), 67–89. https://doi.org/10.3798/tia.1937-0237.14028

Collier, R. B., & Collier, D. (1991). *Shaping the political arena: Critical junctures, the labor movement, and regime dynamics in Latin America*. Princeton University Press.

Collins, J. (2014). New left experiences in Bolivia and Ecuador and the challenge to theories of populism. *Journal of Latin American Studies*, 46(1), 59–86. https://doi.org/10.1017/S0022216X13001569

Córdoba, D., & Jansen, K. (2014). The return of the state: Neocollectivism, Agrarian politics and images of technological progress in the MAS era in Bolivia. *Journal of Agrarian Change*, 14(4), 480–500. https://doi.org/10.1111/joac.12036

Coronil, F. (1997). *The magical state: Nature, money, and modernity in Venezuela*. University of Chicago Press.

Crouch, C. (2005). Models of capitalism. *New Political Economy*, 10(4), 439–456. https://doi.org/10.1080/13563460500344336

De la Torre, C. (2013). El tecnopopulismo de Rafael Correa: ¿Es compatible el carisma con la tecnocracia? *Latin American Research Review*, 48(1), 24–43. https://doi.org/10.1353/lar.2013.0007

Díaz-Cuéllar, V. (2017). The political economy of mining in Bolivia during the government of the Movement Towards Socialism (2006-2015). *The Extractive Industries and Society*, 4(1), 120–130. https://doi.org/10.1016/j.exis.2016.12.011

Di John, J., & Putzel, J. (2009). *Political settlements: Issues paper*. Governance and Social Development Resource Centre, University of Birmingham.

Eaton, K. (2014). Recentralization and the left turn in Latin America: Diverging outcomes in Bolivia, Ecuador, and Venezuela. *Comparative Political Studies*, 47(8), 1130–1157. https://doi.org/10.1177/0010414013488562

Escobar, A. (2010). Latin America at a crossroads: Alternative modernizations, post-liberalism, or post-development? *Cultural Studies*, 24(1), 1–65. https://doi.org/10.1080/09502380903424208

Evans, P. (1979). *Dependent development: The alliance of multinational, state and local capital in Brazil*. Princeton University Press.

Evans, P. (1995). *Embedded autonomy: States and industrial transformation*. Princeton University Press.

Evans, P. (2010). Constructing the 21st century developmental state: Potentialities and pitfalls. In O. Edigheji (Ed.), *Constructing a democratic developmental state in South Africa potentials and challenges* (pp. 37–58). HSRC Press.

Evans, P. B., & Heller, P. (2015). Human development, state transformation and the politics of the developmental state. In S. Leibfried, E. Huber, M. Lange, J. D. Levy, F. Nullmeier, & J. D. Stephens (Eds.), *The Oxford handbook of transformations of the state* (pp. 691–713). Oxford University Press.

Faguet, J. P. (2012). *Decentralization and popular democracy: Governance from below in Bolivia*. University of Michigan Press.

Farthing, L. (2020). An opportunity squandered? Elites, social movements, and the Bolivian government of Evo morales. In S. Ellner (Ed.), *Latin America's Pink Tide: Breakthroughs and shortcomings* (pp. 193–216). Rowman and Littlefield.

Felicien, A., Schiavoni, C. M., Ochoa, E., Saturno, S., Omaña, E., Requena, A., & Camacaro, W. (2020). Exploring the 'grey areas' of state-society interaction in food sovereignty construction: The battle for Venezuela's seed law. *The Journal of Peasant Studies*, *47*(4), 648–673. https://doi.org/10.1080/03066150.2018.1525363

Fernandes, S. (2010). *Who can stop the drums? Urban social movements in Chávez's Venezuela*. Duke University Press.

Fontaine, G., & Fuentes, J. L. (2011). Transición hacia el centralismo burocrático. In *Estado Informe Cero 1950–2010 del país* (pp. 247–262).

Frank, A. G. (1969). *Capitalism and underdevelopment in Latin America*. Monthly Review Press.

Grugel, J., & Riggirozzi, P. R. (2012). Post-neoliberalism in Latin America: Rebuilding and reclaiming the state after crisis. *Development and Change*, *43*(1), 1–21. https://doi.org/10.1111/j.1467-7660.2011.01746.x

Haslam, P., & Heidrich, P. (2016). *The political economy of natural resources and development: From neoliberalism to resource nationalism*. Routledge.

Helleiner, E. (2021). *The Neomercantilists: A global intellectual history*. Cornell University Press.

Hochstetler, K. (2021). *Political economies of energy transition: Wind and solar power in Brazil and South Africa*. Cambridge University Press.

Hochstetler, K., & Keck, M. (2007). *Greening Brazil: Environmental activism in state and society*. Duke University Press.

Humphreys Bebbington, D., & Huber, C. (2017). *Political settlements, natural resource extraction, and inclusion in Bolivia* (Effective States and Inclusive Development Program Working Paper 77). Global Development Institute, University of Manchester.

Jiménez, M. (2021). Contesting autocracy: Repression and opposition coordination in Venezuela. *Political Studies*. doi:10.1177/0032321721999975

Johnson, C. (1982). *MITI and the Japanese miracle: The growth of industrial policy: 1925–1975*. Stanford University Press.

Karl, T. L. (1997). *The paradox of plenty: Oil booms and petro-states*. University of California Press.

Kohl, B., & Farthing, L. (2012). Material constraints to popular imaginaries: The extractive economy and resource nationalism in Bolivia. *Political Geography*, *31*(4), 225–235. https://doi.org/10.1016/j.polgeo.2012.03.002

Kröger, M. (2011). Promotion of contentious agency as a rewarding strategy: Evidence from the MST-paper industry conflicts in Brazil. *Journal of Peasant Studies*, *38*(2), 435–458. https://doi.org/10.1080/03066150.2011.559016

Kurtz, M. J. (2009). The social foundations of institutional order: Reconsidering war and the "resource curse" in third world state building. *Politics & Society*, *37*(4), 479–520. https://doi.org/10.1177/0032329209349223

Larrabure, M. (2018). Post-capitalist development in Latin America's left turn: Beyond peronism and the magical state. *New Political Economy*, *24*(5), 587–604. https://doi.org/10.1080/13563467.2018.1472564

Larrabure, M., Levy, C., Cameron, M. A., Foweraker, J., Lavinas, L., & Spronk, S. J. (2021). Roundtable: The Latin American state, Pink Tide, and future challenges. *Globalizations*. https://doi.org/10.1080/14747731.2021.1925813

Leftwich, A. (2005). Politics in command: Development studies and the rediscovery of social science. *New Political Economy*, *10*(4), 573–607. https://doi.org/10.1080/13563460500344542

Levitsky, S., & Roberts, K. M. (Eds.). (2011). *The resurgence of the Latin American left*. Johns Hopkins University Press.

López Maya, M. (2003). Movilización, institucionalidad y legitimidad en Venezuela. *Revista Venezolana de Economía y Ciencias Sociales*, 9(1), 211–226.

Macdonald, L., & Ruckert, A. (Eds.). (2009). *Post-neoliberalism in the Americas*. Palgrave Macmillan Press.

Massi, E., & Singh, J. N. (2018). Industrial policy and state-making: Brazil's attempt at oil-based industrial development. *Third World Quarterly*, 39(6), 1133–1150. https://doi.org/10.1080/01436597.2018.1455144

McKay, B. (2018). The politics of convergence in Bolivia: Social movements and the state. *Third World Quarterly*, 39(7), 1247–1269. https://doi.org/10.1080/01436597.2017.1399056

McKay, B. M. (2017). Agrarian extractivism in Bolivia. *World Development*, 97, 199–211. https://doi.org/10.1016/j.worlddev.2017.04.007

Mezzadra, S., & Neilson, B. (2017). On the multiple frontiers of extraction: Excavating contemporary capitalism. *Cultural Studies*, 31(2–3), 185–204. https://doi.org/10.1080/09502386.2017.1303425

Mijares, V. (2017). Soft balancing the titans: Venezuelan foreign-policy strategy toward the United States, China, and Russia. *Latin American Policy*, 8(2), 201–231. https://doi.org/10.1111/lamp.12128

Negoita, M., & Block, F. (2012). Networks and public policies in the global south: The Chilean case and the future of the developmental network state. *Studies in Comparative International Development*, 47(1), 1–22. https://doi.org/10.1007/s12116-012-9097-4

North, L., & Grinspun, R. (2016). Neo-extractivism and the new Latin American developmentalism: The missing piece of rural transformation. *Third World Quarterly*, 37(8), 1483–1504. https://doi.org/10.1080/01436597.2016.1159508

Perreault, T., & Valdivia, G. (2010). Hydrocarbons, popular protest and national imaginaries: Ecuador and Bolivia in comparative context. *Geoforum*, 41(5), 689–699. https://doi.org/10.1016/j.geoforum.2010.04.004

Postero, N. (2006). *Now we are citizens: Indigenous politics in post-multicultural Bolivia*. Stanford University Press.

Prebisch, R. (1950). *The economic development of Latin America and its principal problems*. United Nations.

Purcell, T. F. (2017). The political economy of rentier capitalism and the limits to agrarian transformation in Venezuela. *Journal of Agrarian Change*, 17(2), 296–312. https://doi.org/10.1111/joac.12204

Purcell, T., Fernandez, N., & Martínez, E. (2017). Rents, knowledge and neo-structuralism: Transforming the productive matrix in Ecuador. *Third World Quarterly*, 38(4), 918–938. https://doi.org/10.1080/01436597.2016.1166942

Ramírez, F. (2016). Political change, state autonomy, and post-neoliberalism in Ecuador, 2007–2012. *Latin American Perspectives*, 43(1), 143–157. https://doi.org/10.1177/0094582X15586563

Rich, J. (2020). Organizing twenty-first-century activism: From structure to strategy in Latin American social movements. *Latin American Research Review*, 55(3), 430–444. https://doi.org/10.25222/larr.452

Riggirozzi, P. (2020). Social policy, inequalities and the battle of rights in Latin America. *Development and Change*, 51(2), 506–522. https://doi.org/10.1111/dech.12571

Rosales, A. (2018). China and the decaying of socialist rentierism in Venezuela: Instability and the prevalence of non-interventionism. *Third World Thematics: A TWQ Journal*, 3(4), 552–568. https://doi.org/10.1080/23802014.2018.1496797

Rosales, A. (2020). Structural constraints in times of resource nationalism: Oil policy and state capacity in post-neoliberal Ecuador. *Globalizations*, 17(1), 77–92. https://doi.org/10.1080/14747731.2019.1614722

Ross, M. L. (2015). What have we learned about the resource curse? *Annual Review of Political Science*, 18, 239–259. https://doi.org/10.1146/annurev-polisci-052213-040359

Ruggie, J. G. (1982). International regimes, transactions, and change: Embedded liberalism in the postwar economic order. *International Regimes*, 36(2), 379–415. doi:10.1017/S0020818300018993

Saad-Filho, A. (2020). Varieties of neoliberalism in Brazil (2003–2019). *Latin American Perspectives*, 47(1), 9–27. https://doi.org/10.1177/0094582X19881968

Sánchez, F., & Polga-Hecimovich, J. (2019). The tools of institutional change under post-neoliberalism: Rafael Correa's Ecuador. *Journal of Latin American Studies*, 51(2), 379–408. https://doi.org/10.1017/S0022216X1800072X

Sánchez-Ancochea, D. (2009). State, firms and the process of industrial upgrading: Latin America's variety of capitalism and the Costa Rican experience. *Economy and Society*, 38(1), 62–86. https://doi.org/10.1080/03085140802560520

Sánchez-Ancochea, D. (2021). The surprising reduction of inequality during a commodity boom: What do we learn from Latin America? *Journal of Economic Policy Reform*, *24*(2), 95–118. https://doi.org/10.1080/17487870.2019.1628757

Silva, E. (2009). *Challenging neoliberalism in Latin America*. Cambridge University Press.

Silva, E. (2017). Reorganizing popular sector incorporation: Propositions from Bolivia, Ecuador, and Venezuela. *Politics & Society*, *45*(1), 91–122. https://doi.org/10.1177/0032329216683166

Spanakos, A. P. (2011). Citizen Chávez: The state, social movements, and publics. *Latin American Perspectives*, *38*(1), 14–27. https://doi.org/10.1177/0094582X10384206

Swedberg, R. (2018). How to use Max Weber's ideal type in sociological analysis. *Journal of Classical Sociology*, *18*(3), 181–196. https://doi.org/10.1177/1468795X17743643

Tarlau, R. (2013). Coproducing rural public schools in Brazil: Contestation, clientelism, and the landless workers' movement. *Politics & Society*, *41*(3), 395–424. https://doi.org/10.1177/0032329213493753

Urbaneja, D. (2013). *La renta y el reclamo: Ensayo sobre petróleo y economía política en Venezuela*. Alfa.

Vaillancourt, Y. (2009). Social economy in the co-construction of public policy. *Annals of Public and Cooperative Economics*, *80*(2), 275–313. https://doi.org/10.1111/j.1467-8292.2009.00387.x

Vega Ugalde, S. (2016). La política de economía popular y solidaria en Ecuador. Una visión de su gubernamentalidad. *Otra Economía*, *10*(18), 77–90. https://doi.org/10.4013/otra.2016.1018.07

Velasco, A. (2015). *Barrio rising: Urban popular politics and the making of modern Venezuela*. University of California Press.

Veltmeyer, H. (2013). The political economy of natural resource extraction: A new model or extractive imperialism?. *Canadian Journal of Development Studies/Revue canadienne d'études du développement*, *34*(1), 79–95. https://doi.org/10.1080/02255189.2013.764850

Vergara-Camus, L., & Kay, C. (2017). Agribusiness, peasants, left-wing governments, and the state in Latin America: An overview and theoretical reflections. *Journal of Agrarian Change*, *17*(2), 239–257. https://doi.org/10.1111/joac.12215

Virgüez, M. D. M. C., & Mijares, V. M. (2020). Cómo fallan los Petroestados: Análisis del caso Venezuela. *Cuadernos del Cendes*, *37*(103), 35–62.

Wang, X. (1999). Mutual empowerment of state and society: Its nature, conditions, mechanisms and limits. *Comparative Politics*, *31*(2), 231–249. https://doi.org/10.2307/422146

Wolff, J. (2016). Business power and the politics of postneoliberalism: Relations between governments and economic elites in Bolivia and Ecuador. *Latin American Politics and Society*, *58*(2), 124–147. https://doi.org/10.1111/j.1548-2456.2016.00313.x

Woo-Cumings, M. (Ed.). (1999). *The developmental state*. Cornell University Press.

Yaffe, H. (2015). Venezuela: Building a socialist communal economy? *International Critical Thought*, *5*(1), 23–41. https://doi.org/10.1080/21598282.2014.996178

Yu, J., & He, Z. (2011). The tension between governance and state-building. *Journal of Chinese Political Science*, *16*(1), 1–17. https://doi.org/10.1007/s11366-010-9127-x

What are they doing *right*? Tweeting right-wing intersectionality in Latin America

Paulo Ravecca [ID], Marcela Schenck [ID], Bruno Fonseca [ID] and Diego Forteza [ID]

ABSTRACT
Despite the contributions of intersectional approaches, the academic and political left is challenged by competing interests in class, gender, race, and other axes of inequality and power. The disconnect between research on political economy, on the one hand, and on culture and subjectivity, on the other, is stark in Latin American studies. In contrast, an emerging feature of the global radical right is the gathering of these dimensions in simultaneous attacks to different strands of progressive politics and scholarship. The enemy is defined in economic *and* cultural terms: thus, feminism is frequently referred to as an extension of communism while Marxism is understood as part of cultural conspiracies to destroy healthy families and normal lifestyles. We call this phenomenon right-wing intersectionality (RWI). Through a mixed-methods approach, the article explores how RWI manifests in 20 leading influencers, activists, and politicians. The research included the systematic content analysis of 30,858 tweets.

Introduction: analysing the Latin American far-right beyond indignation

This article builds on our curiosity around the capacity of the Latin American far-right to persuade and inspire. In a political context where conservatives seem to be reclaiming the public debate with significant gains, we focus on one specific and important feature of their most extreme wing: the simultaneous attack on the left, feminism, and the social diversity agenda. We argue that such an attack both mirrors and reverses 'intersectionality' and thus call this political narrative right-wing intersectionality (RWI).[1]

Intersectionality (Crenshaw, 1989; Viveros Vigoya, 2016) is a social science approach that entails the acknowledgment and exploration of the multidimensional character of power and the connections between race, class, gender and other axes of social positioning and inequality.[2] As such, it has complexified the critical analysis of society and politics. Studies on intersectionality have also had an intimate relationship with progressive activisms, and they are not shy about their normative dimensions.[3]

What we call RWI *mirrors* intersectionality because it mobilizes and talks about 'intersections' between cultural, economic and social issues. However, it also *reverses* intersectionality normatively by embodying a conservative form of activism that defends racial, gendered and class hierarchies and attacks the different theories and movements that challenge them. In other words, the intersectional political agenda of the Latin American far-right is radically opposed to the one associated with scholars and activists of intersectionality as we know it.

The narrative under analysis combines the current conservative angst around feminism (Dragiewicz, 2008; Faludi, 1991; Segato, 2018; Van Wormer, 2008) with cold-war style of anticommunist rhetoric (Ravecca, 2015; Scirica, 2014).[4] Its main targets are the left, feminism, the LGBTQ movement and the gains they have achieved in the last years, particularly in the context of the so-called pink tide (i.e. the series of progressive governments that led the region at the outset of the twenty-first century).[5] Through RWI's lenses all forms of progressive politics are considered as a transnationally organized *and unified* enemy that undermines the very fabric of 'Western Civilization'.

Our study on RWI expands and complexifies the analysis of the Latin American right and the elites (Chiasson-LeBel, 2019; North & Clark, 2018; Eaton, 2014; Luna & Rovira Kaltwasser, 2014). This is because, first, we focus our attention on the ideational dimension of politics, particularly the ideological innovations within the regional far-right; and second, because this narrative is usually practiced by nonmainstream political actors such as evangelical pastors, Catholic opinion leaders as well as young social media influencers. These radical voices sometimes collaborate with the conservative establishment in its fight against the left, but sometimes challenge the former for being too moderate and soft. In any case it is important to keep in mind that RWI is about electoral politics as much as it is about culture.[6]

One of the most salient features of RWI is that it is expressed both in religious and secular languages. The use of scientific jargon against feminism makes the attack palatable for broader audiences. This is an important feature of how 'intersections' (in this case between religion and science) are mobilized by the far-right. Movements such as *Con mis hijos no te metas*[7] in Perú or *Escola sem Partido*[8] in Brazil are at the forefront of this battle and have successfully entered the institutional arena, affecting public policy and legislation. This public legitimization of RWI's extreme views has been facilitated by social media.[9] For example, WhatsApp and Twitter have been instrumental for its dissemination in Latin America. Indeed, some features of these platforms are particularly welcoming to the extreme perspectives of RWI.

This article begins by further conceptualizing RWI, then we situate it within right-wing politics in Latin America and expand on the centrality of the notion of gender ideology in its script. Finally, we present our findings. The study shows how the far-right uses RWI to influence public debates, leverage political power, and impact public opinion. We also explore how RWI is used to create new political identities that resonate with (widening) publics, and how this is done through Twitter.

The empirical analysis employs a mixed-methods approach. The study's sample includes 30,858 tweets by 20 leading activists and politicians from Argentina, Brazil, Chile, Colombia, Costa Rica, Dominican Republic, Ecuador, Mexico, Paraguay, Perú, and Uruguay. We show the intersectional character of RWI by identifying the presence of, and correlation between, theoretically significant terms as well as the emotions attached to them. The exploration was conducted for each one of the individuals, but we also offer an aggregated analysis of the whole sample.

The evidence validates our argument and clearly illustrates how far-right actors tackle economic, cultural, *and* social issues while attacking the left and feminism simultaneously (i.e. RWI). To further specify the findings and deepen the analysis in qualitative terms, we focus on the discourse of three activists. Furthermore, throughout we interpretatively (Carver, 2020; Geertz, 1997; Ravecca, 2019) engage with tweets that exemplify RWI. We conclude that RWI is both theoretically and politically significant and suggest that, in order to make sense of the emerging far-right movement in Latin America, we need to put indignation aside for a moment, and engage its ideological innovations.

An effective conservative narrative maneuver: right-wing intersectionality (RWI)

Scholarship on intersectionality has become extensive, nuanced, and in fact it has produced an entire subfield within the social sciences (Crenshaw, 1989; Mügge et al., 2018; Nash, 2017; Phoenix & Pattynama, 2006). The term refers to 'the relationships among multiple dimensions and modalities of social relations and subject formations' (McCall, 2005, p. 1771). Thus, the intersectional perspective involves the acknowledgment and exploration of the multidimensionality of power and of the interconnections between race, class, gender, and other axes of social positioning and inequality. The approach opened up key notions of the social sciences such as power and oppression, expanding the very conception of politics beyond any narrow or one-dimensional container (be it the economy or formal institutions). For this reason, it has been perceived as an important intervention in the politics of knowledge production.

Debates about intersectionality revolve around the separability or inseparability between the social dimensions that are analytically 'intersected' (Gunnarsson, 2017); the appropriate methodological strategies for analysis (McCall, 2005); the multiple geographies of the approach's genealogy (Viveros Vigoya, 2016) and the role in it of black feminisms, women of colour feminisms and Latin American feminisms (Gonzalez, 1988; Lugones, 2008; Viveros Vigoya, 2015; 2016); the relationship between scholarship and social movements (Viveros Vigoya, 2016); as well as the potential neoliberal co-option and use of intersectionality as a tool for diversity management (Puar, 2007). Our intention is *not* to participate in the debates *about* the approach. Instead, this article aims to deploy the category of intersectionality in a novel way. Concretely, we want to highlight a conservative narrative that actively intersects different axes of social positioning in – for many people – inspiring ways. We recognize that naming part of the right as intersectional might be shocking and yet we consider that our project honours the spirit of the approach, that is, the critical dismantling of power relations and dynamics of oppression.

Intersections can be mobilized in different ways.[10] The intersectional nature of RWI lies in that the opponents and the issues at stake take an *inter*-sectional form. In its narrative there is a straightforward connection between economic and non-distributive issues. Thus, the defence of private property, the resistance against redistributive policies, the promotion of the traditional family, and the assertion of the 'natural' difference between men and women, to name a few typical themes, become part of a unified political agenda. RWI conceives social hierarchies as the moral anchor of society and defends them by attacking the theories and movements that challenge them.

RWI practices an us-versus-them kind of politics. The 'us' gathers liberal and Christian attributes and sensibilities. The enemy is a mixture of Marxism, feminism, and other 'radical' views. Under the eye of RWI, socialists, antiracists, and feminists fabricate objects to critique (patriarchy), exaggerate problems (racism) and assault natural/fair structures (*the* family, capitalism). In the process they collectively undermine the fundamentals of a well-ordered society (biological differences, the market economy, law and order, etc.). While the 'us' is depicted as a freedom fighter, the 'them' is constructed as totalitarian. In this simple narrative there is so much at stake in the fight that defeat is not an option, and the right-wing outrage becomes more and more intense.[11]

The intersectional narrative of RWI also moves along the spectrum between separability and inseparability: Marxism and feminism are sometimes described by right-wing activists as natural allies, implying that they are thought of as two separate entities. But other times RWI assumes a more mobile form of intersectionality in which socialism and feminism become the same and fluid political chameleonic 'thing'. In this context, temporality matters and becomes political: Feminism is at times denounced as the new Marxism or as the way socialism has been resuscitated, following the collapse of the Soviet Union.[12] Some right-wing intellectuals have put these insights very explicitly in writing (without calling them RWI obviously); salient examples are Aguayo and Rosas (2019) as well as Márquez and Laje (2017). We find it interesting that whereas progressives are still dealing with the tensions between the traditional left and emerging political agendas (Ravecca & Upadhyay, 2013), some right-wing movements, leaders and thinkers seem to have overcome such a divide.

RWI in the context of the Latin American right

The progressive governments of the 2000s not only failed to meet the expectations of their supporters but also generated widespread frustration – though for different reasons, obviously – on both sides of the ideological spectrum (Abbot & Levitsky, 2020; Dabène, 2020). The right has been able to protect its interests in the region (North & Clark, 2018). Furthermore, during the pink tide the right went through learning processes (Chiasson-LeBel, 2019). Luna and Rovira Kaltwasser (2014) offer a general examination of the Latin American right and focus on three forms of political engagement: interest representation through nonelectoral channels, electoral politics through nonpartisan electoral vehicles, and party building.

In the same volume Eaton (2014) focuses on the first type, analysing strategies that target state institutions, strategies that focus on civil society, and strategies that emphasize identity formation. According to the author, in recent years the right has incorporated forms of political action typical of the left, for example, backing social movements, partaking in protests, and facilitating other forms of direct action. In his view, it is the likelihood of losing the battle along class lines that sustains the right's efforts 'to shift the terms of struggle toward territorial and sectoral identities, political frames that give it a much better chance of success against the left' (Eaton, 2014, p. 77). In this analysis, class seems to be the 'real' or main terrain for conflict.

We want to offer an alternative view. We agree that 'the right has innovated in its search for effective strategies in an era of left dominance' (p. 77) and, in fact, this is the context within which we situate the emergence of RWI. However, in our perspective ideology, public narratives, as well as the different axes of power (race, gender, morality, and so on) need to be taken seriously if our aim is to understand right-wing politics in their fullness. For these purposes, we situate RWI in the landscape of the right's effort to affect the terrain of culture and produce hegemony (Gramsci, 2008; Laclau & Mouffe, 2004). RWI is a salient way in which the right crafts political identities. Furthermore, this is not at all disconnected from electoral strategies and public policy outcomes.

We also disagree with Luna and Rovira Kaltwasser (2014, p. 369) in that the 'old battle line of secular versus religious' is 'less relevant' today. Such a battle has experienced changes but is at the centre of the current Latin American political *milieu*. In fact, one of the pathways towards empowerment for the right has been a Christian conservative reaction (Kourliandsky, 2019; Vaggione & Campos Machado, 2020) which, in Brazil for instance, combines the attacks against the Workers Party with anti-feminist backlash.[13] Religion is in fact a key component of RWI. However, religious fundamentalism has two other rather unexpected companions: science and liberalism. RWI's rhetoric combines the engulfing power of religious illumination with the concreteness of positivist science. Appeals to liberalism are weaponized and jammed into the defence of conservative values. In this way, RWI cunningly gathers a coalition of diverse voices and is strategically silent about the frictions between them.

RWI organizes the political terrain through simple associations that remove any sense of complexity from the picture. The political landscape gets divided between 'us' (i.e. healthy families, decent and hard-working people, straight and religious individuals, gender-conforming men and women who respect nature) and 'them' (i.e. radical feminists, subversive leftists, atheists, and LGBTQ people). The latter are narrated as esoteric, complicated, crazy, immoral, and dangerous. RWI's articulations of the natural, normal, and desirable serve to pathologize and vilify. The stark division between friends and foes is done in emotionally charged ways and sometimes invokes conspiracy theories.

RWI defends inequality and oppression by claiming that they do not exist and that the social justice activists are the ones breaking the harmony of a functioning system. To do this political work, RWI mobilizes the prejudices provided by the hierarchies it protects, thus feminists are portrayed as hysterical and foolish, union members are described as lazy and parasitic, while gays and lesbians are depicted as a dangerous influence for kids, and so on. These groups are not perceived as just 'broken' people, but also as highly toxic, as they undermine the very fundamentals of manhood, womanhood, and decency. They are corrupt and, what is much worse, they have the ability to corrupt policies, bodies, and souls.

RWI incarnates a patriarchal, macho way of engaging in political and intellectual debate. As we will show in detail later, its activists punch-with-words and galvanize troubling aspects of the human condition such as the inclination to humiliate and degrade as well as the pleasure of dominating and being above the other. There are, for example, countless online posts, published mostly by young activists, that describe a conservative influencer 'owning', 'destroying', 'humiliating', and 'defeating' a leftist or a feminist. The terms are brutal, war-like, and often sexualized.

At the same time, RWI's activists dispute notions of guilt, victimhood, and innocence. They claim that their opponents weaponize their self-identification as victims to harm society. In an effective narrative maneuver, feminists and leftists turn into perpetrators deserving punishment: the dissolute woman who kills the baby in her womb without remorse, the minorities that take advantage of the state, the gays who are actually child molesters, the lazy rabble that enjoy a good life on the backs of hard-working citizens.

RWI, gender ideology, and freedom

The best-seller *El libro negro de la nueva izquierda. Ideología de género o subversión cultural* (*The Black Book of the New Left. Gender Ideology or Cultural Subversion*) by Agustín Laje and Nicolás Márquez has become a sort of far-right manifesto in Latin America and Spain. Its authors are praised and followed by other activists who, in countless seminars and interviews, introduce them as 'the terror' of feminists and leftists.

The book's scholarship is rather poor, and yet, it is a remarkable political artefact (Goldentul & Saferstein, 2020), so its prominence within right-wing politics in the region is not surprising.[14] Through a mélange of liberalism and conservatism as well as of religious and scientific references, the text simultaneously attacks feminism, socialism as well as entire groups, in particular LGBTQ people. Because of its clear-cut conservative intersectionality, from our point of view it epitomizes RWI. Note that, already from its title, the book equates gender ideology to cultural subversion. Thus, a notion widely employed by the murderous Latin American dictatorships of the 1970s and 1980s to name and degrade leftists (subversion) is now 'updated' in the fight against feminists. The book in this way gathers different issues and times in a unified right-wing narrative.

This book is not alone in its take on gender ideology, which has become topical within the Latin American right. The Vatican was of course a pioneer in distorting the expression 'gender ideology' to use it against the feminist movement and theory.[15] The (re-signified) term became popularized in the context of the conservative discontents around the rise of the so-called agenda of new rights (i.e. abortion, same sex marriage and adoption, and transgender rights).[16] According to the proponents of the concept, feminism brings ideology where it should not be – the private space and the family. The notion of gender ideology also serves the purpose of discrediting feminist scholarship. The naturalness of the sexual difference, of the traditional family and even of heterosexuality are defended against the bulk of academic research that proves gender identity to heavily rely on cultural dynamics (Corredor, 2019). Such reaction sometimes meshes with a generic attack on the humanities and the social sciences, both of which are frequently said to fail the positivist test of scientific objectivity and are thus rendered useless and (precisely) 'ideological'.

This rhetoric directly links gender ideology to 'cultural Marxism' and claims that both are pervasive in universities and public education in general.[17] One of the main and seemingly universal conservative anxieties is that radical views are supposedly being imposed on students of all ages, so teachers and teaching are thought of as central in the ideological battle. The figure of Antonio Gramsci and his concept of hegemony are frequently referenced to show how the left has consciously penetrated academia and popular culture.

Key, from our perspective on RWI, is that far-right activists from across Latin America consistently claim that gender ideology (feminism) and class struggle (Marxism) are intertwined evils (or even the same evil) that distort(s) reality and endanger(s) society (see empirical analysis below). The conceptual conflation between feminism and Marxism makes the latter immanently queer while any form of feminism becomes socialist. In short, the agenda of cultural reform is said to have been coopted by 'sexualized communism' (Márquez & Laje, 2017, p. 169) where class struggle mingles with a 'liberticidal pansexualism' (2017, p. 185). Feminism and Marxism become dangerous even regarding issues or areas they do not tackle or which they traditionally had quarrels about.

RWI portrays feminism as the new totalitarianism (Corredor, 2019). In fact, its activists argue that we are on the verge of a gender dictatorship that resembles the Marxist dictatorship of the proletariat (see, for example, pages 109 and 152 of *The Black Book of the New Left*). The use of the term dictatorship is significant, especially in Latin America where there is a recent history of democracy breakdowns, state terrorism and massive human rights violations. Interestingly, the main representatives of RWI often deny these violations. Feminism is also associated with extremism and Nazism and in fact feminists are frequently called feminazis. Obviously in this context feminism is perceived as more violent than *machismo*.

While good, decent women reject gender ideology, feminists do *everything* wrong. By protesting sexist events, they violate the liberal right to freedom of speech. By promoting abortion rights, they violate the sacred right to live. By asking for gender sensitive public policy, they become a heavy burden for taxpayers. They are portrayed as very cunning and dangerous, yet at the same time they are also stupid and the perfect target of mockery. The narrative inconsistencies are not necessarily a sign of weakness as RWI gathers all critics and criticisms of feminism and affect the terms of the conversation. In this way extreme (and on occasion frankly bizarre) views become more and more popular in Latin America.

Through attack and rejection RWI implicitly recognizes the disruptive egalitarian nature of feminism. The right is worried about feminism because it questions one of the main power structures that regulates our collective lives: patriarchy. But there is much more to this than what is seen at first sight. Besides the depth and complexity of patriarchy itself (Segato, 2018), the robust scholarship on intersectionality and other forms of critical theory have shown that domination is an integrated process. This means that power is not divided into the disciplines in which academics are trained. And, given that political economy, culture, and subjectivity are not separated, once we start denaturalizing hierarchy, we cannot predict where such process will end. Questioning hierarchy at one level might slip into other levels or realms. The implication of this is that *any* form of activism that questions oppression is potentially radical in the very sense of Marx – i.e. going to the root of the issues. In their own – proto-fascistic – way, RWI activists and politicians understand this very well. It therefore makes sense that if questioning subordinations is a democratic gesture, RWI attempts to remove gender, class, and race from democratic contestation.

Given its heavy investments in inequality, RWI has a complicated relationship with democracy itself. Indeed, when the far-right 'defends' democracy, its enemies become redundant. In the following sections we explore how RWI works on Twitter.

Tweeting RWI

3.96 billion people use social media today (We are social and Hootsuite, 2020b). That is more than half of the world's population. Over the last decade, researchers have noticed that these networks have become pivotal spaces for political deliberation (Tumasjan et al., 2010; 2011). Twitter[18] is particularly relevant in this landscape. Despite not being as popular as the other big platforms, it has been identified as the social media for politics. Twitter has lowered barriers for participation (Anduiza et al., 2009) and it is used to campaign, coordinate protests, as well as disseminate and discuss news (Ausserhofer & Maireder, 2013).

Twitter works particularly well for the far-right.[19] Analysing the US, Hawley (2018) explains that this platform amplifies fascistic voices through (1) their interactions with celebrities or influencers and their millions of followers, thus targeting lurkers[20]; (2) the use of one or more anonymous account(s) to 'troll'[21] and magnify messages; and (3) the circulation of shocking claims while framing their violence as honest or fun. To this, we would like to add that Twitter's brief and speedy format stimulates simplification and reduces the space for reflexive and detailed thought.[22] Clearly, if we think about politics *a la* Habermas, in terms of collective deliberation, Twitter's use of language does not seem to lead to such an exercise of thoughtfulness.

In North and Latin America alike, Twitter has been instrumental for the far-right's preaching to widen its audience by circumventing the conservative establishment. The latter gets frequently accused of being either too soft or even complicit with the left. Against moderating filters and widely shared values such as civil dialogue and respect for diversity, the new voices of the right declare war on political correctness. Obviously, this cultural battle does not require – and indeed rejects – long and brainy elaborations and nuanced argumentation. As we will show below, it is instead waged through brief messaging, intense emotion, and often grotesque themes and imagery. In this context, transgression and aggression are frequently praised as good in and of themselves, or even as cathartically cleansing. This style of communication has reached the mainstream as it is being legitimized and even practiced by well-established politicians such as Donald Trump and Jair Bolsonaro who consistently equate honesty to cruelty.

Methodological strategy

We conducted a systematic content analysis of 30,858 tweets by 20 prominent Latin American influencers, activists, and politicians (see Table 1). Besides being active in Twitter these individuals are remarkable contributors to right-wing politics in different arenas such as social movements, journalism, and/or electoral politics. All the accounts and their tweets were public at the moment of the study, and they were collected using the rtweet package of the R cran statistical software (Kearney, 2019). For each account, the maximum limit of tweets collected was 3200. Retweets were removed in order to identify and analyse original material. This explains variations in time range and number of tweets. Additionally, we considered tweets up to 26 February 2020 – when the first case of COVID-19 was reported in Latin America – to neutralize the massive effect that the pandemic has had over the public conversation within the region.

Two kinds of analysis were conducted: A correlation coefficient calculation for pairs of words and a sentiment analysis of each tweet. To calculate the correlations among words we used the phi coefficient. It corresponds to Pearson correlation applied to two binary variables, so its interpretation is similar. Phi coefficient reflects how more likely it is that two words would appear together, or not, rather than one of them appearing without the other:

$$\varphi = \frac{(n_{00}n_{11} - n_{01}n_{10})}{\sqrt{n_{1.}n_{0.}n_{.1}n_{.0}}}$$

	Y = 1	Y = 0	Total
X = 1	n_{11}	n_{10}	$n_{1.}$
X = 0	n_{01}	n_{00}	$n_{0.}$
total	$n_{.1}$	$n_{.0}$	n

For the sentiment analysis we used the 'bag of words' approach in which each tweet is considered as a combination of its individual words, so it is treated as a single document. The sentiment in the tweet is calculated as the sum of the sentiment of the words that compose it. The dictionary used for the analysis was the NRC Word-Emotion Association Lexicon. This lexicon assigns the following emotions to a set of words: anger, anticipation, disgust, fear, joy, sadness, surprise, and trust. For our purposes only the larger distinction between positive and negative sentiments has been considered.

To jointly visualize correlation and sentiment we have used graphs. In these graphs, each node represents a word and the width of the link between them reflects the phi coefficient. Each link is coloured indicating the mean sentiment score of the tweets in which the connected words occurred jointly. Only pairs of words that registered a correlation greater than 0.15 and that individually exceeded an absolute frequency threshold (defined according to the number of tweets of each account) were graphed. Green and red indicate positive and negative emotions respectively, while grey denotes neutrality. Note that the colours only appear in the digital version of the article and that the words in the graphs are in the original form in which they were written.

We noticed that the dictionary assigns sentiments to keywords of the narratives under analysis and this could add bias. As an example, abortion has a negative connotation and president or family a positive one. To fix this issue, we calculated an adjusted sentiment score removing the terms that appeared in the graphs. No significant differences in the results were identified so we show the graphs using the standard lexicon. Throughout the research we did a comprehensive and detailed qualitative content analysis of the tweets. We also studied other interventions and features of the 20 subjects such as interviews, YouTube posts, press articles, and institutional affiliations.

In the following section, we show the results for the whole sample (in Spanish)[23] and for three activists from Argentina (Nicolás Márquez), Brazil (Sara Winter) and Perú (Christian Rosas). In all cases these are leading figures of far-right activism in their countries. The rationale of focusing on

Table 1. Names, Twitter accounts, countries, personal and account profiles of the influencers, activists and politicians analysed.

Name	Twitter account	Country	Short profile description	Number of tweets	Time frame	Followers, up to August 2020
Jair Bolsonaro	@jairbolsonaro	Brazil	Retired military officer. 38th president of Brazil since January 1, 2019.	2449	2019-01-25 to 2020-02-26	6,672,511
Olavo de Carvalho	@opropriolavo	Brazil	Self-promoted philosopher, political pundit, astrologer, and journalist.	3044	2019-03-04 to 2020-02-26	456,053
Agustín Laje	@AgustinLaje	Argentina	Political Scientist, social media influencer and author. Founding Director of Fundación Centro de Estudios LIBRE. Author of *El libro negro de la Nueva Izquierda*.	970	2019-03-24 to 2020-02-26	337,247
Sara Winter	@_SaraWinter	Brazil	'Pro-life' activist and social media influencer involved in far-right politics and in the Bolsonaro government. Leader of the radical far-right group 'Brazil's 300'.	2867	2016-10-21 to 2020-02-26	268,378
Emmanuel Danann	@DanannRock	Argentina	Right-wing influencer, media personality.	444	2013-01-11 to 2020-02-26	104,476
Fernanda Betancourt	@FerBetancourt9	Mexico	Founder and activist of the Daughters of the MX.	1631	2019-12-02 to 2020-02-26	100,384
Vanesa Vallejo	@vanesavallejo3	United States–Colombia	Economist and journalist. Editor in Chief and columnist of PanAm Post: https://es.panampost.com	698	2019-08-02 to 2020-02-26	98,277
Nicolás Márquez	@NickyMarquez1	Argentina	Lawyer, journalist, and author of *El libro negro de la Nueva Izquierda*.	2568	2017-12-26 to 2020-02-26	72,025
Carlos Leal	@CarlosLealMx	Mexico	MP of the Partido Encuentro Social of the state of Nuevo León. Promoter of the 'parental pin'.	2458	2018-04-17 to 2020-02-26	70,561
Christian Camacho	@ccamacho88	Mexico	Right-wing political advisor and influencer.	1859	2018-11-01 to 2020-02-26	26,595
Juan Polanco	@JuanPolancoB	Dominican Republic	Coordinator of Pro-life Youth Dominican Republic. Founding Coordinator of the Centre for Research of Liberty and Family.	1079	2019-04-20 to 2020-02-26	18,298
Amparo Medina	@Amparo_Medina	Ecuador	President of Pro-life Ecuador, social media influencer, and activist against sexual and reproductive rights.	367	2020-01-03 to 2020-02-26	18,240
Fabricio Alvarado	@FabriAlvarado7	Costa Rica	Journalist. Former MP and presidential candidate. General Secretary of the New Republic Party.	893	2013-07-13 to 2020-02-26	9718
Belén Lombardi	@BeluLombardi_	Argentina	Catholic social media influencer and pro-life activist.	2539	2019-01-19 to 2020-02-26	8580*

(Continued)

Table 1. Continued.

Name	Twitter account	Country	Short profile description	Number of tweets	Time frame	Followers, up to August 2020
Jorge Márquez	@jorgemarquezuy	Uruguay	Founder of the evangelical Church Life Mission for the Nations.	1783	2017-09-17 to 2020-02-26	6355
Bryan Albariño	@BryanAlbarino	Paraguay	Right-wing activist.	1470	2018-04-07 to 2020-02-26	5240
Álvaro Dastugue	@AlvaroDastugue	Uruguay	MP of the National Party and pastor of the evangelical Church Life Mission for the Nations.	1505	2015-04-28 to 2020-02-26	5214
Pamela Pizarro	@pizarro_pamela	Chile	Pro-life activist. Executive Director of Care Chile Foundation.	758	2012-05-18 to 2020-02-26	5129
Christian Rosas	@xtian_rosas	Peru	Leader of Don't Mess with my Children.	1280	2011-01-23 to 2020-02-26	3987
Aarón Lara	@LicAaronLara	Mexico	President of the Iberoamerican Congress for Life and Family.	196	2017-08-09 to 2020-02-26	1127

*Around 40,000 when the account was censored in May 2020. https://aconteciendo.com/2020/05/02/censura-twitter-cerro-la-cuenta-de-la-lider-juvenil-y-pro-vida-belu-lombardi/
Source: Own elaboration (2020).

specific individuals to further the analysis is that this procedure allows us to engage with the narrative under study in more detail and, so to speak, at a microlevel.

Graphing RWI

To get an overview of the whole sample, we produced a graph in which all individuals/Twitter accounts in Spanish are included and have the same relative weight (Figure 1). To achieve this, we replicated a procedure 1000 times in which 500 tweets were randomly sampled for each account. In each replicate sentiment analysis (sentiment score and adjusted sentiment score) correlations were calculated. Finally, the overview was achieved considering the average of all the replicates. Since the statistics were computed from a conglomerate of different accounts, making it less likely to obtain high values of association, the correlation threshold considered was of 0.05.

In Figure 1 life is linked to family, god, right, and freedom. These connections are framed in positive emotions. The graph thus displays the core of the conservative narrative: the traditional family conceived as the basis of society and where children are safe and grow up healthy – and normal. Complementarily, the right to life is understood as the opposition to abortion (the word appears connected to women, right, and favour[24] framed in negative emotions). The consistent intertwinement of these views with Christian beliefs, and sometimes explicit references to God, reveals the intimate relationship between RWI and Christian conservatism. The opposition to feminism is the main motif in all the 20 far-right figures under study, but as the following tweet by Belén Lombardi exemplifies, this battle is intersectional in the way we defined this term above:

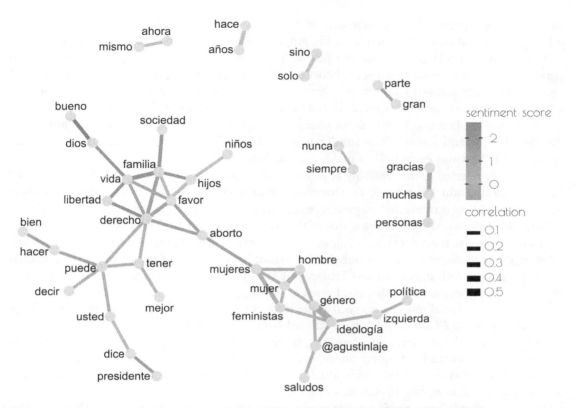

Figure 1. Correlation graph of whole sample (Spanish only)*. Source: Own elaboration (2020).

*Includes words that jointly verify a correlation greater than 0.05 (links) and reach a minimum absolute frequency of 100 among all Spanish users' samples of tweets. Correlation degree is indicated by the width of the links and average sentiment score is indicated by their colour.

> I am pro-life, Catholic, anti-feminist and pro-family. I am in favor of the military and the security forces, and against prostitution and gender ideology. If you don't like it, you can block me, but I'm not going to shut up because you don't like the way I think. Expressing myself is my right. (09/20/2019, 13:37)

The statement has distinct intersectional elements as the promotion of Christian values becomes a battle against feminism, which is also a campaign for law and order. As in countless other occasions, there is an appropriation of the liberal right of free speech used – rather paradoxically – to disqualify any critique or disagreement. Furthermore, the tweet aggressively challenges enemies of free self-expression while legitimizing authoritarian practices. Any keen observer knows what being generically 'in favor' of the military actually means in a Latin American country. As we already pointed out, under the eye of RWI the world is divided between violent feminists who try to censor ('them') and those decent people who have ordered lives and support the military ('us').

Feminism is the main obsession of RWI. As noted above, the terms abortion and women represent a negative nexus in Figure 1 and, unsurprisingly, the latter is linked to feminists. The correlation between gender and ideology is the strongest, and the latter is also linked to feminists and to (the) left. This is expected given the already analysed centrality of the notion of gender ideology in RWI and in the narrative of the radical right in general. We will see that when the level of analysis is more specific, the intersectional – and vitriolic – character of the narrative becomes more robust but, even at this aggregated level, the graph provides a clear mental map of RWI.

The narrative also targets transgender people. The fixity of sex and identity is asserted once and again – that the only valid marriage is between a ('real') man and a ('real') woman goes without saying. The right seems to understand very well that these issues are relevant and that they affect society as a whole. This is revealed in a tweet by the president of the evangelical Iberoamerican Congress for Life and Family about transgender rights in Uruguay: 'We will not allow laws[25] that threaten life and family. #RepealtheTransgenderLaw. We will defend Latin America' (07/22/2019, 16:37). This also exemplifies a highly transnationalized agenda.[26]

We already referred to the centrality of Agustín Laje, one of the authors of *The Black Book of the New Left*, within Latin American RWI. This prominence is revealed by the fact that he is so profusely named by his fellow activists that @agustinlaje appears in the graph.[27] This explains the neutral tone of the set of connections between the words, as the tweets that talk about Laje's books and conferences have a more positive tone. And here is Laje in his own words: 'I defend life of the fetus and his mother, I abhor gender ideology, I vindicate our glorious armed forces, I support the repression of criminals and I sympathize with Bolsonaro and Trump' (10/31/2019, 11:03). The similarity of many of these tweets is striking which shows that RWI operates through stubborn iteration. These narratives are also present in powerful movements such as the Brazilian *Schools without Party* or the transnational *Don't Mess with my Children* which have affected both public debate and policy.

There are views, assertions, and concepts, however, that are prominent even though they get diffused in the thousands of tweets under analysis. We realized this by diving into the material: we studied the discourse of each individual in depth, focusing on the main concepts illustrated by the graphs and analysing the content of each tweet. This brought about findings that demand attention. In what follows, we focus on three examples: the Argentinian intellectual Nicolás Márquez, co-author of *The Black Book of the New Left*; Sara Winter, a Brazilian activist and the female influencer with more followers than all of the women in the sample; and, finally, from Perú, Christian Rosas, a leading voice of *Don't Mess with my Children*.

Nicolás Márquez (@NickyMarquez1, Argentina)

As pointed out before *The Black Book of the New Left*, which Márquez coauthored with Laje, works as a manifesto for RWI. And even though Laje is the most famous and influential of the two, Márquez is a relevant voice within the Argentinian far-right and joined the NOS party in 2020, in the context of the debate about the legalization of abortion. Furthermore, Márquez seems to be the perfect example of RWI. His aggressive rhetoric gathers gender ideology and the left, connecting them to death, murder, and terrorism. He viciously targets Victoria Donda (@vikidonda), a progressive congresswoman whose parents were disappeared by the State in the 1970s. In several rather cruel tweets, Márquez explicitly relates the 'terrorist' past of Donda's parents as leftist militants to her pro-choice advocacy. The feminists are the *Montoneras* (guerrilla forces) of today who want to legalize genocide (as he calls abortion on some occasions). Thus, it is not surprising that in Figure 2 the word abortion is linked to homicide, crime, and child, which is also connected to kill.

Márquez claims that feminism is authoritarian. The graph shows this through the connection between the words gender and dictatorship. At the same time, he endorses the real – and brutal – right-wing authoritarian regime that ruled Argentina between 1973 and 1983 and 'disappeared' thousands of citizens, a fact that he denies (the hashtag 'they weren't 30.000' – #nofueron30mil – in reference to the number of people killed by the dictatorship is used as part of his rhetoric). Because of his open support for State terrorism – as shown in the graph, he calls it 'war' – he has been

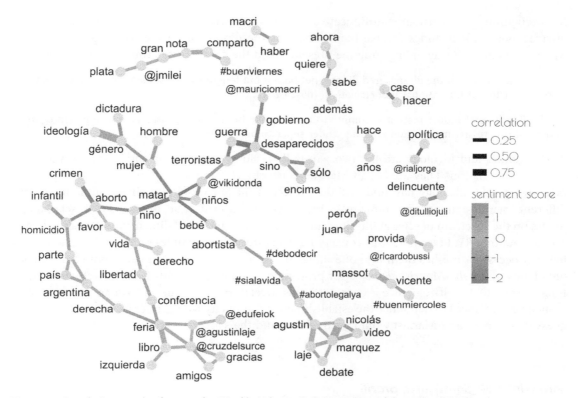

Figure 2. Correlation graph of tweets by Nicolás Márquez*. Source: Own elaboration (2020).
*Includes words that jointly verify a correlation greater than 0.15 (links) and reach a minimum absolute frequency of 30 among Nicolás Márquez's tweets. Correlation degree is indicated by the width of the links and average sentiment score is indicated by their colour.

labelled as fascist or even a Nazi. His reply has been that he is not a Nazi (that he even criticizes Nazism in his books) and that, in fact, feminists are the new Nazis. This is not just an angry metaphor: he considers that the left today is at least as dangerous as Hitler. This might sound confounding for many readers, yet the expression feminazi has recently become popular.

Márquez's comments on international politics places him farther right than the Argentinian conservative establishment:

> Jair Bolsonaro promised a free market and to eradicate gender ideology: the opposite of the 'de-government' of @mauriciomacri [former right-wing President of Argentina], marked by statism and gender ideology as cultural priority. Brazil in two weeks has overcome us (with all merit) in the world context. (01/01/2019, 23:11)

Jair Bolsonaro and Donald Trump are mentioned in many of the tweets under analysis as two of the few presidents that deserve respect. It therefore makes sense that the link between @mauriciomacri and government is coloured in red in Figure 2. It also makes sense that Javier Milei (@jmilei) is mentioned explicitly by Márquez. A rising figure in the far-right's culture and a legislative representative in Argentina since 2021, Milei is also an example of a successful passage from the RWI's influencers' sphere to the electoral arena.

A typical anxiety of the extreme right is the influence that the left exercises through public education and the cultural industries. A hashtag used by Márquez to talk about this is 'Educational

Indoctrination' (#AdoctrinamientoEducativo). As we see in the following two tweets this notion is intersectional as it includes diverse themes such as the discussion of the recent political past – which is of course a way of engaging the present – and the controversy around 'gender ideology':

> If you were told that the disappeared did not put bombs but fought for the student bus pass, you have been a victim of Educational Indoctrination. (05/25/2018, 0:11)

> The Educational Indoctrination is coming to an end. The healthy and conservative youth stands up against progressivism, abortion and the gender superstition. (05/25/2018, 0:19)

Again, gender and ideology are the two words that, along with nicolás and márquez, show the strongest correlation. They are key in Márquez's narrative where time itself is filled with political meaning: gender ideology has 'updated' the project of the left which is a chameleonic force with different manifestations and moments. We have mentioned that intersectional scholarship moves on the spectrum of separability/inseparability of the intersected dimensions. We also already pointed out that RWI resembles this conceptual structure, as it sometimes separates its enemies and in other occasions meshes them into one single 'thing'. In one tweet, Márquez denounces the sodomy lobby and *lesbo-Marxist elements* for protesting a talk he gave with Laje at the Buenos Aires Book Fair of 2018 (self-reference is constant in his tweets). He also added a hashtag 'media silence' (#SilencioMediatico) to denounce the establishment's complicity with gender ideology. Who would guess that lesbian and Marxist would become one and the same concept!

Sara Winter (@_SaraWinter, Brazil)

Sara Winter narrates her story and identity in the terms of a repented feminist who, through a process of enlightenment and personal growth, has become pro-life.[28] She worked for the Bolsonaro government and has supported paramilitary activity in Brazil. Winter's tweeting activity – and highly publicized political actions – fully illustrate RWI as they simultaneously attack the left and feminism while supporting not only Bolsonaro but also Trump (see Figure 3). The internationalized scope of her views is also expressed in negative terms: resembling the gesture of Márquez but from the other side of the border, Winter scorns Argentina for advancing in the direction of legalizing abortion (hence, the link between the words argentina and abortion in the graph). Her discourse obviously targets feminism and the feminist movement too.

We already noticed that the theme of gender ideology has prominence within RWI. The extreme tones of Winter's views in this regard are sharp. For example, she claims that 'effeminate' men search for ideologies such as feminism to justify their lack of masculinity and 'that is evident when we look at leftist militancy' (2/9/2018 18:09). She also condemns Judith Butler, the prominent US queer theory scholar, as the creator of a conceptual perversion. In her narrative, childhood is perceived as a victim of feminism which is connected through gender ideology to pedophilia. Gender ideology takes away the innocence or even the life of kids: it permits killing babies and raping children as well as changing their sex.

The prominence of the theme of the left is clear in Winter's discourse. In a narrative move that resembles the American Alt-right and the neofascists in Europe, she gathers the mainstream media, the left, and corruption. In her own words Globo, the giant media firm, 'promoting a campaign against fake news is like Hitler complaining about Nazism, Marx complaining about communism or Lula complaining about corruption #vaisarinha' (28/7/2018 00:27). As Márquez does, Winter claims to be a victim of mainstream media's hostility.

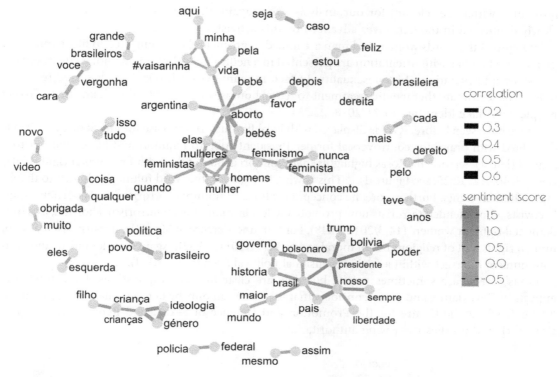

Figure 3. Correlation graph of tweets by Sara Winter*. Source: Own elaboration (2020).

*Includes words that jointly verify a correlation greater than 0.15 (links) and reach a minimum absolute frequency of 38 among Sara Winter's tweets. Correlation degree is indicated by the width of the links and average sentiment score is indicated by their colour.

The left is the enemy of the people and of moral, religious, and scientific truth. It even corrupts the good intentions around 'inclusion'. Such is the theme of the following tweet which expresses RWI so clearly that it does not need further interpretation:

> The left likes inclusion
>
> Inclusion of Gender Ideology in the heads of children
>
> Inclusion of Marxism in the heads of university students
>
> Inclusion of abortion in healthcare policies
>
> And inclusion of public money in their bank accounts. (07/24/2019, 14:33)

Christian Rosas (@xtian_rosas, Perú)

Considering only his followers on Twitter, Rosas can hardly be considered a powerful influencer. However, this man who defines himself with the words Christian, conservative and political scientist is the spokesperson for *Don't Mess with my Children* in Perú, a conservative advocacy group with regional reach, and he is also very active both in social and traditional media.[29] Furthermore, he is a political operator of the right who has expressed support for both Alberto Fujimori as well as his daughter Keiko Fujimori. Given his role within the regional conservative movement, Rosas' posts on Twitter are relevant for our analysis. Once again, the conceptual contours of RWI are clearly delineated in the narratives advanced by this activist.

In Figure 4 the words woman and man are linked in green, and are connected to life, family, and marriage. The links with orientation are presented in a neutral tone, but this cannot be mistaken for a positive interpretation of homosexuality. In fact, in many tweets Rosas defends *sexual re*-orientation as a legitimate therapeutic treatment to 'cure' homosexuality.[30] He also claims that LGBTQ people have 'fake identities' (9/21/2018, 23:35).

As we have seen before, RWI is displayed with local flavours. In this case the attack on feminism is combined with praise for controversial former President Alberto Fujimori and his military victory against (leftist) 'terrorism'; Rosas highlights that Fujimori achieved this with few human rights violations (8/8/2012, 12:25; see Figure 4).[31] This is why, in Figure 4, the word fujimori is linked to thanks and to human rights. Furthermore, he conceptually links 'communist terrorism' and abortion rights: 'Activists who defended terrorists now promote the legalization of natal terrorism, abortion, as a fundamental right for women' (14/3/2012 14:48). For him, the 'defense of life of the unborn' is a matter of human rights, not of religious but of moral order (22/12/2011, 13:32). Again, anti-feminism and anti-communism intersect within a multidimensional political agenda (i.e. RWI).

Rosas' tweets are sometimes messy, but they are clear in their implications. He consistently appeals to Christianity and Jesus, considers that marriage can only be heterosexual, attacks feminist NGOs (such as the Centre for the Promotion and Defence of Sexual and Reproductive Rights, Promsex), and justifies right-wing authoritarian rule.

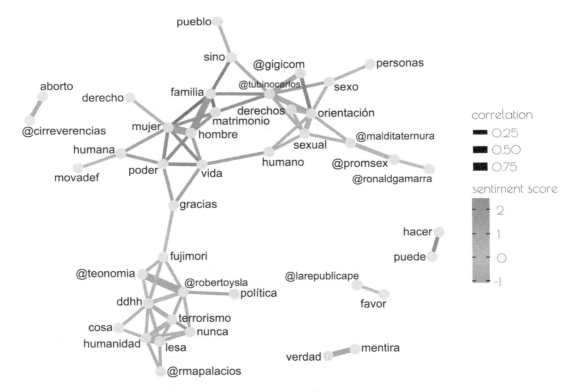

Figure 4. Correlation graph of tweets by Christian Rosas*. Source: Own elaboration (2020).

*Includes words that jointly verify a correlation greater than 0.15 (links) and reach a minimum absolute frequency of 20 among Christian Rosas' tweets. Correlation degree is indicated by the width of the links and average sentiment score is indicated by their colour.

Conclusion

Twitter allows the far-right to circumvent the political establishment's communicative filters and etiquette, to widen audiences, and to spread extreme views. In Latin America, the platform has been instrumental for the consolidation of a conservative perspective that attacks feminism and the left simultaneously while weaving economic, cultural, and social themes into a single narrative. We have tried to capture the multidimensionality of this discourse through the conceptual category of right-wing intersectionality. RWI appropriates the rhetoric of rights to forward a right-wing agenda with authoritarian edges, framed by 'traditional' Christian values. Sometimes these moves are synthesized in the umbrella category of gender ideology. RWI might not be an exclusively Latin American phenomenon and yet the narratives that we have analysed have a clear regional flavour.

RWI shows that it is time to accept that culture and discourse are not a distraction from class-based conflict. RWI is *a multilayered, integrated, and holistic reactionary project*. This innovation in the terrain of right-wing politics mirrors the main insight of scholarship on intersectionality: that power is not divided into the silos of political economy, culture, gender and so on. Despite its crude simplifications, RWI incarnates an effective understanding of how power and hegemony work. Of course, RWI also reverses intersectionality in normative and ideological terms as it weaponizes 'intersections' to defend hierarchy and undermine progressive causes.

While progressive parties in office became ideologically frigid and technocratic, made enormous concessions to neoliberalism, and abandoned the radical political horizons attached to the left, RWI reclaims ideology and emotions, challenges the liberal political establishment, and claims for itself the transformative power and radicalness of politics, reenchanting political life but in a dangerous direction. These features are key to understanding its capacity to inspire. Furthermore, RWI reactivates antidemocratic tendencies within liberalism and dominant common-sense. Thus, it is not surprising that self-identified centrist citizens sometimes seem more concerned about protecting the freedom of expression of fascistic movements and individuals than about the (sometimes physical) violence that they inflict on their opponents and on democracy itself.

In contrast with the heavy jargon of intersectionality (Robertson, 2017) RWI is didactic, clear, simple. The power of simplification is a huge asset in a cultural environment that rejects complexity, philosophy, and nuance, and where technology, development and good management are the new mantras for mainstream left and right alike. How a discourse that emphasizes complexity can compete with one that oversimplifies is a question that remains open. Can progressives communicate the democratic value of complexity in ways that do not backfire on their causes?

RWI's violent and antidemocratic politics demand attention from activists and scholars alike. By contrast it highlights the need to reimagine emancipatory politics beyond the straitjacket of 'rights', nation States, and liberal institutions. At least we can be sure of this: RWI requires engagement beyond indignation.

Notes

1. We employ the notion of political narrative in the plain sense of a political perspective being articulated through language. We are aware of the complexity of the notion of narrative and of the recent explosion of narrative approaches within the social sciences (Ravecca & Dauphinee, 2018).
2. See also Combahee River Collective (2015), Coll Planas and Cruells (2013), Gunnarsson (2017), Henning (2015), Lugones (2008), McCall (2005), Nash (2017), Platero (2012), and Viveros Vigoya (2015).
3. As we will see the dual condition of being academic and activist is used by right-wing actors to criticize feminism and other critical approaches. An anonymous reviewer raised this relevant issue.

4. The blend is not entirely new and in fact RWI updates old attempts of depicting the women's movements as a trojan horse for communism (Valobra, 2014).
5. This includes policy and legislative changes (Pérez Bentancur & Rocha-Carpiuc, 2020).
6. We thank an anonymous reviewer for making this relevant point.
7. *Don't Mess with my Children* has branches in different countries, see for example: https://conmishijosnotemetas.pe/; https://conmishijosnotemetas.com.ar/#!/-inicio/
8. *Schools without Party*: https://www.escolasempartido.org/
9. The role of the latter in the politics of the region seems to be increasing (Segado-Boj et al., 2015; Aruguete & Calvo, 2018).
10. We thank Mara Karina Silva for this clear and concise articulation of RWI. We also want to acknowledge Yesola Kweon for showing to us other potential definitions and approaches to the phenomenon.
11. On the relevance of emotions on contemporary political life, see Gioscia and Wences (2017).
12. Occasionally RWI narrates a patriarchal tale about women being fooled and used by the evil forces of communism, so vaguely defined that it includes international organizations and NGOs. After all, the story *has to be* about a struggle between men, even when women overflow the streets, build movements, and develop powerful theoretical interventions that advance critical theory.
13. Vaggione and Campos Machado (2020) propose the category of neoconservatism as an adept framework to understand the current landscape of conservative politics; we do not dispute the usefulness of the category, but we are interested in highlighting the intersectional character of such a landscape. See all contributions to *Politics & Gender*'s online symposium about the conservative backlash in Latin America (Biroli & Caminotti, 2020).
14. The book re-arranges or fabricates historical facts to match its script. It is populated by inaccurate interpretations of feminist and critical theory authors (amusingly, it quotes 'Foucault for beginners'). It is poorly written, authors' names are misspelled throughout the text, and citations and references are wrongly presented. The research is weak, and its sources are not reliable. The lack of well-crafted arguments is compensated by repeating the same ideas once and again in rhetorically formulaic ways.
15. The concept was originally coined to critically explore gendered dynamics, encompassing intersectional approaches (see Collins, 1990).
16. For a detailed analysis of the notion of gender ideology see Cornejo-Valle and Pichardo (2017) and Corredor (2019). In 1998 the Episcopal Conference of Peru published one of the first texts in Latin America that advocates for this 'anti-gender' perspective.
17. In this regard RWI incorporates and resembles the narratives of the American Alt-Right (Hawley, 2017; Woods, 2019).
18. Twitter is a platform for microblogging messages of up to 280 characters (called tweets) that allows the user to instantly share ideas, photos, or videos. It was launched on 13 July 2006 and, since then, has grown constantly: currently, it has 166 million daily users (The Washington Post, 2020). According to the latest We Are Social and Hootsuite Report (2020a), three Latin American countries are among the 20 with more Twitter penetration worldwide (Brazil, Mexico, and Argentina). The same report states that Twitter's audience self-identifies predominantly as male (62%).
19. This resembles the experience of the American Alt-right (Hawley, 2018; Froio & Ganesh, 2018),
20. A lurker is someone who participates in a virtual community only in a receptive way.
21. A troll is someone who tries to provoke other users in a virtual community.
22. This linguistic compression brings to mind the concerns that philosopher Herbert Marcuse expressed decades ago about the generalized imposition of 'a syntax in which the structure of the sentence is abridged and condensed in such way that no tension, no 'space' is left between the parts of the sentences' (Marcuse, 1991, p. 86).
23. For the aggregated analysis, it was only possible to work with the accounts in the same language. We chose to show the Spanish graph because Spanish speakers were the majority of the sample.
24. This is because the expression 'being in favor of abortion' and 'being in favor of life' or 'family' are profusely used in the tweets under study.
25. Law 19.684 recognizes and protects transgender's people rights.
26. This video in Spanish is very revealing in such regard: https://www.youtube.com/watch?v=6gng8Z-DHg4
27. Laje's influence is strong in Twitter and beyond. He was one of the main speakers of the second South American Congress for Life and Family.

28. This narrative strategy anchored in regret for a shameful past seems common among anti-feminist female leaders which is an interesting topic for future research.
29. For a description of Rosas' relevance, see Iglesias (2018), Cariboni (2018) and Rousseau (2020). For an analysis on *Don't Mess with my Children* and its role in the national campaign against the Ministry of Education's new National Curricula for Basic Education in Peru, see Meneses (2019) and Rousseau (2020).
30. This is one of the links that can be mistaken because of the lexicon's bias: the adjusted version of the graph reveals negative emotions.
31. In fact, Fujimorism baked the mobilization against the inclusion of 'gender' in basic education (Meneses, 2019).

Acknowledgements

The theoretical framework of this research was presented by Paulo Ravecca at the 'Pink tides, right turns in Latin America Seminar' (Université du Québec en Outaouais, Gatineau, Quebec, June 2019) organized by Charmain Levy and Manuel Larrabure. More recent versions of the work were thoroughly debated at the faculty seminar of the Instituto de Ciencia Política (Universidad de la República, Montevideo, September 2020) as well as at the 2021 world congresses of the American Political Science Association, the Canadian Association for Latin American and Caribbean Studies, the International Public Policy Association, the International Political Science Association, and the Latin American Studies Association. We gratefully acknowledge the extensive and rich feedback and suggestions we received in these conversations. Finally, we thank the anonymous reviewers for their helpful and constructive engagement with our research.

Disclosure statement

No potential conflict of interest was reported by the author(s).

ORCID

Paulo Ravecca http://orcid.org/0000-0002-9754-9520
Marcela Schenck http://orcid.org/0000-0002-8526-3736
Bruno Fonseca http://orcid.org/0000-0002-2327-9695
Diego Forteza http://orcid.org/0000-0002-3818-6467

References

Abbot, J., & Levitsky, S. (2020). The left turn and citizenship: How much has changed? In M. Balán, & F. Montambeault (Eds.), *Legacies of the left turn in Latin America. The promise of inclusive citizenship* (pp. 370–407). Notre Dame University Press.

Aguayo, G., & Rosas, C. (2019). *Ideología de género. El nuevo intento por desnaturalizar el plan eterno de Dios*. Editorial Peniel.

Anduiza, E., Cantijoch, M., & Gallego, A. (2009). Political participation and the internet: A field essay. *Information, Communication & Society*, *12*(6), 860–878. https://doi.org/10.1080/13691180802282720

Aruguete, N., & Calvo, E. (2018). Time to #protest: Selective exposure, cascading activation, and framing in social media. *Journal of Communication*, *68*(3), 480–502. https://doi.org/10.1093/joc/jqy007

Ausserhofer, J., & Maireder, A. (2013). National politics on twitter. *Information Communication & Society*, *16*(3), 291–314. https://doi.org/10.1080/1369118X.2012.756050

Biroli, F., & Caminotti, M. (2020). The conservative backlash against gender in Latin America. *Politics & Gender*, *16*(1), E1. https://doi.org/10.1017/S1743923X20000045

Cariboni, D. (2018). El género es el nuevo demonio. In *Revista noticias, Dic. 22nd*, 16–20.
Carver, T. (2020). Interpretative methods. In D. Berg-Schlosser, B. Badie, & L. Morlino (Eds.), *The SAGE handbook of political science* (Vol. 1, pp. 406–422). SAGE.
Chiasson-LeBel, T. (2019). Neoliberalism in Ecuador after Correa. *European Review of Latin American and Caribbean Studies/Revista Europea de Estudios Latinoamericanos y del Caribe, 108*(108), 153–174. https://doi.org/10.32992/erlacs.10500
Coll Planas, G., & Cruells, M. (2013). La puesta en práctica de la interseccionalidad política: el caso de las políticas LGTB en Cataluña. *Revista Española de Ciencia Política, 31*, 153–172.
Collins, H. (1990). *Black feminist thought: Knowledge, consciousness, and the politics of empowerment*. Unwin Hyman.
Combahee River Collective. (2015). The combahee river collective statement. Retrieved from the Library of Congress, https://www.loc.gov/item/lcwaN0028151/
Cornejo-Valle, M., & Pichardo, J. I. (2017). La "ideología de género" frente a los derechos sexuales y reproductivos. El escenario español. *Cadernos Pagu, 50*, https://doi.org/10.1590/18094449201700500009
Corredor, E. (2019). Unpacking "gender ideology" and the global right's antigender countermovement. *Journal of Women in Culture and Society, 44*(3), 613–638. https://doi.org/10.1086/701171
Crenshaw, K. (1989). *Demarginalizing the intersection of race and sex: A black feminist critique of antidiscrimination doctrine, feminist theory, and antiracist politics* (pp. 139–167). University of Chicago Legal Forum 1989.
Dabène, O. (2020). Uses and mises of the "left" category in Latin America. In M. Balán, & F. Montambeault (Eds.), *Legacies of the left turn in Latin America. The promise of inclusive citizenship* (pp. 347–369). Notre Dame University Press.
Dragiewicz, M. (2008). Patriarchy reasserted: Fathers' rights and anti-VAWA activism. *Feminist Criminology, 3*(2), 121–144. https://doi.org/10.1177/1557085108316731
Eaton, K. (2014). New strategies of the Latin American right. Beyond parties and elections. In J. P. Luna, & C. Rovira Kaltwasser (Eds.), *The resilience of the Latin American right* (pp. 75–93). Johns Hopkins University Press.
Faludi, S. (1991). *Backlash: The undeclared war against women*. Three Rivers Press.
Froio, C., & Ganesh, B. (2018). The transnationalisation of far-right discourse on twitter: Issues and actors that cross borders in Western European democracies. *European Societies, 21*(4), 513–539. https://doi.org/10.1080/14616696.2018.1494295
Geertz, C. (1997). *La interpretación de las culturas*. Gedisa.
Gioscia, L., & Wences, I. (2017). Sentir la política. *Crítica Contemporánea. Revista de Teoría Política, 7*, 2–6.
Goldentul, A., & Saferstein, E. (2020). Los jóvenes lectores de la derecha argentina. Un acercamiento etnográfico a los seguidores de Agustín Laje y Nicolás Márquez. *Cuadernos del Centro de Estudios de Diseño y Comunicación, 24*(112), 113–131.
Gonzalez, L. (1988). Por um feminismo Afro-latino-americano. http://www.letras.ufmg.br/literafro/ensaistas/24-textos-das-autoras/1445-lelia-gonzalez-por-um-feminismo-afro-latino-americano
Gramsci, A. (2008). *Selections from the prison notebooks*. (Q. Hoare & G. Nowell, Trans., Eds.). International Publishers. (Original work published 1971).
Gunnarsson, L. (2017). Why we keep separating the 'inseparable': Dialecticizing intersectionality. *European Journal of Women's Studies, 24*(2), 114–127. https://doi.org/10.1177/1350506815577114
Hawley, G. (2017). *Making sense of the alt-right*. Columbia University Press.
Hawley, G. (2018, March 15). Is the alt-right collapsing? Talk sponsored by Berkeley's Center for Right-Wing Studies, UC Berkeley. https://www.youtube.com/watch?v=McqA5wmI5fQ
Henning, C. E. (2015). Interseccionalidade e pensamento feminista: as contribuições históricas e os debates contemporâneos acerca do entrelaçamento de marcadores sociais da diferença. *Mediações, 20*(2), 97–128.
Iglesias, N. (2018, June 21). ¡Dios nos libre! El movimiento con mis hijos no te metas. La diaria. https://ladiaria.com.uy/opinion/articulo/2018/6/dios-nos-libre/
Kearney, M. (2019). Rtweet: Collecting and analyzing Twitter data. *Journal of Open Source Software, 4*(42), 1829. https://doi.org/10.21105/joss.01829
Kotef, H. (2020). Violent attachments. *Political Theory, 48*(1), 4–29. https://doi.org/10.1177/0090591719861714
Kourliandsky, J. (2019). Democracia, evangelismo y reacción conservadora. *Revista Nueva Sociedad, 280*, 139–146.

Laclau, E., & Mouffe, C. (2004). *Hegemonía y estrategia socialista: Hacia una radicalización de la democracia*. Fondo de Cultura Económica.

Lugones, M. (2008). Colonialidad y género. *Tabula Rasa*, 9(9), 73–102. https://doi.org/10.25058/20112742.340

Luna, J. P., & Rovira Kaltwasser, C. (eds.). (2014). *The resilience of the Latin American right*. The Johns Hopkins University Press.

Marcuse, H. (1991). *One-dimensional man: Studies in the ideology of advanced industrial society*. Beacon Press.

Márquez, N., & Laje, A. (2017). *El libro negro de la nueva izquierda: Ideología de género o subversión cultural*. Pesur Ediciones.

McCall, L. (2005). The complexity of intersectionality. *Signs: Journal of Women in Culture and Society*, 30(31), 1771–1802. https://doi.org/10.1086/426800

Meneses, D. (2019). Con mis hijos no te metas: un estudio de discurso y poder en un grupo de facebook peruano opuesto a la «ideología de género». *Anthropologica*, 37(42), 129–154. https://doi.org/10.18800/anthropologica.201901.006

Mügge, L., Montoya, C., Emejulu, A., & Weldon, S. L. (2018). Intersectionality and the politics of knowledge production. *European Journal of Politics & Gender*, 1(1-2), 17–36. https://doi.org/10.1332/251510818X15272520831166

Nash, J. (2017). Intersectionality and its discontents. *American Quarterly*, 69(1), 117–129. https://doi.org/10.1353/aq.2017.0006

North, L., & Clark, T. (2018). *Dominant elites in Latin America: From neo-liberalism to the 'pink tide'*. Palgrave Macmillan.

Pérez Bentancur, V., & Rocha-Carpiuc, C. (2020). The postreform stage: Understanding backlash against sexual policies in Latin America. *Politics & Gender*, 16(1), E3. https://doi.org/10.1017/S1743923X20000069

Phoenix, A., & Pattynama, P. (2006). Intersectionality. *European Journal of Women's Studies*, 13(3), 187–192. https://doi.org/10.1177/1350506806065751

Platero, R. L. (2012). *Intersecciones: cuerpos y sexualidades en la encrucijada*. Edicions Bellaterra.

Puar, J. (2007). *Terrorist assemblages: homonationalism in queer times*. Duke University Press.

Ravecca, P. (2015). Our discipline and its politics. Authoritarian political science: Chile 1979–1989. *Revista de Ciencia Política*, 35(1), 145–178. https://doi.org/10.4067/S0718-090X2015000100008

Ravecca, P. (2019). *The politics of political science. Re-writing Latin American experiences*. Routledge.

Ravecca, P., & Dauphinee, E. (2018). Narrative and the possibilities for scholarship. *International Political Sociology*, 12(2), 125–138. https://doi.org/10.1093/ips/olx029

Ravecca, P., & Upadhyay, N. (2013). Queering conceptual boundaries: Assembling indigenous. *Marxist, Postcolonial and Queer Perspectives. Jindal Global Law Review*, 4(2), 357–378.

Robertson, E. (2017, September 30). Intersectional-what? Feminism's problem with jargon is that any idiot can pick it up and have a go. *The Guardian*. https://www.theguardian.com/world/2017/sep/30/intersectional-feminism-jargon

Rousseau, S. (2020). Antigender activism in Peru and its impact on state policy. *Politics & Gender*, 16(1), E5. https://doi.org/10.1017/S1743923X20000070

Scirica, E. (2014). Comunistas y anticomunistas: redes políticas y culturales en Argentina y Chile durante la guerra fría (circa 1960). *Anuario del Instituto de Historia Argentina*, 14, http://www.memoria.fahce.unlp.edu.ar/art_revistas/pr.6728/pr.6728.pdf

Segado-Boj, F., Díaz-Campo, J., & Lloves-Sobrado, B. (2015). Líderes latinoamericanos en twitter. Viejas costumbres para nuevos medios en tiempos de crisis políticas. *Revista Latina de Comunicación Social*, 70, 156–173.

Segato, R. (2018). A manifesto in four themes. *Critical Times*, 1(1), 198–211. https://doi.org/10.1215/26410478-1.1.198

Tumasjan, A., Sprenger, T., Sandner, P., & Welpe, I. (2010). Predicting elections with twitter: what 140 characters reveal about political sentiment. *Proceedings of the Fourth International AAAI Conference on Weblogs and Social Media*, 4(1), 178–185. https://ojs.aaai.org/index.php/ICWSM/article/view/14009

Tumasjan, A., Sprenger, T., Sandner, P., & Welpe, I. (2011). Election forecasts with twitter: How 140 characters reflect the political landscape. *Social Science Computer Review*, 29(4), 402–418. https://doi.org/10.1177/0894439310386557

Vaggione, J., & Campos Machado, M. (2020). Religious patterns of neoconservatism in Latin America. *Politics & Gender*, 16(1), E2. https://doi.org/10.1017/S1743923X20000082

Valobra, A. (2014). "Mujeres-sombra" y "Barbudas": Género y política en el Primer Congreso Latinoamericano de Mujeres, Chile – 1959. *Anuario del Instituto de Historia Argentina, 14*, 1–17. http://www.memoria.fahce.unlp.edu.ar/art_revistas/pr.6729/pr.6729.pdf

Van Wormer, K. (2008). Anti-feminist backlash and violence against women worldwide. *Social Work & Society, 6*(2), 324–337.

Viveros Vigoya, M. (2015). L'intersectionnalité au prisme du féminisme latino-américain. *Raisons Politiques. Les langages de l'Intersectionnalité, 58*(2), 39–55. https://doi.org/10.3917/rai.058.0039

Viveros Vigoya, M. (2016). La interseccionalidad: una aproximación situada a la dominación. *Debate Feminista, 52*, 1–17. https://doi.org/10.1016/j.df.2016.09.005

The Washington Post. (2020, April 30). Twitter sees record number of users during pandemic, but advertising sales slow. *The Washington Post*. https://www.washingtonpost.com/business/economy/twitter-sees-record-number-of-users-during-pandemic-but-advertising-sales-slow/2020/04/30/747ef0fe-8ad8-11ea-9dfd-990f9dcc71fc_story.html

We Are Social and Hootsuite. (2020a). *Digital 2020. Global digital overview*. https://wearesocial.com/digital-2020

We Are Social and Hootsuite. (2020b). *Digital 2020. July Global Statshot report*. https://wearesocial.com/blog/2020/07/more-than-half-of-the-people-on-earth-now-use-social-media

Woods, A. (2019). Cultural Marxism and the cathedral: Two alt-right perspectives on critical theory. In C. M. Battista, & M. R. Sande (Eds.), *Critical theory and the humanities in the age of the alt-right* (pp. 39–60). Palgrave Macmillan.

Is Jair Bolsonaro a classic populist?

João Feres Júnior, Fernanda Cavassana and Juliana Gagliardi

ABSTRACT
Is Brazil's president Jair Bolsonaro a classic populist? This article tries to answer this question by testing whether the political discourse of Bolsonaro fits the tenets of two major theories of populism: Mudde and Kaltwasser's and Laclau's. We analyse the entire text of his presidential campaign platform to find that Bolsonaro's discourse has almost no room for a 'concept of the people' or of nation, a fact that problematizes the bulk of the literature on populism, including its major theories. Conversely, his discourse is structured around the concept of corruption, which is tightly linked with a strong anti-left and anti-PT sentiment. It is corruption that connects the different regions (themes) of his discourse. We then run a computerized similarity analysis to confirm the central placement of corruption regarding the whole of his discourse and its different regions.

Introduction

In October 2018, a somewhat obscure politician called Jair Bolsonaro[1] was elected president of Brazil, capturing 55.01% of the valid votes, on the ticket of a very small party with no solid funds or structure. Presenting himself as an outsider of the political establishment and a champion in the fight against corruption, his extreme-right stance on crime, minority rights, gender and racial equality, democracy, etc., and his raucous persona have earned him the epithets of 'populist' (Schipani & Leahy, 2018), 'populist conservative' (Londoño & Andreoni, 2018), 'right-wing populist' (Faiola & Lopes, 2018), 'far-right populist' (Phillips & Phillips, 2018), and 'crude and thuggish populist' (Times, 2018) in the international press. Even academics such as Rovira Kaltwasser, Nadia Urbinati, and Lawrence Rosenthal have referred to him as an extreme right-wing populist (Charleaux, 2018). But can he truly be called a populist?

In this article, we contend that Bolsonaro is not a 'classic' populist, or, putting it in another fashion, that using the classic concept of populism to grasp his discourse and role in contemporary Brazilian politics may miss important innovations introduced by Bolsonaro. We will attempt to demonstrate that, contrary to what the bulk of the literature on populism argues, the concept of 'the people' has a marginal role in his political discourse, while the concept of corruption lies at the centre of it, articulating diverse discursive areas such as morals, economics, foreign relations, etc., with Bolsonaro's strong anti-left stance. First, however, we will review the literature on populism, particularly the conceptualizations proposed by Cas Mudde and Cristóbal Rovira Kaltwasser, and by Ernesto Laclau, given that the former tries to cover different aspects of the concept and is based on a comprehensive review of the literature and the latter is arguably the most philosophically sophisticated take on the matter to date. We will also examine the contribution of Ricardo Mendonça and Renato Caetano, who adhere to the recent trend of explaining populism through its visual presentation, chiefly on social media. This new approach expands the possibilities for understanding present-day politics, while preserving key aspects of the previous theory of populism, as we intend to show. Second, we will analyse the text of Jair Bolsonaro's political platform for the 2018 presidential election in search of key concepts, discursive regions, and articulations.

In terms of methodology, the literature review will make use of textual analysis with the aim of organizing ideas rather than capturing the hidden meanings and articulations of discourse. The analysis of Bolsonaro's discourse will be done by a combination of techniques with the aid of a computer program called Iramuteq (R interface for Multidimensional Analysis of Texts and Questionnaires),[2] which facilitates the statistical analysis of texts extracted from interviews and documents such as Bolsonaro's campaign platform. With the goal of identifying different regions (themes) of Bolsonaro's discourse, we employed the Descending Hierarchical Analysis (DHA) algorithm, called ALCESTE (Contextual Lexical Analysis of a Set of Text Segments),[3] and the Similarity Analysis algorithm, which divides the corpus into semantic contextual units and compares them according to the lexemes they contain.

The problematic concept of populism

Statements about the lack of clarity and cohesion of the concept of populism are commonplace in the academic literature (Kaltwasser et al., 2017a; Laclau, 2005; Mudde & Kaltwasser, 2017; Taggart, 2000). Mudde and Kaltwasser see it as 'an essentially contested concept ... a perfect example of conceptual confusion' (Mudde & Kaltwasser, 2017, p. 2). In her contribution to the literature, Margaret Canovan refuses to propose a general theory of populism. After surveying a trove of empirical cases and arriving at a typology of populisms,[4] she concludes that the types are 'not reducible to a single core' (Canovan, 1981, p. 298).

In the introductory chapter to the Oxford Handbook of populism, Kaltwasser et al. present a bibliometric analysis of articles published in leading political science journals that covers the historical development of the literature over the last decades (Kaltwasser et al., 2017b). English-written political science started publishing on populism in the 1950s. The literature expanded until the 1970s but hit the doldrums in the 1980s. In the 1990s, a new expansion started, which lasts until the present date (Kaltwasser et al., 2017b, p. 9). This most recent wave includes, under the umbrella-concept of populism, diverse political phenomena such as the rise of neoliberal political leaders in Latin America in the late 1980s and early 1990s, the subsequent appearance of leftist charismatic figures such as Evo Morales and Hugo Chaves, the growth of nationalist right-wing movements in Europe throughout the period, the appearance of leftist political forces in the continent such as Podemos in Spain and SYRIZA in Greece, the electoral victories of Donald Trump in the United States and of Jair Bolsonaro in Brazil, just to mention some major references. Despite this rich collection of cases, one cannot avoid the conclusion, after surveying the Handbook, that the authors assembled for that enterprise do not share a common concept of populism, something that Taggart had already concluded 20 years earlier while examining the academic contributions of Isaiah Berlin, Edward Shils, Torcuato Di Tella, and Ernesto Laclau (Taggart, 2000).

Even the secondary literature on populism, which is comprised of texts that focus on assessing and organizing academic works on the theme, has not reached a consensus on the best way to classify different theories of populism. As we have already said, Canovan proposes a typology based on empirical cases. While analysing the scholarship on populism in Brazil, Jorge Ferreira presents a classification based on the schools of thought from which different theories of populism spring: liberalism, modernization theory, and Marxism. After surveying the literature, Mudde and Kaltwasser propose a theoretically oriented typology, but contrary to that of Ferreira, theirs is not genealogical but focused on the inner workings of each approach to the study of populism. Also differing from Ferreira's typology, whose scope is limited to a particular country case, Brazil, Mudde and Kaltwasser's is designed with the ambition of serving as a template for the study of populism anywhere.

It is worthwhile looking into Mudde and Kaltwasser's typology in more detail, not only because it is based on the most complete survey of the literature produced so far but also because of the theoretical potential they attribute to it. According to the authors, there is the popular agency approach, which understands populism as a democratic phenomenon that springs from the people's engagement in politics; the socioeconomic approach, which sees populism as a brand of fiscal irresponsibility practiced by rulers to amass popular support; the political psychology approach, which focus on the 'folkloric style of politics' practiced by leaders who display unprofessional political behaviour with the aim of attracting media attention and popular support (Mudde & Kaltwasser, 2017, pp. 3-4); and their ideational approach, which defines populism as

> a thin-centered ideology that considers society to be ultimately separated into two homogeneous and antagonistic camps, 'the pure people' versus 'the corrupt elite', and which argues that politics should be an expression of the *volonté générale* (general will) of the people. (Mudde & Kaltwasser, 2017, p. 6)

We could stop at this point and validate whether Mudde and Kaltwasser's approach fits the figure of Jair Bolsonaro in order to answer our original question about the appropriateness of calling him a populist. Nonetheless, that would make this essay a simple exercise in a conceptual application, in other words, our contribution would be theoretically trite. But there is a productive way of enriching our theoretical reflection that, at the same time, contributes to further the analysis of a case in point: testing not only the approach proposed by Mudde and Kaltwasser but also Ernesto Laclau theory of populism. In fact, we intend to show that they are strikingly similar and that the approach proposed by the organizers of the *Oxford Handbook* is a theoretically watered-down version of Laclau's theory of populism. Let's see why.

Leaning on the contributions of Antonio Gramsci theory of hegemony, Ferdinand Saussure's structural linguistics, and Jacques Lacan's psychoanalytic theory, Laclau has set himself to reshape the theory of populism, thus turning the concept from a merely descriptive and often disparaging term into a thick theoretical construct with the potential of capturing key elements of contemporary democratic politics (Laclau, 2005). In this task, he often counted on the collaboration of Chantal Mouffe (Laclau & Mouffe, 1985).

Laclau clearly rejects 'attempts to identify the social base of populism', such as in Margaret Canovan's typology (Canovan, 1981), as a vain search for the universal substance of the concept, as if it could only pertain to specific social actors or even social classes.

> the inanity of the whole exercise of trying to identify the universal contents of populism becomes evident: as we have seen, it has repeatedly led to attempts to identify the social base of populism – only to find out a moment later that one cannot but continue calling 'populist' movements with entirely disparate social bases. (Laclau, 2005, p. 15)

According to the Argentine thinker, populism surfaces in moments of crisis of the democratic system, when the institutions are unable to satisfy the individual demands of the citizens. Such situations foster the establishment of solidarities among groups of people with different demands – a movement of mobilization Laclau calls 'the equivalence of demands'. The populist leader then erupts in the political arena, galvanizing the mobilized masses through a discourse that is seen by his adversaries as ridden with demagoguery and manipulation (Laclau, 2006, pp. 57–58). In other words, the struggle for hegemony heightens to a point in which dichotomous solutions come to dominate the discursive realm of politics (Laclau, 2006, pp. 56–57). In this context, the populist is the political project that appropriates the idea of 'the people' as its chief discursive point of reference in the contest between two opposing solutions.

Laclau's adhesion to Gramsci's concept of hegemony leads him to privilege ideological struggle and the role of discourse in it (Laclau & Mouffe, 1985, pp. 137–138). Applying concepts borrowed from structural linguistics to political discourse, he sees political identities as formed in an exclusively relational fashion (Laclau, 1990, p. 207). Thus, the 'birth' of populism is also the birth of antipopulism: its political antipode. It is important to notice that this formalistic way of conceiving the constitution of political identities leads him to the conclusion that they in fact have no obligatory semantic content. In this regard, Laclau goes beyond Saussure's contention that all signifiers must correspond to something signified and adheres to the post-structuralist notion of the empty signifier.[5] The expression 'the people' employed by populist discourse, in his perspective, belongs just to this category of concepts: it conveys whatever content the actual struggling political forces manage to project upon it.

This conception is cogent with Carl Schmitt's reflection on the nature of the political as essentially conflictual. According to this German philosopher, 'the specific political distinction ... is that between friend and enemy' (Schmitt, 1976, p. 26). Laclau himself does not cite Schmitt very often as a source, contrary to his intellectual partner Chantal Mouffe, who has creatively received Schmitt's concept of the political.[6] But the similarities between Laclau's theory of populism and Schmitt's concept of the political are plentiful. According to Schmitt, the distinction between friend and enemy is eminently public and not private. Moreover, this distinction is of a special kind because it cannot be reduced to or discarded by substantive distinctions such as those of ethnic, cultural or religious nature. These substantive distinctions do exist in the private realm, but they only become political by irrupting in the public arena, a process that corresponds to becoming the focal point of antagonism between belligerent political factions (Schmitt, 1976, pp. 25–27). Thus, for Schmitt, as for Laclau, the content of what is political is not fixed.

The floating semantics of populism is a key aspect of Laclau's theory, and one that allows him to give the concept a positive and progressive aspect, differently from the bulk of the academic literature that over decades has portrayed populism as a menace to democracy, to liberal institutions, and even to responsible economic policy. Laclau understands populism as a potential conduit for democratic renewal through the inclusion in the public realm of demands and groups of people that had been previously out of it. In a well-functioning liberal democratic context, these groups and their demands are held outside of the public space by the capacity of the state to meet the needs of individuals. Hence, these demands are extinguished at the administrative level and the individual does not establish solidarity liaisons with other individuals (equivalence) in order to publicly demand the state (Laclau, 2005, p. 89).

Although the notion of an empty signifier forces Laclau to conclude that the content of the concept of the people in populist discourse varies widely, 'from communism to fascism' (Laclau, 2006, p. 57), it is undeniable that his main contribution is to show the democratic logic lodged inside movements and figures deemed populist. His article on the Latin American centre-left movements (later called Pink Tide by some commentators), which focuses on the case of Hugo Chavez, is a clear example of such an attempt to give populism a good name. Instead of trying to exempt Chavez from been called a true populist thus assuming that the epithet 'populist' is an imprecation, Laclau confirms that the Venezuelan leader is populist and tries to show that his populism was the only democratic way out of Venezuela's ossified, corrupt, and oligarchic political regime (Laclau, 2006, p. 60). The comparison he makes with other Latin American countries such as Brazil, Argentina, Chile, and Uruguay is revealing of his mode of thinking: since they accomplished a democratic transition that brought about a regime able to accommodate popular demands, populism did not surface (Laclau, 2006, p. 60). If Laclau was still alive, he probably would feel pressed to explain how his theory could accommodate recent events, such as the electoral victory and popularity of Jair Bolsonaro in Brazil.

Now, after briefly surveying Laclau's theory of populism, one can clearly see how Mudde and Kaltwasser's ideational approach can be interpreted as an attempt to translate it into descriptive terminology. The 'thin-centered' ideology refers to the floating semantic aspect they and Laclau identify in populist discourse, chiefly in the definition of 'the people' but also in other concepts that populate it. The reference to the notion of society as 'separated into two homogeneous and antagonistic camps' in Mudde and Kaltwasser's definition fits perfectly Laclau's description of the dichotomization of politics brought about by the emergence of populism. Their contention that by presenting itself as true representative of the people, populism creates its antipode, the elite, the anti-populist faction, it is also coherent with the Schmittian flavour of Laclau's theory. Finally, and most importantly, despite the effort of these authors to propose an abstract concept of populism, they all agree that populism is an ideology inexorably grounded in a notion of 'the people'. Thus, the concept of populism has a necessary content, 'the people', even if it is an empty shell that can receive different semantic fillings.

The central role given to the notion of 'the people' in populist rhetoric is pervasive in the rest of the literature. Authors of the first wave, such as Edward Shils saw the opposition between the people and the elite as the main feature of populism (Shils, 1956, pp. 100–101). Among the main features of populism, Isaiah Berlin identifies a disposition to speak in the name of the majority (Venturi et al., 2001, pp. 173–178). Taggart, who is one of the Handbook's organizers, claims that most common feature of populism is the assertion that it is for the people' (Taggart, 2000, p. 91). Even Canovan, one of the founders of the new generation of studies of populism, cannot refrain from affirming the centrality of the people in the concept's semantics: 'Populism in modern democratic societies is best seen as an appeal to "the people" against both the established structure of power and the dominant ideas and values of the society' (Canovan 1999, p. 2).

Recent contributions to the theory of populism have contended that the analysis of the phenomenon should not be restricted to language and discourse. Also leaning on Laclau's theory, Maria Casullo explores the visual presentation of populist leaders on social media to argue that their bodies function as a primary signifier within populist communication (Casullo, 2018). Her approach to populism was borrowed by Ricardo F. Mendonça and Renato Duarte Caetano and applied to the case of Jair Bolsonaro to argue that his visual presentation (1) mirrors the people, (2) displays extraordinary features and (3) appropriates symbols of power (Mendonça & Caetano, 2021).

Mendonça and Caetano agree with the argument that the literature on populism has paid almost exclusive attention to discourse while neglecting its visual aspects, a fair point to make if we consider the importance of visual-centric social media in today's political communication. By interpreting images published on Bolsonaro's Instagram account, the authors conclude that his unsophisticated visual self-presentation is a caricature of the demeanour of graveness expected from a president, concluding that this 'performance hyperbolizes the transgressive aspect of populism, producing a vertiginous and pleasurable ambiguity toward the figure of the leader' (Mendonça & Caetano, 2021, p. 212).

In the next section, we will examine the case of Jair Bolsonaro and see how it relates to the elements of the theories of populism examined above.

Bolsonaro and the people

Jair Bolsonaro was born to a lower middle-class family with an Italian and German background in the Ribeira Valley of the State of São Paulo. At the age of 33, he retired from the army as a captain, after almost being expelled from the corporation for being caught planning a terrorist attack to a water supply facility of the city of Rio de Janeiro. That same year, 1988, Bolsonaro was elected to the city council of Rio de Janeiro, amassing votes from low-ranking military personnel and their families.[7] His first electoral success can be credited to the popularity gained as the leader of a movement demanding a pay raise for the lower ranks of the army and the graduates of military schools. Bolsonaro has been a professional politician since then, moving through several parties before settling in the Partido Progressista (PP), a medium-size right-wing party deeply embroiled in corruption scandals. He was first elected federal deputy in 1990, a post he held on to through six consecutive elections, always keeping a low profile and a low level of engagement in parliamentary activity until he was elected president in November 2018.

In the following paragraphs, we will interpret Bolsonaro's political discourse using as a source the document containing his political platform in the 2018 presidential election.[8] We will follow an anticlimactic order of analysis and address first the most important question pertaining to the appropriateness of branding Bolsonaro a populist: the concept of the people.

The Bolsonaro campaign adopted a moto that later become the slogan of his presidency: Brazil above all and God above everyone. There is clearly no reference to the Brazilian people in the moto, but to Brazil as a nation. One could hypothesize that this reference to nation is, in fact, an indirect reference to the Brazilian people, but that interpretation is unwarranted, as we intend to show.

The entire document of the platform contains 81 slides (not pages), each one containing a few slim paragraphs. Contrary to most of the platforms of competitive candidates in Brazil's presidential elections, which traditionally are detailed documents covering most areas of policy under the jurisdiction of the executive branch of government, Bolsonaro's is a political pamphlet written in a crude belligerent style. Just to provide the reader with a basis for comparison, the document containing the platform of Fernando Haddad, his main opponent in the 2018 election, has four times as many words as his.[9] Their visual styles are also strikingly different. While Haddad's platform is presented as a neat policy paper, comprised exclusively of text organized in coherent topics linked by rational argumentation, Bolsonaro's resembles a PowerPoint presentation made by an elementary school student, mixing texts boxes in different styles and colours with images of all sorts, from tables and figures to the hands of Christ, all done with the intent to appear crude, coarse, and at the same time virulent.

More importantly, in the entire document, there are only six references to the Brazilian people, and none of them is semantically loaded. Three of those references are very trite: one in the chapter entitled 'Free press', which states that 'our people should be free to think, get information, opine, write, and choose their future'; a second one in a chapter entitled 'All will be done according to the law', simply declaring that the constitution was written by the representatives of the people; and a third one found in the chapter called 'Zero-base budget', which states that the people's money (the public budget) will be spent according to priorities and goals.

The other three are a bit more loaded with meaning. Two occurrences of the term 'people' appear in the chapter entitled the 'New Ministry of Foreign Affairs' (Novo Itamaraty). The first affirms that the Ministry must serve the values of the Brazilian people. The defense of conservative values is a core element of Bolsonarian discourse. These are values often associated with being Christian and being a heterosexual member of a family. The defense of such values is repeatedly articulated with the image of the menace posed by leftist ideologies, like in this passage of the same document, in the chapter called 'Our flag is green-yellow':

> In the last 30 years cultural Marxism and its derivations, like Gramscism, have colluded with the corrupt oligarchies to sabotage the values of the Nation and of the Brazilian family.

That looks like a school-book quote of populist discourse. It contains the radical opposition between two warring parties (Bolsonarism and the left); there is a clear rejection of elites (named as oligarchies); and it speaks in the name of the Nation and of the Brazilian family. But there is no reference to the people. This is different from saying that 'the people' is an empty signifier. In the case of Bolsonarian discourse, 'the people' is rarely articulated as a central category loaded with predicates. One could object that the word 'nation' found in the quotation above, is playing the role of 'the people' and hence that Bolsonaro's discourse is typically populist. However, a search for 'nation' in the document yields a meagre result: six occurrences in passages that are shallow in terms of meaning and do not provide a clear link with the concept of 'the people'.

Bolsonarian discourse dramatically construes a leftist scarecrow against which it articulates its stance as a champion of conservative, individualistic, God-fearing values. The second reference to 'the people', found in the chapter on Foreign Relations, follows this strategy of demonizing the left:

> We will stop honoring murderous dictatorships and stop despising, or even attacking, important democracies such as the United States, Israel, and Italy. We will neither celebrate spurious trade agreements nor share the patrimony of the Brazilian people with international dictators.

The passage is an anti-left diatribe commonly found in Bolsonarian discourse. The left, more precisely the Workers Party (PT) and its representatives,[10] is accused of trying to make Brazil communist. The independent stance of Brazilian foreign policy regarding the United States and Europe, and the goal of becoming a key representative of the Global South in the arena of international relations, championed by Minister Celso Amorim under Lula's presidency, are interpreted as signs of communism, and the PT is portrayed as a major force behind the Forum of São Paulo, which according to Bolsonarism is an international league of countries bent on exporting communism all over the planet: the Forum is cited five times in the document. As for the meaning of 'the people', the message is also trite: Brazilian foreign policy must be conceived according to the interests of the Brazilian people. As in the previous passages examined above, here 'the people' is not named as an agent but solely as a holder of propriety and wealth.

Finally, the first reference to 'the people' in the document states that in order to be truly free, 'the Brazilian people has to rid itself of the corrupt politicians ... there must be less space for populists and their lies'. The message here is that, by voting Bolsonaro, the people will free the country of political corruption. There isn't much to say about the semantics of 'the people' in this passage either, but it could be argued that the semantic inaneness we found in this particular concept actually applies to the whole of Bolsonaro's discourse. After all, if Mudde and Kaltwasser are right and populism is a thin-centred ideology, then vague and imprecise concepts must abound in it. But that is not the case. There is a concept that indeed abounds in the document, giving meaning to several of its passages. And that is 'corruption'.

The word 'corruption' is used 26 times in the platform, and it has the important function of bringing together the different parts of Bolsonaro's discourse. It connects morals with domestic politics, with militarism, with a strong anti-left stance, and with economic performance. In his diatribes, Bolsonaro equates corruption with theft. Above all, a good politician is one that does not embezzle public moneys or propriety. Although this anti-Machiavellian move of equating private morals with political morality might appear crude from an intellectually sophisticated viewpoint, its simplicity and intuitive power have enormous popular appeal, particularly for an electorate that for decades has been bombarded by a press coverage focused on the exploitation of political corruption scandals (Azevedo, 2017; Feres Júnior, 2020).

There is a second moralist layer in Bolsonaro's discourse, this one related to the advocacy of conservative Christian values, such as heteronormativity, traditional gender roles, prohibition of abortion, etc. But those issues are not treated explicitly in terms of 'moral corruption'. The simple language of Bolsonarian ideology seems to limit the usage of the word corruption to the realm of politics. Indeed, in current ordinary Brazilian Portuguese, the word corruption means chiefly political corruption. Meanings such as moral corruption, corruption of the soul, corruption of customs are rarely used unless one is intent on sounding erudite. In the text of the platform, domestic politics is described as utterly plagued by corruption 'in the last decades'.

Bolsonaro branded the modus operandi of Brazil's democratic regime 'old politics', while presenting himself as the herald of a new way of doing politics. The fact that elected presidents trade cabinet nominations for political support in parliament, a natural procedure in multiparty systems with proportional representation all over the democratic world (Abranches, 1988; Figueiredo & Limongi Neto, 1999), is seen by Bolsonaro and his followers as a form of corruption. Again, applying individual morals to politics, Bolsonaro brands this practice 'tit-for-tat', clearly suggesting that it is a kind of thievery. Following the simple logic of Bolsonarian discourse, besides being conservative, the good politician is the one that sticks to his guns, who does not budge to pressure, who does not negotiate his principles with adversaries – the gender language here is intentional.

Bolsonaro built his entire political career around the defense of the interests and principles of the military. A staunch admirer of the dictatorial regime that ruled Brazil from 1964 to 1985, a denialist when it comes to human rights abuse during that period, he does not save words to praise the alleged no-frills honesty, spiritedness, and love of nation of the military. Again, the concept of corruption is key to integrating his pro-military stance into the rest of the discourse. For the Brazilian reader, the reference to 'the last decades' in the passage commented above suggests that under the Military Dictatorship (1964–1985), there was no corruption, and, consequently, that corruption only appeared after the return of the democratic regime. Relying on this idyllic image of the military, Bolsonaro has resorted to them in an attempt to bypass the process of negotiating with political parties a support coalition in Congress, which would require him to use nominations as a bargaining asset. Instead, he has placed a record number of military personnel, both active-duty and reserve, in posts all over his administration.

The occupation of bureaucratic posts of the executive branch by the military under Bolsonaro is truly staggering. In January 2015, the first month of Dilma Rousseff's second term, there were 2600 military employed in the presidency, 2200 in the Ministry of Infrastructure, 500 in the Ministry of Science and Communications, 500 in the Ministry of Foreign Relations, and 1500 others distributed throughout the cabinet. In less than 2 years of government, Bolsonaro managed to raise these numbers to 15,100 military persons employed only in the presidency, 11,000 in the Ministry of Mining and Energy, 10,000 in the Ministry of Science and Communications, 8300 in the Ministry of the Environment, 7300 in the Ministry of Public Health, and 16,000 others in different places of his cabinet.[11] This calculation discounts public servants actually engaged in military functions. In sum, the executive branch under Bolsonaro employs almost ten times as many military persons in non-military functions as it employed under Dilma.

In fact, the study shows that the total number of military persons employed and their distribution throughout the cabinet vary little from the beginning of the records, January 2013, until May 2016, when Dilma was deposed. This number grew moderately under Michel Temer's government (2016–2018) and then exploded with Bolsonaro. As of 2021, the president's cabinet had 11 Ministers of State that are military out of 26, including the Minister of Health, an active-duty general that does not have a medical degree responsible for leading the country's public health system efforts to fight the Covid-19 pandemic.

This strategy of populating his government with military personnel aims at consolidating the support of the military in case of political instability. It is a move to display a type of power that is not acquired through democratic means and serves to keep the regime under threat.[12] Bolsonaro thus actualizes the idea, very much present within the military establishment, that the military must preserve the power to intervene in the political arena in case of strife – the so-called *poder moderador*.[13]

Beyond the power politics of militarization, or combined to it, the resource to the military symbolizes an administration that does not budge to the 'old politics' of negotiation. In other words, it coheres with Bolsonaro anti-corruption stance. In November 2019, one year after his electoral victory, he left Partido Social Liberal (PSL), previously an insignificant party used by his group just for the sake of meeting the legal requirements of Brazil's electoral laws.[14] Until early 2022, the president remained without a party membership, a highly unusual choice in Brazil's political history. In sum, by rejecting the association with institutional politics, both through the regular means of party negotiation or through simple party membership, Bolsonaro continues to present himself as a champion in the war against corruption.

Bolsonaro's economic platform was written by the Chicago Boy Paulo Guedes, who has been his Minister of Economy since the election. The text of the platform blames Brazil (sic) for never having truly adopted 'liberal[15] principles'. According to the chapter entitled 'Economic Liberalism', 'corrupt politicians and populists left the legacy of a high budget deficit, explosive fiscal conditions, low economic growth, and high unemployment rate'. The title in the following page of the document speaks for itself: 'The problem is the legacy of inefficiency and corruption left behind by the PT'. Again, 'corruption' links up the ultra-liberal economic viewpoint of Bolsonarism with *antipetismo* – a neologism that has become commonplace in Brazilian political parlance and conveys a strong and irrational hatred for Lula, the Workers Party, its politicians, and ideas (Davis & Straubhaar, 2020; Ribeiro et al., 2016).

The importance of the concept of 'the people' in Bolsonarian discourse pales before the central role played by 'corruption'. It is not a coincidence that 'elite' is also rarely used by the president and his followers – the platform has no reference to elites. With his rude behaviour, poor command of the Portuguese language and of speech in general, and resistance to reasoned argumentation, Bolsonaro does present himself as an authentic representative of the simple man. That would be a true sign of populism, according to much of the literature. After all, Mudde and Kaltwasser have placed the people-elite opposition at the core of their concept of populism, and Laclau has affirmed that the public irruption of populism necessarily comes with the symmetric event of the public irruption of anti-populism. However, Bolsonaro's strategy of presentation is not connected to a glorification

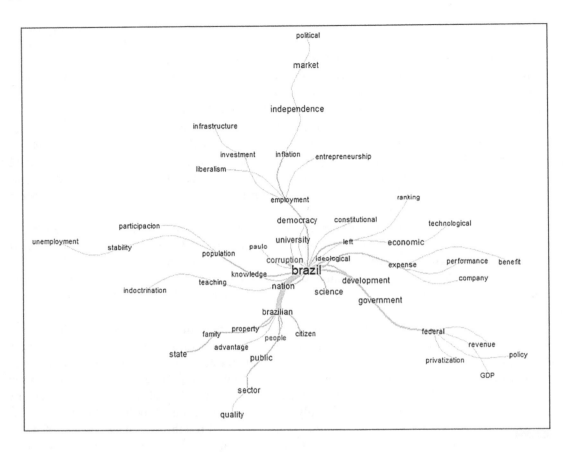

Figure 1. Similarity analysis of the text of the platform.

of the people in tandem with a denunciation of an exploitative elite. The absence of a clear anti-elite stance might have to do with the strong support he has received from business elites – agricultural, industrial, commercial, and financial –, or maybe with the fact that his opponent of choice, the PT with Lula at the helm, is a party with a strong popular appeal, and thus can hardly be described as an elite.

Another probable reason that is strongly connected with the support Bolsonaro receives from business is his adherence to neoliberal economic principles, a commitment that has his Minister of Economy, Paulo Guedes, as a guarantor before the 'market'. A pundit of neoliberalism, Guedes was formerly a banker and a columnist of newspaper O Globo. His weekly articles were nothing more than neoliberal diatribes praising the virtues of the market and lambasting the fiscal irresponsibility of elected politicians of the left. Actually, the Bolsonaro is a neophyte to small-state ideology (Almeida, 2019; Cesarino, 2019). Throughout his career as a federal representative, he either was aloof or opposed neoliberal reforms but adhered to this ideology during the campaign in a clear move to capture the support of business elites for his candidacy against the 'populist' left. In his campaign platform, the word 'populism' appears three times, always used to attack the left and its alleged proclivity to waste public money. Again, 'corruption' appears as a linking concept that connects 'populism', here articulated through an economic approach, with the other areas of Bolsonarian discourse: 'corrupt politicians and populists have left us the heritage of high public deficit … '.[16]

The centrality of the word corruption can be further confirmed by a similarity analysis of the platform text, done with the help of the software Iramuteq, which plots a tree-shaped graph composed of related words. This type of analysis takes into account co-occurrences of words and, thus, helps identify the structure of a textual corpus.

Then, to further strengthen our argument, we utilized a web-based tool to obtain data from Bolsonaro's official accounts on Facebook, Instagram, Twitter, and YouTube during his first 6 months in office. Together his 6 accounts published 2339 posts during the period, and their content confirm what we had found before. The word 'people' was used only 51 times, and most of them in a general, semantically thin, manner. This finding shows that the marginal role given to the concept of the 'people' in Bolsonaro's campaign platform, revealed above, also characterizes his social media communication after elected president (Figure 1).

The centrality of the word corruption is second only to 'Brazil', a term that is obviously employed in all discursive regions. The proximity to the centre always denotes that 'corruption' is not specific to any region (theme) but is present all over the text.

Conclusion

Mendonça and Caetano are right in saying that Bolsonaro presents himself as coarse and rude. However, like many authors before them, they resort to the analytical shortcut of taking populism from the outset as a thing-in-the-world, a phenomenon, and then discuss its theoretical implications. The correct contention is that the literature on populism has focused on discourse while neglecting visual data does not do away with the conceptual problems of populism and does not prove that Bolsonaro is a true populist. In fact, the authors take an opposite path: they assume that Bolsonaro is a populist and then go on to show that his alleged populism has a consistent visual element.

Mendonça and Caetano make a convincing effort to show that a large number of the images Bolsonaro's page posted on Instagram contain elements that the broader literature associates with populism, particularly the display of his body in close physical proximity with common people and crowds (Mendonça & Caetano, 2021, p. 221). In sum, if they are right and our analysis is sound, the 'people' are rarely mentioned in Bolsonaro's textual communication but visual references to them abound in the posts on his social media pages. This apparent paradox might be explained as different elements of a communication strategy that encompasses textual and visual media, which in turn do not have to mirror each other entirely in terms of content. Instead, their relation might be complementary. That is a hypothesis that calls for more analytical work in order to be confirmed, nonetheless.

It is true that the bulk of the literature on populism has been focused on describing it as a discourse, including the contributions of Mudde and Kaltzwaser and of Laclau. In plain terms, Bolsonaro's politics can better be described as a collection of ultra-conservative, neoliberal, right-wing stances loosely integrated around a crude anti-corruption fervour. These stances are defended through a belligerent strategy of high polarization against an enemy whose description varies from regular democratic political institutions, such as Congress and the Supreme Court, to party politics, to the political left, and to Lula and the PT, more specifically. It is tempting to equate this description to Laclau's conception of populism a gyrating politicizing machine for naming enemies. But as we have shown above, Bolsonaro is fiercely engaged in moving key political issues (such as women's rights, health choices, education rights, etc.) to the private realm. His insistent attempts to reduce politics to individual religious morals are, in fact, the opposite of the inclusive democratizing energy what Laclau identified in populism. Depoliticization is one of his key political strategies.

The Bolsonarian discourse is indeed thin, something that Mudde and Kaltwasser see as a chief characteristic of populism, but the semantic depth of concepts in it varies a great deal. As we have shown above, the concept of corruption ties many loose ends of his overall political discourse. In his very apt critique of Joe Biden's anti-corruption agenda in international relations, Benjamin Fogel argues that instead of fighting populism, American-backed anti-corruption crusades like the Lava Jato Operation ended up creating the proper conditions for the installation of 'authoritarian populist' governments (Fogel, 2021). According to the author, '[a]nticorruption populism is a form of politics based on promoting national salvation from the plague of corruption through a messianic figure located outside of the system, who will "cleanup politics"' (Fogel, 2018).

This seems to be a good short summary of the process that led to Bolsonaro's electoral success, but with a small pitfall. In this short essay, Fogel never really explains how Bolsonaro fits the populist shoe. On the contrary, he assumes from the outset that Bolsonaro's populism is a matter of fact, which is the exact point that we have been problematizing in this article. Fogel concludes that the populist, this charismatic outsider, promises 'to sweep the system clean purging the corrupt elite that dominate the country' (Fogel, 2018). Again, another seemingly fitting description of recent Brazilian political history, but, as we have shown here, the stress on the elite-people opposition is a classical tenet of the literature on populism but hardly a good description of Bolsonaro's anti-corruption crusade, which chiefly targeted the most popular Brazilian political party, the PT, and the most popular Brazilian political leader, Lula (Samuels & Zucco, 2018).

The wave of popularity that led to Bolsonaro's electoral victory seems to have been fuelled by process of equivalence, the way it is described by Laclau. Business elites, the masses of poor evangelicals, the white middle-class of the South and Southeast regions, medical doctors, engineers, and college graduates in general, they all came together in support of his ticket. This disparate amalgam of Brazilians was not united, however, by a common ideal of 'the people' or of 'nation', but by the anti-corruption and anti-political fervour Bolsonaro displayed. It was his condemnation of politics, understood by the common people as an utterly corrupt activity, his condemnation of the PT, portrayed by the news media as the champion of political corruption, that did the trick of bringing them all together.

Another dissonance between the Bolsonaro phenomenon and the theories of populism we have been surveying is related to the polarization brought about by politicization, which in Schmittian terms are one and the same process. Thus, if Bolsonaro was a textbook populist, then his appearance in the scene would trigger the appearance of the anti-populist, which in this case would be the PT. But history doesn't fit this hypothetical narrative. Antipestismo was not created by Bolsonaro or by the alt-right movements that sprouted in Brazil after the June 2013 wave of protest. It has existed since PT has become a formidable political force (Samuels & Zucco, 2014).

An enthusiast of the theory of populism could still argue that Laclau's narrative is not lost here. It was exactly because the governments led by PT stopped delivering economic development that demands from disparate sectors of Brazilian society got together behind Bolsonaro with the aim of changing the political status quo. The analysis of this hypothesis would require that we identify what demands were those, whether they were real or perceived, how was the process of politicization of these new demands, etc.

After all, is Bolsonaro a true populist? Based on the analysis we have done so far, the answer is: he displays many behavioural features that the bulk of the literature ascribes to populism (such as coarseness, aggressiveness, authoritarianism, and disregard for institutions), but, at the same time, his discourse lacks key elements of the concepts of populism proposed by this same literature, such as a central role for the concept of 'the people', and, as a consequence, for the opposition between people and elite, or even the quasi-absence in this same discourse of strong national sentiment.

The literature on populism is extensive and fast-growing. However, or maybe because of it, its lacks cohesion and conceptual coherence. Many authors treat populism as a thing-in-the-world just in need of systematic description, as if such a thing preexisted its theory. On the contrary, we believe that a complex object of knowledge such as populism is the very product of its theorization. Its validity depends not only on the theory's internal logic, but on the painstaking job of testing cases and building generalizations and typologies.

The analysis of Bolsonaro's case done in this article shows that, if Mendonça and Caetano are right, there might be an interplay between textual and visual communication strategies that enables Bolsonaro to present himself as someone close to the people without having to deal with the people within the parameters of textual rational argumentation. We have also argued that Bolsonaro seems to operate in a manner that is the opposite of that of the populist defined by Laclau: instead of promoting the politicization of demands that were previously kept out of the public realm, Bolsonaro insists on reducing previously politicized issues to the private realm of individual morals. There is much to be said about this dialectic of politicization and depoliticization regarding Bolsonaro and probably many other political figures nowadays deemed populist. However, this must be left for a future contribution.

Notes

1. Jair Bolsonaro was elected to the city council of Rio de Janeiro in 1988, the same year he retired from the army as a lieutenant, after leading a movement for raising the salary of low-ranking military and orchestrating the bombing of a water treatment plant that serves the city of Rio de Janeiro. His first electoral success can be credited to the popularity he acquired as a leader of low-ranking military men and their families. Bolsonaro has been a professional politician since then, moving from party to party before settling in the Partido Popular (PP), a medium-size right-wing party deeply embroiled in corruption scandals. He was first elected federal deputy in 1990, a post to which he was re-elected five more consecutive times, always relying on the vote of conservative military and people that resented the end of the military dictatorship. Bolsonaro kept a low profile and a low level of engagement in parliamentary activity throughout his parliamentary career, something of which he seems to be proud, Congress approved only two bills sponsored by him throughout the 27-years period of his career as a federal deputy.
2. IRAMUTEQ (*Interface de R pour les Analyses Multidimensionnelles de Textes et de Questionnaires*) is an open-source computer program developed by Pierre Ratinaud (2009), based on the statistical software R, that allows for an array of statistical analysis of textual corpora (Ratinaud, 2009; Camargo & Justo, 2013).
3. ALCESTE (Reinert, 1990) is a program created by M. Reinert, whose algorithm was later incorporated by IRAMUTEQ, among other types of statistical analyses of text (Reinert, 1990).
4. Based on historical evidence, Canovan identifies the following types: farmers' populism, peasants' populism, intellectuals' populism, populist dictatorship, populist democracy, reactionary populism, and politicians' populism.
5. This move is possible by conceiving the struggle for hegemony from a Lacanian perspective of an endless strife for representing the real by the symbolic. According to Laclau: 'The representation of the unrepresentable constitutes the terms of the paradox within which hegemony is constructed' (Laclau, 2005, p. 66).

6. Mouffe tried to domesticate Schmitt's conception of the political and apply it to the understanding of the workings of liberal democracy by arguing that the antagonistic nature of politics could be mediated by institutions and thus must not be equaled to a destructive, war-like competition for the annihilation of one's enemy (Mouffe 1999, 2000).
7. The capital of Brazil from the late eighteenth century to 1960, the city of Rio de Janeiro still retains several active military installations such as garrisons, schools, forts, etc.
8. All candidates for president in Brazil are obliged by law to deposit a document containing their political platform in the Supreme Electoral Court.
9. The document containing the electoral platform of Fernando Haddad, of the Workers Party (PT), has a total of 210,594 characters while Bolsonaro's has only 51,683. For Haddad's platform check https://drive.google.com/file/d/1eI6Zqs4v0XqzbmfHVS9NNrppNwzLJE5x/view. For Bolsonaro's platform check https://divulgacandcontas.tse.jus.br/candidaturas/oficial/2018/BR/BR/2022802018/280000614517//proposta_1534284632231.pdf, last accessed in 3 March 2021.
10. The PT won four consecutive presidential elections, starting in 2002, when Lula became president. He then was re-elected in 2006 and helped elect one of his Ministers, Dilma Rousseff, president in 2010. Dilma then won the 2014 presidential election but had her term interrupted in 2016 by a controversial impeachment process.
11. These numbers were extracted from the Transparency Portal of the Federal Government, and organized by the cabinets of Senator Alessandro Vieira (Cidadania) and representative Tabata Amaral (PDT). More information can be found at: https://preview.flourish.studio/5202872/T2tMbc_otm_djTbBa5TjnxQZeGuOssq8WLnbmc8pYL764Sti6FBP6nHeyHEnDT6q/. Last access in 11 March 2021. Realização: Senador Alessandro Vieira (Cidadania/SE) e Dep. Tabata Amaral (PDT/SP) Source https://preview.flourish.studio/5202872/T2tMbc_otm_djTbBa5TjnxQZeGuOssq8WLnbmc8pYL764Sti6FBP6nHeyHEnDT6q/. Last checked in 11 March 2021.
12. Bolsonaro has explicitly threatened or hinted at a military take over several time after becoming president. For some examples, see https://piaui.folha.uol.com.br/materia/vou-intervir/; https://istoe.com.br/bolsonaro-faz-ameaca-aberta-de-golpe-agora-so-falta-o-fuzil/; https://anovademocracia.com.br/noticias/14988-inspirado-por-trump-bolsonaro-ameaca-golpe-em-2022.
13. For the relation between military intervention in Brazilian politics and the notion of *poder moderador* see https://jus.com.br/artigos/82698/um-poder-moderador.
14. It is required by law that all candidates to elected public offices in Brazil have a party membership.
15. The word is here used in its continental sense, which is more cogent to the meaning of libertarian or neoliberal.
16. President Bolsonaro continues to call Lula and the PT populists, blaming them for allegedly being fiscally unresponsible, as in his recent reaction to a speech Lula gave after being exonerated of three convictions by the Supreme Court. See https://valor.globo.com/politica/noticia/2021/03/10/bolsonaro-reage-a-lula-defende-gestao-da-pandemia-e-diz-que-petista-faz-campanha.ghtml.

Disclosure statement

No potential conflict of interest was reported by the author(s).

Funding

This work was supported by FAPERJ, under the *Cientista do Nosso Estado*; by CNPq, under the *Produtividade* Scholarship; and by CNPq and CAPES under the *Institutos Nacionais de Tecnologia*, as part of the *Instituto da Democracia e da Democratização da Comunicação*.

ORCID

João Feres Júnior ⓘ http://orcid.org/0000-0002-5830-0458
Fernanda Cavassana ⓘ http://orcid.org/0000-0003-1668-3160
Juliana Gagliardi ⓘ http://orcid.org/0000-0003-1085-0271

References

Abranches, S. (1988). Presidencialismo de coalizão: o dilema institucional brasileiro. *Dados: Revista de Ciências Sociais*, *31*(1), 3–55.
Almeida, R. d. (2019). Bolsonaro presidente: Conservadorismo, evangelismo e a crise brasileira. *Novos estudos CEBRAP*, (38), 185–213.
Azevedo, F. A. (2017). *A Grande Imprensa e o PT (1989–2014)*. Editora UFSCar.
Camargo, B. V., & Justo, A. M. (2013). IRAMUTEQ: um software gratuito para análise de dados textuais. *Temas em Psicologia*, *21*(2), 513–518. https://doi.org/10.9788/TP2013.2-16
Canovan, M. (1981). *Populism* (1st ed). Harcourt Brace Jovanovich.
Canovan, M. (1999). Trust the people! Populism and the two faces of democracy. *Political Studies*, *47*(1), 2–16.
Casullo, M. E. (2018). *The populist body in the age of social media: A comparative study of populist and non-populist representation*. International Political Science Association Conference.
Cesarino, L. (2019). Identidade e representação no bolsonarismo: Corpo digital do rei, bivalência conservadorismo-neoliberalismo e pessoa fractal. *Revista de Antropologia*, *62*(3), 530–557. https://doi.org/10.11606/2179-0892.ra.2019.165232
Charleaux, J. P. (2018, October 17). Which is extreme right: And why it applies to Bolsonaro. *Nexo*.
Davis, S., & Straubhaar, J. (2020). Producing Antipetismo: Media activism and the rise of the radical, nationalist right in contemporary Brazil. *International Communication Gazette*, *82*(1), 82–100. https://doi.org/10.1177/1748048519880731
Faiola, A., & Lopes, M. (2018, October 4). 'Just like Trump': Bolsonaro leads Brazil's presidential race with right-wing populist pitch. *The Washington Post*. https://www.washingtonpost.com/world/the_americas/just-like-trump-bolsonaro-leads-brazils-presidential-race-with-right-wing-populist-pitch/2018/10/04/c4ba3728-c65c-11e8-9c0f-2ffaf6d422aa_story.html
Feres Júnior, J. (2020). *Cerco midiático: O lugar da esquerda na esfera "publicada*. Friedrich Ebert Stiftung.
Figueiredo, A. M. C., & Limongi Neto, F. P. (1999). *Executivo e legislativo na nova ordem constitucional* (1a. ed.). Editora FGV.
Fogel, B. (2018). Against 'anti-corruption'. *Jacobin* 10.
Fogel, B. (2021). The problem with anti-corruption. *Jacobin* 2.
Kaltwasser, C. R., Taggart, P. A., Espejo, P. O., & Ostiguy, P. (2017a). *The Oxford handbook of populism* (1st ed., Oxford handbooks). Oxford University Press.
Kaltwasser, C. R., Taggart, P. A., Espejo, P. O., & Ostiguy, P. (2017b). Populism: An overview of the concept and the state of the Art. In C. R. Kaltwasser, P. A. Taggart, P. O. Espejo, & P. Ostiguy (Eds.), *The Oxford handbook of populism* (pp. 1–26). Oxford University Press.

Laclau, E. (1990). *New reflections on the revolution of our time.* Verso.
Laclau, E. (2005). *On populist reason.* Verso.
Laclau, E. (2006). La deriva populista y la centroizquierda latinoamericana. *Nueva sociedad,* (205), 56–61.
Laclau, E., & Mouffe, C. (1985). *Hegemony and socialist strategy: Towards a radical democratic politics.* Verso.
Londoño, E., & Andreoni, M. (2018, October 29). Brazil election: How Jair Bolsonaro turned crisis into opportunity. *The New York Times.* https://www.nytimes.com/2018/10/29/world/americas/jair-bolsonaro-brazil-profile.html
Mendonça, R. F., & Caetano, R. D. (2021). Populism as parody: The visual self-presentation of Jair Bolsonaro on Instagram. *The International Journal of Press/Politics, 26*(1), 210–235. https://doi.org/10.1177/1940161220970118
Mouffe, C. (1999). *The challenge of Carl Schmitt, Phronesis (London, England).* Verso.
Mouffe, C. (2000). *The democratic paradox.* Verso.
Mudde, C., & Kaltwasser, C. R. (2017). *Populism: A very short introduction, very short introductions.* Oxford University Press.
Phillips, T., & Phillips, D. (2018, October 7). Far-right populist Jair Bolsonaro leads as Brazil goes to vote. *The Guardian.* https://www.theguardian.com/world/2018/oct/07/brazil-presidential-election-far-right-populist-jair-bolsonaro
Ratinaud, P. (2009*). IRAMUTEQ: Interface de R pour les Analyses Multidimensionnelles de Textes et de Questionnaires.* Retrieved 12 de março de 2021. http://www.iramuteq.org
Reinert, M. (1990). Alceste une méthodologie d'analyse des données textuelles et une application: Aurelia De Gerard De Nerval. *Bulletin of Sociological Methodology/Bulletin de Méthodologie Sociologique, 26*(1), 24–54. https://doi.org/10.1177/075910639002600103
Ribeiro, E., Carreirão, Y., & Borba, J. (2016). Sentimentos partidários e antipetismo: condicionantes e covariantes. *Opinião Pública, 22*(3), 603–637. https://doi.org/10.1590/1807-01912016223603
Samuels, D., & Zucco, C. (2014). Lulismo, Petismo, and the future of Brazilian politics. *Journal of Politics in Latin America, 6*(3), 129–158. https://doi.org/10.1177/1866802X1400600306
Samuels, D. J. and C. Zucco (2018). *Partisans, antipartisans, and nonpartisans: Voting behavior in Brazil.* Cambridge University Press.
Schipani, A., & Leahy, J. (2018). Brazil remains priced for perfection in the eyes of investors. *Folha de S. Paulo.*
Schmitt, C. (1976). *The concept of the political.* Rutgers University Press.
Shils, E. (1956). *The torment of secrecy; the background and consequences of American security policies, Heinemann books on sociology.* W. Heinemann.
Taggart, P. A. (2000). *Populism, concepts in the social sciences.* Open University Press.
Times, The New York. (2018, October 21). Brazil's sad choice (editorial). *The New York Times.* https://www.nytimes.com/2018/10/21/opinion/brazil-election-jair-bolsonaro.html
Venturi, F., Haskell, F., & Berlin, I. (2001). *Roots of revolution: A history of the populist and socialist movements in 19th century Russia* (Rev. ed.). Phoenix Press.

Neo-structuralist bargain and authoritarianism in Nicaragua

Miguel González

ABSTRACT
This paper examines the relations between the FSLN government in Nicaragua and the social actors that have mobilized against it, especially Indigenous, *campesino* and Afro-descendant activisms during the second Ortega administration. These relationships are interpreted from the perspective on a 'neostructuralist bargain' which allowed the FSLN, since 2007, to embrace neoliberal policies under an environment of relative social cohesion and economic growth. That bargain came to an end in 2018 when the government – facing a political crisis – resorted to the use of force and authoritarian practices to contain the mounting social discontent. The limited realization of Indigenous and Afro-descendant rights and the ongoing transformation of agrarian structures that marginalizes peasant economies, coupled with the FSLN's promotion of extractive forms of capitalist accumulation, all tested the bases of the bargain, while also revealed unprecedented articulations of collective agency by subaltern actors.

Introduction

In 2007 Daniel Ortega, Secretary General of the FSLN (Sandinista Front of National Liberation) was signed into office to serve for a second presidential administration, almost 17 years after being defeated in general elections by a right-wing coalition, the National United Opposition (UNO, for its Spanish acronym) led by Violeta Chamorro. The election of Ortega back to the country's presidency was possible due to a carefully articulated strategy to regain power. That strategy included both economic and political elements: politically, it involved the construction of a national alliance with a variety of very dissimilar actors, including the Catholic and Protestant churches, former *contra* insurgents, and Afro-Indigenous political organizations. Economically, the FSLN fostered an inter-class alliance with sectors of the Nicaraguan capitalist class, which had recouped economic and political strength during the almost two decades of right-wing liberal and conservative administrations that espoused neoliberal economic policies and political liberalization (Cuadra, 2016, p. 98).

Close and Martí i Puig, suggest that the election of the FSLN to the Nicaraguan presidency is to be inscribed within the overall 'pink tide' that characterized Latin American politics in the 2000s, in part as an expression of popular discontent with neoliberal governments elected at the dawn of the twenty-first century (2009, p. 31). However, Ortega, *strictu sensu*, was not a newcomer to the pink tide. After overthrowing the Somoza dictatorship in 1979, his party governed Nicaragua under a platform of socialist orientation and faced an exhausting counterrevolutionary war supported by the United States (Sklar, 1988).

Recent social science scholarship on Nicaragua focuses on the contested legacy of *Sandinismo* and the Sandinista Revolution (Collombon & Rodgers, 2018; Figueroa et al., 2021; Hale, 2017), on the changes in the regime type (Martí i Puig & Serra, 2020), agrarian transformations (Martí i Puig & Baumeister, 2017), and social movements and protest in the context of the 2018 political crisis (Cortés Ramos et al., 2020; Cruz-Feliciano, 2021; Tittor, 2018).

To add to this scholarship, my contribution engages with the overall orientation of the FSLN's development discourse and strategy since 2007, which I associate with Latin American neostructuralism, as well as social responses from subaltern sectors. I propose that the evolution of the second Ortega administration can be conceptualized within the overall trend of neostructuralism/neo-developmentalism that has characterized the 'pink tide'. Neostructuralism, according to Leiva (2008), 'hoists the highly seductive notion that international competitiveness, social integration, and political legitimacy can synergistically be attained by swimming along, not against, the swift currents unleashed by globalization' (*xx*). Under this approach, neostructuralist governments embraced a far-reaching agenda inspired by policies of social inclusion – particularly of the most marginalized sectors of the population – combined with functional and pragmatic alliances with sectors of the transnational and domestic capital. This model remains within the parameters of neoliberalism but is premised under the idea that is possible to pursue a 'new "globalization with a human face"' (Leiva, 2008, p. xx).

Although neostructuralist governments offered a vast array of limited mechanisms of participation and inclusion to popular classes, these governments have struggled to contain collective social responses to the adverse effects of neoliberal policies. Larrabure (2020) proposes to conceptualize neostructuralist's strategy to counteract the increasing social mobilization in terms of a socio-political 'bargain'.

> In this bargain vulnerable sectors of society are granted material gains and opportunities for limited consultation, but in return, social movements are asked to give up their ambitions for more direct and participatory forms of democracy and non-market forms of social organization. (p. 10)

My essay explores whether Ortega's second administration can be understood as a neostructuralist bargain, and asks to what extent the mobilization of Indigenous, *campesino* and Afro-descendant actors against Ortega's neoliberal policies might be interpreted as an indication of the limits of that bargain. Theoretically, the essay hypothesizes that the neostructuralist authoritarian variation of the FSLN post-2018, was the regime's response to a crisis of legitimacy. The political crafting of this neostructural authoritarian adaptation was not very different from *cupulism* – 'a top-down, "pact making" style of governance' which has deep roots in Latin American politics of vertical decision making, often through closed-door negotiations between centralist political parties (Carruthers & Rodríguez, 2009, p. 743).

The second Ortega administration initially defined itself as a praiseworthy model of social unity and cooperative relations between the capitalist class and popular sectors of the country (FSLN, 2006). However, this model only worked as long as the FSLN was able to dispense among its political bases the generous Venezuelan aid, and on its ability to sustain an ongoing elitist negotiation scheme with the local capitalist class on issues related to continuity of the neoliberal accumulation model. When the aid declined, social opposition grew while the accommodation with the capitalist class rapidly deteriorated (Feinberg, 2018, p. 7). In response, Ortega resorted to authoritarian practices to stem social discontent against his model of limited participation.

This analysis does not underestimate the political support the FSLN has within important segments of the Nicaraguan population, even despite the enduring current political crisis. Nor does it try to suggest that its most loyal supporters are so because they depend on clientelist political mechanisms that are organized and controlled through the state power. For a certain time, the second Ortega administration succeeded in expanding public spending, significantly increased public sector employment, launched pro-poor social assistance programmes that contributed to reducing extreme poverty, and increased consumption (Rocha, 2019, pp. 61–62). In that sense, even temporarily, Ortega succeeded in reversing the adverse social impacts of two decades of liberal and conservative governments that preceded his administration (Schmook et al., 2022, p. 16).[1] This explains, at least partially, the continued popular support for the FSLN, the galvanization of its most loyal bases and, at least during Ortega's first term (2007–2011), the expansion of his electoral base.

The research approach leading to this paper is for the most part qualitative, though I also draw from historical sources. In terms of the methodology, I have relied on documentary research such as newspapers and reports produced by independent and official media, as well as by academic works. I have also conducted fieldwork at various moments in between 2016 and 2018, when I was able to complete interviews with Indigenous, peasants, and Afro-descendant activists and carried out ethnographic observations at different locations on the Nicaraguan Caribbean Coast.

The FSLN's come back and the making of neostructuralism

Contrary to other Latin America leftist political organizations elected to office in the 2000s, the year 2007 connoted for the FSLN a second coming after it had undergone electoral defeat in 1990s, and three unsuccessful attempts to regain power in the 1990s and early 2000s. The FSLN has conceptualized its new administration as a 'second epoch' of the Sandinista Revolution, an era when the hopes and aspirations of the Nicaraguan people would be finally realized under new political conditions, not characterized by war and confrontation but by peace and reconciliation (Martí i Puig, 2010, p. 92).

The Nicaragua of the 2000s is a very different society than it was in 1979. In broad terms, the 1980s Sandinista Revolution had instituted a *de-facto* single party system – despite claims to political pluralism –; it faced a debilitating US-backed counterrevolutionary war that ended in peace agreements and open elections in 1990; and it had sought to promote – with poor results – a 'mixed economy' in which the state played a central role in accumulation and social redistribution, along with private agents (Weeks, 1987). Cuadra captures the significance of the economic and political changes Nicaragua experienced since 1990:

> the transition from the political project of the revolution to a liberal democratic regime; the pacification of the country and the reconstruction of society after the conflict; and the change from the economic model of the revolution to one characterized by the free market and the reinsertion of the country into a globalized economy. (2016, p. 95)

Therefore, since 1990 the country begun an economic and political transition to a liberal democracy through a multiparty system and the formalities of the rule of law (Álvarez & Vintró, 2009), initiated a social process of incorporation of former insurgents to civil life (Rueda Estrada, 2015), and embedded economic neoliberalism (Close, 1999).

The FSLN that was defeated in 1990 is not the same party governing Nicaragua today. After confronting internal dissidence in mid 1990s, Ortega imposed a centralized leadership with zero tolerance to criticism from within his own party (Martí i Puig, 2010). With respect to the power sharing and electoral competition, in 1999 Ortega crafted a political pact with the then governing

PLC (Liberal Constitutional Party) that involved distribution of state institutions that included the bi-partisan control of the Judiciary, the Electoral Supreme Council, the National Assembly and it also interfered with the rules of succession of the military and police forces. The FSLN could not have built this system of power without the self-interested collaboration of the PLC which also sought to guarantee a long-term power-sharing scheme with the FSLN. The FSLN-PLC *pact* was negotiated secretly and un-democratically and it came into full effect through a constitutional reform passed in 2000. The reform, among other things, included stringent rules for electoral competitors and modifying the minimum percentage through which a party could win the presidency, which was a strategic objective of the FSLN whose electoral support in the previous national elections ranged between 35–40 percent. The reform allowed to gain the Presidency with 35 percent provided the winner had a 5 percent margin over the runner-up (Close et al., 2011).

In economic terms, the FSLN built a corporate powerhouse through alliances with the private sector (Collombon & Rodgers, 2018), while it has also privatized the Venezuelan official cooperation that in the period between 2008 and 2015 amounted to $3.7 billion dollars, at an average of 460 million per year (Feinberg, 2018, p. 7). This aid was diverted to multiple private investment and enterprises, ranging from energy production, agriculture, and infrastructure, to finance and insurance companies (Chamorro, 2016). In 2017 Venezuelan aid had declined to about 31 million (Feinberg & Miranda, 2019, p. 15).

Another element that explains the FSLN's rising influence and orientation toward neostructuralist bargain was the inauguration of a top-down model of social control and limited participation, led by the now Vice-president and Ortega's wife, Rosario Murillo, who instituted the Citizens' Power Councils (*Consejos del Poder Ciudadano*, CPC, for its Spanish acronym) later on renamed as Family Councils (GF, *Gabinetes de Familia*). Symbolically, CPCs have their roots in a model of popular participation promoted by the FSLN during the 1980s within a single-party rule. Under the second FSLN administration, these spaces were reinvented under a new narrative of social inclusion and civil participation but under a limited consultation model. The functioning elements of this model involves the political operatives of the FSLN who are designated by the office of the Vice President to departmental, municipal, and communal levels of government. The CPCs have instituted a clientelist form of citizen participation and serve as consultative bodies whose endorsements are a prerequisite for the poor to receive state's social assistance, such as *hambre cero* and other social assistance programmes (Martí i Puig & Baumeister, 2017, p. 392; Spalding, 2009). By clientelism I refer to a variety of informal practices based on 'patron-client' relationships that have characterized Ortega's second administration with regard to social participation, particularly towards the FSLN's political supporters. O'Donnell referred to clientelism as a broad term to designate 'non-universalistic relationships, ranging from hierarchical particularistic exchanges, patronage, nepotism, and favors to actions that […] would be considered corrupt' (1999, p. 181). Clientelist relationships Ortega has promoted are attuned with a neostructuralist bargain and consist of multiple mechanisms of exchange between party operatives and popular sectors in urban and rural areas aimed at securing continuous support for the FSLN in exchange for material and/or political benefits. These practices expanded to include political rivals, affiliated sectoral organizations (such as teacher and employer unions, university student associations) sectors of the Nicaraguan bourgeoisie, and are intended to contain more autonomous and organic forms of civil participation.

Clientelist forms of social participation differ from other forms of social participation, such as, for example, participatory budgets, due to their intentionality as instruments of social control.

Participatory budgets, as part of a larger attempt to promote inclusive governance, as in the case of Brazil, encourage mechanisms for the inclusion of poor urban dwellers in local development decisions, frequently strengthening public spheres where critical and constructive debates take place (Goldfrank, 2011). In these experiences, as various authors have noted, the exercise of democracy and citizenship rights are stimulated. Contrary to these principles of substantive consultation and democratic engagement, CPCs and GFs offered a limited consultation mechanism and they led to a model of social control embedded in clientelist practices. In other words, Ortega instrumentalized social participation to rally political support among his own political bases but also to circumvent internal democratic life within the FSLN (Rocha, 2019, p. 87).

Once in office, the FSLN pursued an active engagement with country's largest private business association, the Superior Council of Private Enterprises (COSEP, for its acronym in Spanish) with whom it established a 'consensus model' on matters related to labour, social security and environmental legislation which allowed a shared decision-making mechanism with regard to policies on economic growth, macro-economic stability, and taxation. In fact, this 'model' was premised under two conditions: securing pragmatic alliances with the local capitalist class that would allow the continuation of the model of neoliberal accumulation, in exchange for this class not interfering in the political decisions of the FSLN to consolidate a model of limited popular participation and centralizing practices. While the FSLN-COSEP alliance was praised by the business community for providing the optimal conditions for labour-capital relations that allowed the country's overall growth and economic stability over the last decade (at the rate of 4–5 percent per annum since 2007), it also undermined political inclusion, since many decisions were made without substantial consultation neither with the National Assembly – which is controlled by an FSLN majority – nor with independent civil society organizations, including labour unions (Cruz Sequeira, 2020, p. 196; Feinberg, 2018, p. 6). The 'consensus' endorsed by the Nicaraguan capitalist class defined the overall engagement of the Ortega administration towards neostructuralism, while at the same time it fashioned limited participation of those popular sectors – the urban and rural poor and vulnerable, Indigenous, peasants, and pensioners – who were in the path of capitalist neo-developmentalism. The FSLN-COSEP consensus model collapsed at onset of the 2018 political crisis, when Ortega issued a social security reform that was not sanctioned by the domestic capitalist class (Cruz-Feliciano, 2021, p. 11).

It is within this overall economic and political context that a neostructuralist bargain between the FSLN government and the Indigenous, *campesino* and Afro-descendant activisms in Nicaragua is to be understood. Although the social mobilization and country-wide protests that erupted on April 2018 in response to social security reforms were in many regards unprecedented and spontaneous,[2] Afro-indigenous and peasant activisms on the Caribbean Coast gained momentum in response to the incomplete land titling process and the social anxiety sparked by the FSLN administration's approval of the concession to a Chinese consortium (HK Nicaragua Canal Development Investment) to build the interoceanic canal in 2013. In other words, after an initial moment of inclusion and alliance building between the FSLN and organizations on the Coast discontent accumulated, which involved both Indigenous and Afro-descendant activisms and they came into public visibility in the context of the April crisis (Simmons, 2018, p. 32). The discontent on the Coast found an environment of increasing politicization and mobilization at the national level that allowed not only to make historical demands for effective autonomy more visible to the Nicaraguan public, but also to articulate new oppositional alliances with non-indigenous activists and organizations.

Contrary to past right-wing oriented administrations (1990–2006) which were not able to forge a hegemonic bloc of the ruling elite, the FSLN's return to office sought to gradually institute the leadership of its own economic group through a firm grip to state power. Cuadra observes that this strategy was based on three interrelated moves: alliance-building with business sectors particularly from telecommunications, tourism, finance as well as with the higher echelons of the military; seizing political control of state institutions; and social control of community organizations through clientelism, coercion, and intimidation. Cuadra suggests that the Ortega-Murillo group 'has a strong process underway that includes the concentration and accumulation of capital, and the concentration and accumulation of force'. Nonetheless, she also comments 'that it is still too early to affirm that it is a consolidated group and that it has achieved hegemony over the other elites' (2016, pp. 98–99). Neostructuralism – Leiva proposes – requires 'the active promotion of new forms of social coordination beyond those offered by market forces alone' (2008, p. xxi, emphasis from the original). The FSLN found in the political arena the space for this coordination by constructing a series of alliances both with the capitalist class and popular sectors.

Leading to the 2006 general elections, the FSLN built a broad popular alliance that appealed to a larger electoral base, it promised to reinvigorate autonomy and Indigenous collective rights on the coast while at the same time, along with a neostructuralist appeal, it provided assurance to the national bourgeoisie that – if elected to office – the FSLN will not derail the overall orientation of the country's market-based policies, and its continuing insertion into the globalized economy. When launching the FSLN governing platform, Ortega announced: 'Our economic policy aims at diversifying the foreign market, and opening ourselves to where the best opportunities are, to avoid the country's dependence on a single trade bloc, to the detriment of our sovereignty' (FSLN, 2006). In a true sense, the FSLN had foreseen that in order to pursue this path it must ensure cohesion, class conciliation, and coordination among competing interests within a broad-based coalition forces it was appealing to. For neostructuralists

> economic policies – Leiva points out – must be conceived with an explicit awareness about the role that institutions, culture and social capital in economic coordination. Economic growth, social equity and democratic governance and governability require much expanded policy mindset … (2008, p. xxi)

Ortega envisioned crafting such a purpose, with a twist: his government actively sought selective cohesion to gravitate around very few players, restricted democratic governance, and crafted limited consultation alongside a model of social participation controlled from above.

The current political crisis reflects the contradictions of Ortega's conflicting priorities: he did promise social justice through inclusive economic growth though this model was eventually erected on the foundations of authoritarianism and a precarious but – at least initially – functional neostructuralist bargain. It is therefore a paradox that those at the end of the FSLN's ambitious programme regarding inclusive policies, those whom the party promised to 'restitute rights' undermined by decades of neoliberalism – *campesinos*, Indigenous, Afro-communities – are now at the forefront of oppositional forces challenging the Ortega-Murillo regime.

In what remains of the paper I will examine the FSLN relationships with YATAMA (*Yapti Tasba Masraka Asla Takanka*, the Organization of the Peoples of the Mother Earth), the largest Indigenous Miskitu-led political organization on the Coast with whom the FSLN had built an electoral alliance leading to the 2006 presidential elections. Secondly, I will also discuss the Afro-Nicaraguan activism seeking to secure collective rights to ancestral lands, and the right to free, prior, and informed consent. Third, I devote attention to the peasant-led anti-canal movement, the *Movimiento Campesino Anti-Canal*, which in a relatively short time, when the Ortega administration decided to grant a concession for the construction of the interoceanic canal, was able to challenge the regime and its disregard for rural livelihoods and peasant economies. The final section of this paper offers some concluding thoughts regarding the conflicting FSLN's relationships with the Afro-Indigenous and *campesino* movements within the context of a neostructuralist bargain.

Leaving the past behind? The FSLN and indigenous-afro-descendant alliances

> There were problems, it's true; we made mistakes, it's true; of course, we made mistakes! And we have asked for forgiveness for those mistakes we made. We have apologized to the brothers of the Caribbean Coast, we have apologized to the Miskito people; we have also apologized here, in the Pacific, to those who were affected by mistakes we made. Daniel Ortega Saavedra (The People, 18 March 2006)

On 18 March 2006 the then candidate Daniel Ortega apologized to the Miskitu people for abuses his government had committed during the war in 1980s.[3] The apology came in the context of the political campaign in which the FSLN sought to build an electoral alliance with YATAMA – as part of its coalition building strategy *Juntos Nicaragua Triunfa* (Together Nicaragua Triumphs). YATAMA, a Miskitu-led political organization, controls around the 35 percent of the popular vote on the Caribbean Coast – with a stronger support in the Northern region – and had held pragmatic governance agreements with the FSLN in regional governing councils since 2002 (González, 2016). It therefore seemed expected that both the FSLN and YATAMA would seek to galvanize their alliance to advance the long overdue implementation of the autonomy and Indigenous collective rights. After all, they were former enemies during the war who had sought an agreed to a peace agreement in 1985, which allowed the political conditions for the approval of regional autonomy on the Coast in 1987 (Frühling et al., 2007). Regional autonomy granted limited self-government to the inhabitants of the Caribbean Coast in recognition to historical demands for the inclusion of the coastal people – *Miskitu, Sumu-Mayangnas, Rama, Creoles,* and long-term *Mestizo* residents – to exert cultural, political, social, and economic rights over the two autonomous regions established in Law 28, the Autonomy Statute (González, 2008). Because the FSLN lost the presidency in 1990, the same year when the first Regional Autonomous Councils were inaugurated, autonomy could not be implemented by the Sandinistas. In the following two decades, right-wing national administrations pursued an active strategy to undermine autonomy rights, which they thought to be part of an undesirable Sandinista legacy.

Within the framework of a neostructuralist bargain, in 2006 the FSLN promised to reinvigorate autonomy through a wide-reaching platform that included governmental support to the titling of ancestral lands, compliance with the Interamerican Court of Human Right's ruling regarding YATAMA's exclusion from the 2000 municipal elections, and autonomy rights implementation through decentralization and additional power-sharing mechanisms that included both levels of government regional and national (González, 2016). However, for the FSLN to fulfil this ambitious platform, it demanded from YATAMA to renounce to its autonomous organizational practices and to give up to its more radical demands, including the possible eviction of non-indigenous *campesino* settlers from indigenous territories.

The alliance lasted for seven years and ended with mutual accusations about each party's lack of commitment to honour the agreement. YATAMA accused the FSLN of electoral fraud in the 2014 regional elections and decided to leave the alliance. While the agreement was instrumental in advancing the land titling process which resulted in 23 territories being demarcated and titled, effective control over communal property remained a highly contested subject due to the uncontrolled advance and often violent illegal occupation of non-indigenous colonists over indigenous and afro-descendant lands (Bryan, 2019). YATAMA blamed the FSLN government for not pursuing a firm containment to further colonization of indigenous lands, and for promoting a strategy gearing towards 'co-existence' between indigenous and non-indigenous communities which for YATAMA and other coastal organizations equated to 'ethnic cleansing.' As Carlos Gabriel [4] put it:

> The FSLN wanted us to remain silent on these abuses to our territories, but we couldn't do this. It has been our struggle for years. We went to war over land and now we have been asked to stay quiet if we want to keep alive our agreement with Daniel. For me to remain silent is to be complicit with the land takeovers.[5]

In essence, it had become apparent that once in office the FSLN found itself entangled in the complex dilemma of trying to reconcile its promise to respect and enforce Indigenous rights with its needs for continuing building an electoral base within historically political adverse *campesino* population on the coast. In fact, land regularization, social assistance programmes, and service infrastructure in *campesino* populated areas on the Coast have received priority attention by the FSLN government. Coastal organizations interpreted this support to the influx of non-indigenous communities as evidence of the FSLN's lack of commitment to respect indigenous rights and autonomy.

The FSLN's contradictory support to indigenous rights vis-à-vis campesino colonists resonates with a distinctive feature of the bargaining process of neo-developmentalism – and ultimately, omission of power relations – ' ... bargaining takes place not through a formal process tied to a long-term plan of national development, but is rather informal and sometimes ad hoc, merely the outcome of more fluid and sometimes spontaneous political forces' (Larrabure, 2020, p. 11). The narrative of ethnic coexistence could not sit well in a context of continuous abuses against indigenous rights, less so in conditions in which state authorities were reluctant to enforce the legislation on land titling. Instead, while the Ortega government insisted on interethnic conciliation between indigenous and colonists, it offered an unwavering support to capitalist endeavours on other areas of the Coast. The last five years have been particularly worrisome for Indigenous Peoples. Multiple instances of forced displacements have been reported, indigenous and non-indigenous communities have resorted to violence in disputes over land occupations – both legal and illegal – and land trafficking has become rampant, often involving local and regional authorities (The Oakland Institute, 2020).

YATAMA and a small group of human rights organizations on the Coast, such as CEJUDHCAN (the Centre for Justice and Human Rights of the Atlantic Coast of Nicaragua), have been keen in bringing to national attention issues surrounding land dispossession, illegal occupations by non-indigenous colonists in indigenous territories, the lack of implementation of Indigenous land rights, and the truncated political participation both locally and nationally.[6] More particularly, YATAMA has insisted on its demands for reforms to the electoral law, which would allow customary elections of local authorities, therefore challenging liberal-inspired political representation and the meddling of national political parties in communal politics (Salinas & Cerda, 2018).

In summary, in its venture to regain power, the FSLN's second administration agreed to an ambitious platform geared towards autonomy implementation and the realization of Indigenous rights but fell short in its political will and effective actions to deliver on its promises. At the core of these drawbacks is the Ortega administration's unwillingness to withdraw from its passive and/or active endorsement of new land occupation on the Coast, coupled with a strategy aimed at deposing autonomy governing bodies from its decision-making powers by means of judicial manoeuvres and questionable electoral practices. In 2018 Brooklyn Rivera, the main leader of YATAMA, evaluated his party relationship with the FSLN in the following terms: 'What the government is imposing here [on the Coast] is internal colonialism, the domination of the population, the dispossession of the territories, the plundering of the riches and it is destroying us culturally as a community' (Salinas & Cerda, 2018). Ortega's administration found itself at odds in trying to accommodate both Indigenous rights and universalist policies for social inclusion of *campesino* colonists, seeking immediate political gains among non-indigenous inhabitants of the Coast. Nonetheless, such as strategy required Indigenous activist on the coast to temper their demands for land security and the protection of their livelihoods.

Ortega's public commitment to Indigenous rights was tested in the light of an incremental demand of land by *campesino* colonists. Within this context, the language of conciliation sought to appease Indigenous claims but did nothing to devise concrete actions to prevent new illegal occupations by non-indigenous colonists over the newly titled territories. Contradictorily, Ortega's neo-developmentalist pragmatism dictated interethnic conciliation between the dispossessed and impoverished classes but refused to interrupt the extractive capitalist dynamics already operating on the Caribbean Coast. Thus, the FSLN's active promotion of large-scale corporate investment in infrastructure demanded a minimalist conception and partial realization of Afro-descendant and Indigenous land rights within a framework of conditional participation, which made salient a contradiction of Ortega's neostructuralism: not recognizing the disempowering effects of the multiple dynamic of land dispossession over Indigenous communities.

In addition to Indigenous alliances, the FSLN actively pursued an agreement with Afro-descendant communities on the Coast in its endeavour to build a multiethnic coalition for the 2006 presidential elections. The agreement established that FSLN will support land claims and a series of other initiatives to promote socio-economic development and political participation of Afro-descendant communities under an FSLN government. However, to realize this agreement the Ortega devised an elitist model of coalition building that undermined more radical demands and welcomed an accommodation model with prominent members of the Black Creole community, FSLN-sympathizers within communal authorities, and sectors of the Moravian church, a religious institution with deep historical and social roots on the Coast. Once in office, the FSLN actively promoted a model of consociation that substituted official state support for autonomy institutions with a scheme of limited political inclusion of Afro-descendant leaders in the state. Under this model, members of the Creole elite were designated to the state apparatus, including selective appointments to municipal and regional governments, the foreign service, state ministries, the Supreme Electoral Council, the judiciary, and seats at the National Assembly.

Two issues would test Ortega's true commitment to respect Afro-descendant rights while still promoting a neo-developmentalist agenda. First, whether it would be willing to recognize the land claim brought forward by the Bluefields' Creole territorial government to the Land Adjudication Commission (CONADETI, for its Spanish acronym), which included areas under the administration of multiple municipal jurisdictions, including *campesino mestizo* populated communities, and areas of African palm plantations under concession to private investors. More importantly, Creoles' land claim demanded ancestral rights over an area that had been identified as a possible route for the Inter-oceanic canal project. Second, the Ortega regime had legal obligations to consult in good faith with the Rama and Kriol people and with the South Caribbean Autonomous Regional Council about its plan to concession the building of the Canal.[7] The Rama-Kriol, whose territory was titled in 2009, holds ownership over a vast track of land in the southern part of the South Caribbean Coast and the canal project foresees to affect approximately 12 percent of the territory.

Ortega ended up recognizing legal ownership over just 7 percent of the original land claim requested by the Creole community of Bluefields leaving outside the title both the African palm plantations and the area designated for the proposed canal construction. With respect to consultation, early in 2016 the Ortega regime crafted a questionable 'consent' among the Rama-Kriol communities in a fast-track process and without substantive consultation with the concerned communities (González, 2018; Mayer, 2018). It should also be mentioned that Law 840 opened up the possibility for the expropriation of communal lands in the canal projected route, justifying the reform under the argument of national/'public interest'. In fact, the 'consent agreement' signed between the Canal Commission (on behalf of the Nicaraguan state) and the Chinese consortium introduced the concept of 'perpetual leasing' of the identified Indigenous and Creole land, a euphemism for privatization and dispossession. Thus, more radical demands for territorial rights brought by Afro-Indigenous sectors were dismissed under a scheme that favoured selective elitist accommodation, large-scale infrastructure investment, and plantations economies.

Confronting these challenging circumstances, Creole activism has been persistent. Their criticism has questioned the neo-developmentalist agenda endorsed by the FSLN administration and in doing so, they have been able to articulate a vision of development that enliven local needs, livelihood-based, against the extractive, plantation-based model promoted by the government. Creole activism has also made evident the discriminatory and racialized nature of the process of development, as this model marginalizes the need of Black people to decent livelihoods over the need of capitalist productive infrastructure. As John Pedro put it:

> Our claims to the territory are legitimate and they are historically documented. Our Creole community has the right to live with dignity, respect and to seek out protections to our livelihoods. The government talks about grand investments but clearly that means another form of racism because we, poor Black and Indigenous communities, have no decision over those plans. We are excluded.[8]

In its dealing with the demands of the Creole community of Bluefields, Ortega's exposed one of the most troubling limitations of the model of social cohesion promoted by his neostructuralist approach: the selective elitist inclusion of members of the Black community, while at the same time curtailing the most far-reaching demands on land ownership, undermining meaningful consultation with communal authorities, and ultimately favouring the interests of transnational private actors via an increased centralizing decision making by national authorities.

'Injustice is greater than fear': the anti-canal *campesino* movement

The most important challenge to the Ortega regime in the pre-April 2018 crisis came from the anti-canal *campesino* movement, primarily composed by poor rural settlers from 12 municipalities along the proposed canal routed, including peasant-populated areas within the jurisdiction of the southern Caribbean Coast. Moreover, many of the members of the movement came from *campesinos* living in precarious land agreements in the Rama-Kriol territory, whose livelihoods also became threatened by the canal project. *Campesino* anxieties about land insecurity and the impending menace associated with the canal construction were not unfounded: the economic and social impact study commissioned by the Chinese HKND consortium identified substantial impact over population settlements in the proposed canal route. An independent study found that a 'population of nearly 16,500, and several regional or locally unique transportation and communication routes are directly affected by the canal construction' (Muñoz Ardila et al., 2018, p. 1). Lack of consultation on the canal project, the swift passing of Law 840 that granted the concession, direct threats of forced displacement by governmental agencies, and police repression to peaceful protest created conditions for the *campesino* movement to emerge and, in this process, to take central stage in Nicaragua's contentious politics today (Serra, 2016; Tittor, 2018).

The campesino movement was organized around the Council for the Defense of the Land, Water and National Sovereignty (*Consejo Nacional de Defensa de la Tierra, el Lago y la Soberania Nacional*) formed in 2014. Under the slogan 'Nicaragua is worth more than a canal', the Council, which is comprised by representatives of *comarcas* – rural districts – and local communities from potentially impacted municipalities, had held 92 rallies until 2018, including marches to the capital city, sits-in, and other public events. Almost all demonstrations were confronted by police repression, incarceration of the Council's leaders, and intimidations. Since its inception the Council's leadership have insisted on its non-partisan orientation, grassroots/popular foundations, and its nationalist sovereigntist principles. Counteracting the nationalist developmentalist discourse promoted by the government, a peasant leader Carlos Robleto stated:

> The canal project is not an act of national sovereignty as the government wants us to believe. On the contrary, is the opposite: it is selling off our land to a foreigner, it is surrendering our sovereignty. It is a national shame.[9]

Both *campesino* and indigenous/afro activists have also shared common cause on their opposition to the canal project and have held cooperative strategies to show their resistance and opposition against it. Dispossession, capitalist extraction, and the effects of an unequal model of rural development are experienced both by the rural poor and afro-indigenous communities alike.[10] Nonetheless, collaboration has not been an easy enterprise due to the distinctive demands, mobilization strategies, and accusation of 'co-optation' of Indigenous leaders on the part of *campesino* organizations. Indigenous authorities have promoted a discourse toward ancestral lands titling and *saneamiento* – clearing land rights – of illegally occupied indigenous lands by mestizo *campesino* colonists while the peasant movement advocates for the protection of livelihoods, including securing legal ownership to the land in their *de facto* possession. *Saneamiento* of collectively held lands under indigenous ownership seemed to set a course of clash with campesino's demands for acquiring legal rights to own land within indigenous territories. Goett points out to that 'titling brought new systems of territorial governance with far more intimate political and administrative ties to the state than during the neoliberal era' which has been used to 'to tamp down dissent and co-opt community leadership' (Goett, 2018, p. 49). In other words, the canal project made salient and intensified structural inequalities between Indigenous/Afro and *campesino* communities, and state policies promoting neo-developmentalism have been instrumental to this process. The FSLN celebratory neostructuralist discourse on transnational integration and competitiveness through the canal project played down ongoing disruptive dynamics within peasant economies and Indigenous livelihoods, which were already set in motion by capitalist restructuring in rural Nicaragua.

Scholars of Nicaragua's agrarian evolution have pointed out how the second Ortega administration ensured continuity rather than substantial change with post-1990 neoliberal model of rural development (Martí i Puig & Baumeister, 2017). This model favoured medium and large agricultural producers through the promotion of export markets, the consolidation of intermediary commercial groups with ties to traditional business sectors and private-public corporations. It has also targeted social assistance among the rural poor while sustaining 'weaker peasant economies' (Martí i Puig & Baumeister, 2017, p. 394). Over the last two decades there has been a slow process of land concentration in which medium properties in rural Nicaragua expanded, waged labour decreased, and demographic expansion opened both patterns of outward migration and new colonization of the agricultural frontier (Schmook et al., 2022).[11] The FSLN has also curtailed *campesino* autonomy by instituting a system of interest intermediation that prioritizes clientelism over participatory democracy and independent organizing (Martí i Puig & Baumeister, 2017, p. 394).

In sum, oppositional peasant struggles have been formed out of a large sector of rural poor who live out of low productivity economic units, in areas characterized by high poverty and unemployment, precarious tenure conditions and income. Peasant communities have also faced centralized participation and clientelist forms of state-led social support, and the aggressive modernizing/neoliberal development projects promoted by the Ortega government. Studies have proposed that the country is experiencing a *repeasantization* due to the expansion into the agricultural frontiers by poor colonist families devoted to subsistence agriculture. *Campesino* activism has largely been formed out of this re-peasantry process and it has repoliticized neo-developmentalism in a broader sense, by bringing to central stage concerns around peasant economies and social inclusion as opposed as agribusiness and large transport infrastructure the FSLN government prioritized; in addition to reclaiming the language of 'sovereignty' from the narrow-minded nationalist/pro-capitalist discourse deployed by Ortega's second administration.

Rebellion against the FSLN's neostructuralism and authoritarianism

It is not an overstatement to say that prior to the April 2018 crisis the most significant challenge to the Ortega rule came from Indigenous/Afro and *campesino* oppositional struggles. Both social movements and political organizations on the Coast and southern Nicaragua confronted Ortega's government within their own terms and limitations which were both practical (through alliance-building) and structural (by questioning the FSLN exclusionary neo-developmentalist agenda). And while these subaltern expressions emerged in response to distinctive oppressive structural conditions (inequitable rural development, political exclusion, and land dispossession), these conditions had worsened due to the continuity of neoliberal governance and capitalist accumulation promoted by pro-neoliberal governments since the 1990s.

Collective action of Nicaragua's anti-canal campesino movement and Afro-Indigenous activisms emerged within the less likely sectors to mobilize against Ortega's rule: these sectors were the supposed political allies – and agents – of an ambitious social programme inspired by social justice objectives and rights' restitution with regard to longstanding demands on land redistribution and political inclusion. Nonetheless, discontent among Indigenous, *campesino* and Afro-descendant communities heralded a limit of the neostructuralist bargain which hindered meaningful inclusion of subaltern classes in critical decision-making processes on issues that had the potential of negatively impacting on their livelihoods (Larrabure, 2020, p. 21).

For indigenous organizations on the coast – including political parties such as YATAMA – the return of the FSLN to power meant the possibility to advance Indigenous rights and to amend errors of the past. The Ortega administration was not able to keep its promises because it ended up promoting an active neo-developmental state as a mechanism for capitalist accumulation at the expense of self-determination of Indigenous autonomy and regional self-governance. Indigenous-Afro and *campesino* activisms were able to articulate critical voices to the neo-developmentalist agenda carried over by the FSLN, exposed the limits of the neostructuralist bargain, and along the way, decried the authoritarian nature of Ortega's rule.

Non-elite members of the Afro-descendant community went from disappointment with Ortega's dismissive response to their territorial claims, to active engagement in demanding meaningful recognition to ancestral collective rights and free, prior, and informed consultation. In this process they also experienced criminalization, intimidation, and divisive politics aimed at undermining territorial governance and collective decision making. Nevertheless, they have not backed down from governmental coercion nor have they subdued to cooptation strategies. On the contrary, Afro-descendant activists have continued to mobilize politically, engaged in coalition building with *campesino* struggles and have been actively denouncing governmental disrespect for autonomy rights in national and international forums.

Finally, in the period between 2014 and 2018, the *campesino* anti-canal movement launched the most radical and nation-wide initiative of discontent against Ortega's neo-developmentalism. They did so in response to abusive state power and the threats against land dispossession and displacement. They protested in defence of their livelihoods and demanded their voices to be heard. In this process they built unprecedented alliances with indigenous and afro-descendent activist, environmentalists and supportive non-governmental organizations (Serra, 2016). Indigenous, afro, and *campesino* activisms were able to re-signify and expose the contradictions of mainstream neo-developmentalist discourse, questioning its meaning, purpose, and omissions. They were determined in building solidarity of subaltern collective agents against the 'rights restitution' narrative promoted by the interethnic conciliatory discourse of the FSLN government, and by criticizing its centralizing governance and authoritarianism. In this sense, these movements politicized the nationalist 'sovereigntist' discourse deployed by the government, offering instead a racialized, rights-based discourse; a sort of 'sovereignty from below' that articulates concerns for the environment alongside social, redistributive justice.

In the aftermath of the April 2018 crisis the *campesino* anti-canal movement suffered the brunt of police repression and criminalization. Several of his leaders were detained and sentenced to ridiculous term sentences in trails that violated their constitutional rights to due process (Alianza Cívica, 2019). Other leaders sought political asylum in neighbouring countries. The violent response to the crisis reached tragic proportion with the killing of protesters and the deployment of paramilitary that operated under the command of police forces (IACHR, 2018). Ortega's response to mounting social mobilization showed the authoritarian character of neostructuralism in the light of a generalized crisis of legitimacy.

Campesino and Afro-Indigenous activisms on the Coast joined the national protest not because they were part of an US-backed conspiracy plan to overthrow the Ortega government (the '*coup*' official narrative) and certainly not because they were controlled or directed by national opposition parties seeking to destabilize the Ortega administration. They joined forces precisely because they sought to reclaim what Ortega had taken away from them: the possibility to voice their concerns within a restricted model of participation, the lack of security over lands and waters, and ultimately, to uphold their demands to respect Indigenous rights, livelihoods and land redistribution. In the process, Indigenous, Afro and *campesino* actors begun to work with each other and persevered in their demands while shifting to denouncing and resisting the government's increasing authoritarianism and political repression.

Conclusion

In this paper, I have argued that relationships between the FSLN's second administration and Indigenous, *campesino* and Afro-descendant activisms in Nicaragua can be interpreted as a neostructuralist bargain, one in which grassroots democratic activism was sidelined by the FSLN's elite governance model to ensure the country's insertion into globalized extractivism.

I also proposed that the Ortega government's subsequent shift towards authoritarianism and repression was a response to mounting social protest within a crisis of legitimacy rooted in the limits of the said bargain; namely, on its incapacity to internalize demands for autonomy.

Neoliberal globalization, and the possibilities it offered for capital accumulation through an active engagement with the domestic capitalist class within a model of social cohesion, signalled a precarious path Ortega's second administration had chosen to fashion a neostructuralist agenda. When the bargain became untenable and the stakes for the governments' survival were higher, Ortega's government faced an existential crisis and opted up for state repression and authoritarianism. This course of events brought to the ground campaign promises to revitalize regional autonomy, promote Afro-Indigenous collective rights, and the strengthening *campesino* economies. The FSLN authoritarian variation of neostructuralism, I have contended, was built upon the premises of limited participation, selective elitist inclusion, centralizing tendencies in decision-making, and the rejection of more radical demands from popular sectors.

Ortega undermined his alliance with subaltern actors on the Coast not because his government opposed *in principle* to the idea of recognizing Indigenous and Afro-descendant rights but because the goals of advancing redistributive, conciliatory policies in a context of economic globalization were thwarted by a model of limited participation and opposed by the interests of domestic and transnational capitalism, which brought to the point of crisis the neostructuralist bargain. When the bargain faded, the agreement with the capitalist class deteriorated, and discontent from other social sectors increased, the government's resorted to authoritarian practices and repression, which placed the country in a pathway of democratic regression.

In November 2021, Ortega was elected for a new presidential term in elections lacking international credibility, with political opponents held under arrest in questionable legal proceedings, and facing an economic crisis that has caused unprecedented outward emigration of Nicaraguans. Future research could shed light on how Indigenous and Afro-descendant rights, along with campesino's demands for land security are evolving within the context of increased authoritarianism. Theoretically, it will be important to further explore whether the government's recourse to state repression was an inevitable turn to deal with the contradictions of neostructuralism, or whether – in the case of Nicaragua – it was a miscalculation by a political party unable and unwilling to reverse its own authoritarian legacy which began during the early 1980s.

Notes

1. Schmook, and collaborators observe that 'the percent of the population living below the poverty line in 2009 changed from 44.7 percent, down to 39.0 percent in 2015, and back up to 44.4 percent in 2019' (Schmook et al., 2022, p. 16).
2. The civic protest that started in April 2018 was led by university students, pensioners, peasants, and environmental activists and resulted in a level of police repression and human rights violations only comparable to the worst decades of the Somoza dictatorship (1934–1979). According to the Inter-American Human Rights Commission between April and July 2018, 325 people were killed, 200 injured, dozens disappeared, and 700 persons were illegally apprehended and politically prosecuted (later released through a controversial amnesty law that offered immunity to the regime's perpetrators). Also, approximately 65 thousand flee into exile to neighbour Costa Rica, the US, Canada and Europe (see IACHR, 2018). The OAS has been involved in pressuring the Ortega regime into a political agreement with oppositional forces, while both the US government and the EU have imposed sanctions to the inner circle of Ortega, including his wife, sons and senior officers in his administrations (US Treasury Department, 2020). There is a current standoff in political negotiations.
3. The abuses Ortega referred to in his apology were in relation to human rights violations against individuals and communities in the Moskitia region: forcibly displaced communities along the Wangki River, extra-judicial killings and illegal apprehensions conducted by FSLN forces during the military conflict on the Caribbean Coast. Independent sources extensively documented these abuses and the human costs of the war, such as CIDCA (1984); IACHR (1983). The Sandinista-Miskitu conflict has been extensively documented (Hale, 1994). A combination of government human abuses against the local population, threats against ancestral lands, and a nationalist approach to ethnic demands resulted

in the uprising of the local population in 1981. The military confrontation came to an end in 1985 through peace agreements between YATAMA and the FSLN, and the approval of regional autonomy (Frühling et al., 2007).
4. Pseudonymous are used in this article to protect the safety of individuals interviewed.
5. Indigenous elder member of YATAMA's councillors in the North Atlantic regional autonomous council, personal interview, August 2016.
6. In response to a petition from CEJUDHCAN, the Interamerican Human Commission of Human Rights has issued a dozen of precautionary measures to protect the lives and property of Indigenous communities on the Coast (Cunningham, 2017).
7. Chapter 181 of the Nicaraguan political constitution states that: 'Concessions and contracts for the rational exploitation of natural resources granted by the State in the Autonomous Regions of the Caribbean Coast must have the approval of the Council Corresponding Autonomous Regional' (Asamblea Nacional de Nicaragua, 2014, p. 83).
8. John Pedro, member of the Bluefields Communal Government, Bluefields, August 25, 2016. Personal interview.
9. Carlos Robleto, campesino leader, Nueva Guinea, personal interview, 29 August 2016.
10. 'Faced with their mutual destruction some leaders from the Rama-Kriol Territory began to form relationships of solidarity with the mestizo *campesino* anti-canal movement' (Goett, 2018, p. 28).
11. Martí i Puig and Baumeister observe that 'the middle sectors, who owned units either between 35 and 140 hectars or between 140 and 350 hectares, were the ones who benefited the most' (2017, p. 387). Also, citing data from the United States Agency for International Development, Schmook and collaborators indicate that 'in 2011 the richest 9 percent of landowners held 56 percent of farmland in Nicaragua, while an estimated 38 percent of the rural population owned no land at all' (Schmook et al., 2022, p. 18).

Disclosure statement

No potential conflict of interest was reported by the author(s).

Funding

This work was supported by the Social Science Research Council of Canada (SSHRC) under the Small-Travel Grant funding administered by York University.

References

Alianza Cívica. (2019). Condenamos las Agresiones a Lideres del Movimiento Campesino. Comuniqué. Retrieved April 20, 2020, from https://www.alianzacivicanicaragua.com/es/condenamos-las-agresiones-a-lideres-del-movimiento-campesino/

Álvarez, A. G., & Vintró, C. J. (2009). Evolución Constitucional y Cambios Institucionales en Nicaragua (1987-2007). In S. Martí i Puig & D. Close (Eds.), *Nicaragua y el FSLN [1979-2009]: ¿Qué queda de la revolución?* (pp. 169–220). edicions bellaterra.

Asamblea Nacional de Nicaragua. (2014). *Constitución Política de Nicaragua. Texto íntegro con reformas incorporadas a 2014*. Retrieved August 10, 2020, from https://www.poderjudicial.gob.ni/pjupload/archivos/documentos/LA_CONSTITUCION_POLITICA_Y_SUS_REFORMAS(3).pdf

Bryan, J. (2019). For Nicaragua's indigenous communities, land rights in name only. *NACLA Report on the Americas*, *51*(1), 55–64. https://doi.org/10.1080/10714839.2019.1593692

Carruthers, D., & Rodríguez, P. (2009). Mapuche protest, environmental conflict and social movement linkage in Chile. *Third World Quarterly*, *30*(4), 743–760. https://doi.org/10.1080/01436590902867193

Chamorro, C. F. (2016, April 14). The Right to Know about Albanisa [El Derecho a Saber Sobre Albanisa]. *El Confidencial*. https://confidencial.com.ni/the-right-to-know-about-albanisa/

CIDCA. (1984). *Trabil nani: Historical background and current situation of the Atlantic coast.*
Close, D. (1999). *Nicaragua: The Chamorro years.* Lynne Rienner.
Close, D., & Martí i Puig, S. (2009). Introducción: Los sandinistas y Nicaragua desde 1979. In S. Martí i Puig & D. Close (Eds.), *Nicaragua y el FSLN [1979-2009]: ¿Qué queda de la revolución?* (pp. 11–31). edicions bellaterra.
Close, D., Martí i Puig, S., & McConnell, S. A. (2011). *The Sandinistas and Nicaragua since 1979.* Lynne Rienner.
Collombon, M., & Rodgers, D. (2018). Introduction. *Sandinismo 2.0*: Reconfigurations autoritaires du politique, nouvel ordre économique et conflit social. *Cahiers des Amériques Latines, 87*(87), 13–36. https://doi.org/10.4000/cal.8475
Cortés Ramos, A., López Baltodano, U., & Moncada Bellorin, L. (Eds.). (2020). *Anhelos de un nuevo horizonteAportes para una Nicaragua democrática.* FLACSO. https://dialnet.unirioja.es/servlet/libro?codigo=773390
Cruz-Feliciano, H. (2021). Whither Nicaragua three years on? *Latin American Perspectives, 48*(6), 9–20. https://doi.org/10.1177/0094582X211041065
Cruz Sequeira, A. J. (2020). Un breve ensayo sobre la crisis del régimen de Daniel Ortega. In A. Cortés Ramos, U. López Baltodano, & L. Moncada Bellorín (Eds.), *Anhelos de un Nuevo Horizonte: Aportes para una Nicaragua Democrática* (pp. 193–202). FLACSO.
Cuadra, E. (2016). Las Elites y los Campos de Disputa en Nicaragua: Una Mirada Retrospectiva. *Península, XI*(1), 85–101. https://www.sciencedirect.com/science/article/pii/S1870576616000052
Cunningham, M. (2017, July 11–13). *The open paths as an indigenous woman in the defense of the human and territorial rights of the Indigenous Peoples of the North Caribbean Coast autonomous region.* Paper presented at the Simposio sobre Memoria Social de la Autonomía Costeña, VI Congreso Centroamericano de Estudios Culturales, Managua: UCA.
Feinberg, R. (2018). Nicaragua: Revolution or restoration. *Foreign Policy at Brookins.* https://www.brookings.edu/research/nicaragua-revolution-and-restoration/
Feinberg, R. E., & Miranda, B. A. (2019). *La Tragedia Nicaragüense: Del Consenso a la Coerción.* Wilson Centre, Latin American Program. https://www.wilsoncenter.org/article/la-tragedia-nicaraguense-del-consenso-la-coercion
Figueroa, D., Rueda, V., & Villena, S. (2021). El 40 aniversario de la Revolución Sandinista y la crisis política de abril de 2018. *Canadian Journal of Latin American and Caribbean Studies, 46*(3), 325–332. https://doi.org/10.1080/08263663.2021.1970324
Frühling, P., González, M., & Buvollen, H. P. (2007). *Etnicidad y Nación. el desarrollo de la Autonomía de la Costa Atlántica de Nicaragua. 1987-2007.* F&G Editores.
FSLN. (2006). *Programa de Gobierno. Alianza Unidad, Nicaragua Triunfa.* Retrieved August 10, 2020, from http://www.realinstitutoelcano.org/especiales/EspecialEleccionesAmericaLatina2005/nicaragua/ProgramaGobiernoFSLN-UnidadNicaraguaTriunfa.pdf
Goett, J. (2018). Beyond left and right: Grassroots social movements and Nicaragua's civic insurrection. *LASA Forum, 49*(4), 25–31. https://forum.lasaweb.org/past-issues/vol49-issue4.php
Goldfrank, B. (2011). *Deepening local democracy in Latin America. Participation, decentralization, and the left.* Penn State University Press.
González, M. (2008). *Governing Multi-Ethnic Societies in Latin America: Regional Autonomy, Democracy, and the State in Nicaragua 1987-*2007. Doctoral dissertationn, York University, Toronto.
González, M. (2016). The unmaking of self-determination: Twenty-five years of regional autonomy in Nicaragua. *Bulletin of Latin American Research, 35*(3), 306–321. https://doi.org/10.1111/blar.12487
González, M. (2018). Leasing communal lands ... in perpetuity: Post-titling scenarios on the Caribbean Coast of Nicaragua. In L. Baracco (Ed.), *Indigenous struggles for autonomy. The Caribbean Coast of Nicaragua* (pp. 75–98). Lexington Books.
Hale, C. R. (1994). *Resistance and contradiction. Miskitu Indians and the Nicaraguan state, 1894-1987.* Stanford University Press.
Hale, C. R. (2017). What went wrong? Rethinking the Sandinista revolution, in light of its second coming. *Latin American Research Review*; *52*(4), 720–727. https://doi.org/10.25222/larr.269
Interamerican Commission on Human Rights (IACHR). (1983). *Report on the situation on human rights of a segment of the Nicaraguan population of Miskito origin.* IACHR-Organization of American States. Retrieved August 11, 2020, from http://www.cidh.org/countryrep/Miskitoeng/toc.htm

Interamerican Commission on Human Rights (IACHR). (2018). *Gross human rights violations in the context of social protests in Nicaragua*. IACHR-Organization of American States. Retrieved August 12, 2020, from https://www.oas.org/en/iachr/reports/pdfs/Nicaragua2018-en.pdf

Larrabure, M. (2020). Left Governments and Social Movements in Latin America. *The Oxford Encyclopedia of Latin American Politics*. Retrieved February 5, 2022, from https://doi.org/10.1093/acrefore/9780190228637.013.1720

Leiva, F. I. (2008). *Latin American neostructuralism*. University of Minnesota Press.

Martí i Puig, S. (2010). The adaptation of the FSLN: Daniel Ortega's leadership and democracy in Nicaragua. *Latin American Politics and Society*, 52(4), 79–106. https://doi.org/10.1111/j.1548-2456.2010.00099.x

Martí i Puig, S., & Baumeister, E. (2017). Agrarian policies in Nicaragua: From revolution to the revival of agro-exports, 1979–2015. *Journal of Agrarian Change*, 17(2), 381–396. https://doi.org/10.1111/joac.12214

Martí i Puig, S., & Serra, M. (2020). Nicaragua: De-democratization and regime crisis. *Latin American Politics and Society*, 62(2), 117–136. https://doi.org/10.1017/lap.2019.64

Mayer, J. L. (2018). Negotiating consiultation: The duty to consult and contestation of autonomy in Nicaragua's Rama-Kriol territory. In L. Baracco (Ed.), *Indigenous struggles for autonomy. The Caribbean Coast of Nicaragua* (pp. 99–129). Lexington Books.

Muñoz Ardila, A., Rebscher, A., & Hack, J. (2018). An open-data based assessment of expected changes in land use and water availability as a result of the construction of the west segment of the Nicaragua interoceanic canal. *Environments*, 5(1), 14. https://doi.org/10.3390/environments5010014

O'Donnell, G. (1999). On the state, democratization, and some conceptual problems: A Latin American view with glances at some post-communist countries. In G. O'Donnell (Ed.), *Counterpoints. Selected essays on authoritarianism and democratization* (pp. 133–158). University of Notre Dame Press.

Rocha, J. L. (2019). *Autoconvocados y Conectados: Los Universitarios en la Revuelta de Abril*. UCA.

Rueda Estrada, V. (2015). *Recontras, Recompas, Revueltos y Rearmados: Post-guerra y Conflictos por la Tierra en Nicaragua 1990-2008*. Instituto de Investigaciones Dr. Jose María Luis Mora.

Salinas, M. C., & Cerda, A. (2018, November 20). Yatama va a Elecciones Regionales 'bajo protesta.' *Confidencial*. https://confidencial.com.ni/yatama-va-a-elecciones-regionales-bajo-protesta/

Schmook, B., Radel, C., & Carte, L. (2022). Migration as a survival strategy for smallholder farmers facing an authoritarian extractivist regime in Nicaragua. *LASA Forum*, 53(1), 15–20. https://forum.lasaweb.org/files/vol53-issue1/Dossier-3.pdf

Serra, L. (2016). El movimiento social nicaragüense por la defensa de la tierra, el agua y la soberanía. *Encuentro*, 104(104), 38–52. https://doi.org/10.5377/encuentro.v0i104.2861

Simmons, S. (2018). Grito por Nicaragua, un grito desde la Costa Caribe. *LASA Forum*, 49(4), 32–36. https://forum.lasaweb.org/past-issues/vol49-issue4.php

Sklar, H. (1988). *Washington's War on Nicaragua*. Between the Lines.

Spalding, R. J. (2009). Las Políticas contra la Pobreza en Nicaragua. In S. Martí i Puig & D. Close (Eds.), *Nicaragua y el FSLN [1979-2009]* (pp. 351–382). Edicions bellaterra.

The Oakland Institute. (2020). *Nicaragua's failed revolution: The indigenous struggles for Saneamiento*. Retrieved August 10, 2020, from https://www.oaklandinstitute.org/sites/oaklandinstitute.org/files/nicaraguas-failed-revolution.pdf

The People. (2006, March 18). Ortega apologizes to the Miskito people. http://www.radiolaprimerisima.com/noticias/generica/952/ortega-pide-perdon-al-pueblo-miskito/

Tittor, A. (2018). Conflicts about Nicaragua's interoceanic canal project: Framing, counterframing and government strategies. *Cahiers des Amériques latines*, 87, 117–140. https://doi.org/10.4000/cal.8561

US Treasury Department. (2020). *Nicaragua-related Sanctions*. Retrieved August 12, 2020, from https://www.treasury.gov/resource-center/sanctions/Programs/Pages/nicaragua.aspx

Weeks, J. (1987). The mixed economy in Nicaragua: The economic battlefield. In R. J. Spalding (Ed.), *The political economy of revolutionary Nicaragua* (pp. 43–60). Allen & Unwin, Inc.

The gendered political economy of Chile's rebellious discontent: lessons from forty-five years of neoliberal governance

Verónica Schild

ABSTRACT
Chile's unprecedented citizen mobilizations of 2019, and subsequent political developments, have revealed the social and institutional limits of Latin America's paradigmatic case of neo-developmentalism. They have raised critical questions about the nature, reach and effects, of a 30-year progressive program of 'growth with equity' resulting in profound inequalities and political disenchantment for the majority. The article argues for a gendered cultural political economy approach to understand the impact of neoliberalism, best conceived as a governing rationality, that is now facing a generalized crisis of legitimacy. It examines the role of the Constitution of 1980 in enshrining in law neoliberal structural reforms, and setting the political and institutional bases for subordinating the substance of society and individuals to the laws of the market. The article shows that this marketization has transformed fundamental taken-for-granted social relations of reproduction which make markets possible, with harsh effects for the majority of Chilean women..

Introduction

In October 2019, a social uprising of historically unprecedented proportions took place in Chile. On the 15th, what seemed like a localized protest by high school students linked to a 30-peso fare hike in Santiago's Metro detonated a nationwide ongoing rebellion which unfolded outside the control and leadership of 'progressive' political parties. Though for many pundits and experts the massive, diverse, and well-organized expressions of discontent appeared to come out of nowhere, they expressed long-standing grievances.[1] On the 23rd, for example, a demonstration took place in Viña del Mar organized by public sector health professionals and students, including doctors, nurses, physiotherapists, psychologists, and those from other related fields. They denounced the critical underfunding of the public health sector, most dramatically observed at the venerable Fricke hospital. Halfway to the adjacent city of Valparaíso, the demonstrators were met by a similarly large contingent that marched toward Viña, also demanding better resources and work conditions for the Van Buren hospital of that city, as well as for local public clinics. Throughout the route I observed demonstrators being greeted with cheers and applause from the general public lining the streets.[2]

People remained defiant, despite the imposition of a national curfew under the *Ley de Seguridad del Estado*, the use of indiscriminate repression, escalating human rights violations at the hands of the military and the police, and mounting national and international condemnation.[3] Then, on November 15th, the President conceded and signed an agreement negotiated with most sectors of the opposition, the *Acuerdo por la Paz Social y la Nueva Constitución* (Social Peace Agreement and New Constitution), that paved the way to a plebiscite for a new Constitution to be held on October 25, 2020.

Daily marches and sporadic acts of violence would only be halted six months later, in March of 2020, when President Sebastián Piñera imposed tight security measures in response to the unfolding COVID-19 health crisis. What seemed to unify the protesters, despite their diversity of voices and demands, was a generalized sense of malaise and anger at rampant social and economic inequality, injustice, and abuse of power. This spectacle of a cross-section of Chilean society, including women and men, young and old, students and pensioners, public and private sector workers and professionals, marching massively and defiantly with banners claiming '*No son los 30 pesos, son los 30 años!*' (It is not the 30 pesos; it is the 30 years!) and '*Basta ya!*' (Enough already!), put an end to the myth that Chile was 'an oasis in a region in turmoil' – words used by President Sebastián Piñera in his address to the UN General Assembly only weeks before the unrest started, on September 24, 2019.

It was not by chance that the agreement reached between Piñera's government and the opposition forces on November 15, 2019 focused on rewriting the Constitution of 1980. For it was that Constitution which enshrined in law Chile's drastic neoliberal restructuring of the late 1970s and paved the way for its global capitalist integration. Despite a number of amendments to it since 1990, the legal matrix of the 1980 Constitution has remained fundamentally unchanged, and has been the regulatory framework for unfolding neoliberalism as an *entrenched mode of regulation* of society and individuals since 1990. As such, it has increasingly been regarded as the major impediment for any meaningful structural reforms for overcoming the extreme forms of inequality in a whole range of areas affecting the lives of the country's majority. After the plebiscite of October 2020, which approved by a wide margin of 78 percent the demand for a new Constitution to be drafted by an elected, citizens-only Constituent Convention, Chileans went to the polls to elect the Constituent Convention in May 2021. This election was unprecedented because for the first time in the country's political history, of the total 155 representatives to be elected, 17 seats were reserved for representatives of Chile's *pueblos originarios* ('first peoples'), and strict gender parity of candidates and elected representatives was required. The was a resounding rejection of the post-1990 political order and of traditional political parties, and in particular a punishment of the centre-left coalitions that had governed Chile for 24 of the last 30 years along with the two more recent centre-right coalition governments of Sebastián Piñera. In fact, the constituent body that will draft the new Constitution is 'without precedent in terms of social origin, generational, ethnic, and gender composition' of its delegates (Heiss, 2021).

This dramatic fall from grace of a Latin American 'progressive' model of development which had been committed since the end of the dictatorship in 1990 to a programme of 'growth with equity', and of a country which has enjoyed the status of being the region's most stable democracy, raises some urgent questions for analysis. What is the nature of this much celebrated instance of an ostensibly pragmatic 'post-neoliberal' development project premised on political consensus, whose mounting social, environmental, and political limits have been dramatically punctuated by a social rebellion and the demand for a new Constitution? What does this moment tell us about the limits of this project of 'modernization' that has sought for the past 30 years to subordinate society and individuals to the laws of the market in the name of democratic inclusion and 'active' citizenship? Above all, what accounts for the prominent, albeit understudied, role that women have played in mobilizations for change, from urban feminists to popular activists, students and professionals, to labour activists and environmentalists? In this article I propose that rather than being an example of an ostensibly pragmatic 'post-neoliberal' development project, Chile stands as a paradigmatic case of an entrenched neoliberalism which offers lessons about the social limits and political implications of subjecting societies and individuals to the rationality of the market.

The argument

In much of my work I have taken the notion of neoliberalism to be more than a byword for marketization, and have insisted – along with other critical scholars – in understanding neoliberalism in processual terms as unfolding, contradictory projects of neoliberalization in diverse and historically specific forms (Brenner et al., 2010; Peck & Theodore, 2019; Peck et al., 2018). In this article I argue that the present, *generalized crisis of political and institutional legitimacy* in Chile needs to be specifically understood as the outcome of transformations that are associated with the deep-seated social contradictions of entrenched neoliberalism and their effects. In other words, rather than as a paradigmatic case of early neoliberal restructuring, or as a case of post-neoliberal development, post-1990 Chile should be viewed as a specific instantiation of a contradictory and conflict-ridden, entrenched or mature neoliberal 'mode of regulation', to use the apt formulation of Jamie Peck, Neil Brenner and Nik Theodor (2018, p. 2). To this end, a narrow political economy approach is inadequate in helping us grasp the scope and social effects of transformations associated with what Gabriel Palma has aptly called 'the novel reconfigurations of political and institutional power encapsulated by the neo-liberal revolution' (Palma, 2009, p. 840). Addressing the strategy of 'growth with equity' in Chile (and indeed in other Latin American contexts), therefore, requires a complex, historically contextualized understanding of neoliberalism. Moreover, a gender sensitive political economy is necessary for understanding the relation between the social rebellion of October 2019 and the social consequences of a development path that has remained committed to the fundamentals of economic liberalism.

Karl Polanyi nearly 80 years ago argued the need to make sense of the limits of what he called the subordination of 'the substance of society itself to the laws of the market'. I join feminist political economists to contend that a crucial element of what Polanyi meant by the 'substance of society' refers to the social relations that make the very existence of markets possible. In particular, attending to gender relations is fundamental because the project of treating society as a market is a gendered project that invisibilizes all those activities which create the very conditions for the reproduction of society and of life as such, that is, the paid and unpaid activities of social reproduction for which women worldwide are primarily responsible. As the vast literature on feminist political economy has argued, social reproduction 'encompasses the activities associated with the maintenance and reproduction of people's lives on a daily and intergenerational basis' as a *necessary* component of the reproduction of capitalism itself (Ferguson, 2020, p. 31, 27).[4] Furthermore, as feminist political economists have insisted, women have figured prominently in this new regime of accumulation because of their historically unprecedented participation in the wage economy that is the cornerstone of labour flexibilization strategies. Women are also the focus of renewed gender normative regulation efforts by the state through partnership-based social governance mechanisms, so that those who are not already in the labour market, and who qualify for social assistance, constitute the pool of potential workers who are 'readied' for employability (Schild, 2015a).

The regulation, and above all, the 'responsibilization' of subjects is a critical component of entrenched neoliberalism. Over the last three decades Chile's vision of a 'modern' and democratic

Chile has been premised on this market-driven development, and has fostered an active, responsible citizenship that has expected subjects to be 'resilient' individuals who, responsibly and autonomously, take advantage of the 'levers' offered by an enabling state and the market to find personal success and fulfilment. As empowered citizens, Chilean men and women have been *required* to exercise their 'free choice' in accessing health, education, and pensions as private commodities in the market – through debt if need be. Thus, as a distinctive rationality shaped by the ethos of the market, this form of governing 'transmogrifies every human domain and endeavor, along with humans themselves, according to a specific image of the economic' (Brown, 2015, pp. 9–10; Schild, 2007).[5]

However, to understand the implementation, consolidation and reproduction of this project of neoliberalisation, and the present *generalized crisis of political and institutional legitimacy*, we need to consider the centrality of the Constitution of 1980. This is a document whose political origins and intent have been largely ignored in critical political economy and cultural analyses of 'progressive politics'. Yet, as critical legal scholars like Fernando Atria have shown, this 1980 Constitution set the terms for what was both desirable and possible at the national and subnational levels (Atria, 2013). Most fundamentally, it enshrined the market-oriented regulatory transformations, i.e. the privatizations and deregulations associated with the first, so-called 'experimental' phase of neoliberal restructuring, that enabled the global integration over time of Chile's economy. Panitch and Gindin, writing about neoliberalism and the role of the state in the making of global capitalism, have correctly argued that '(n)eoliberal practices did not entail institutional retreat so much as the expansion and consolidation of the networks of institutional linkages to an already globalizing capitalism' (Panitch & Gindin, 2012, p. 15). This regulatory framework also set the political and institutional bases for the national and subnational successful implementation of those 'modernizations' associated with the so-called neo-developmentalist project of 'growth with equity' of the post-1990 period.

In the following pages I use a gendered political economy approach, and focus on the marketization of society's impact on social reproduction, with particularly negative consequences for women.[6] My discussion proceeds in three parts. The first section offers an exploration of the neoliberal policies and legacies of the post-1990 coalition governments of the centre-left and centre-right. It highlights the succession of promises which have been partially met, or have remained unmet, leading to increasing frustration, and to political disaffection and rising discontent. The subsequent section explores the significance of the 1980 Constitution in laying the foundational continuities of the political economy of 'the possible' and neoliberal governance through a constitutional form explicitly designed to enshrine private property rights, to limit political demands, and to drastically reduce the scope for social solidarity. The final section explores fundamental transformations in the political economy, with an explicit focus on social reproduction and the costs for women of a social order premised on the primacy of the market as the space for enabling and enacting an 'active' citizenship.

Chile's agenda of 'growth with equity': a history of promises unmet and rising discontent

Committed to economic 'growth with equity', the succession of centre-left or *Concertación* coalition governments voted in after the end of the dictatorship in 1990 pursued an agenda that saw an increase in social spending, enabling the reduction of poverty and extreme poverty, while also further expanding the export-oriented development model. The legacy of 24 consecutive years, from 1990 to 2014, of 'progressive' governments is contradictory at best. Indeed, under the government of socialist Ricardo Lagos (2000–2006) deregulation and privatizations of public goods were intensified, tariffs were further reduced – securing the country's status as one of the most open economies in the world – and trade relations were expanded, making it the country with the most free trade agreements in the world. Despite what some analysts call a gentler market model, generalized frustration with the failure of progressive governments to address pressing demands for reform in the areas of health, education, and pensions, not to mention changes to labour conditions and wages, mounted steadily. Michelle Bachelet, the much-celebrated so-called feminist Pink Tide leader of Latin America, came to power in 2006 with a promise to address these urgent demands and to 'expand political and economic participation through commissions that would provide a path for socioeconomic change' (Borzutzky & Perry, 2020, pp. 214–215). The failure of Bachelet's government to deliver on these promises was met with mounting social mobilizations and expressions of discontent that cost the *Concertación* the election in 2010. The turn to the right under billionaire businessman Sebastián Piñera's presidency (2010–2014) promised to transform Chile into a developed nation by 2020 by opening its economy even further to the world.

In 2014, Michelle Bachelet and her broad coalition of centre-left parties, the *Nueva Mayoría* (the New Majority), including for the first time Chile's Communist Party (therefore signaling a move to the left of the Chilean progressive spectrum), was returned to power on the promise of addressing the increasing frustrations and demands of broad sectors of society through substantial changes to health, education, and social security. The *Nueva Mayoría* also promised substantial labour reforms and an overhaul of the country's taxation system. Above all, it committed to the project of drafting a new constitution. Although Bachelet's electoral success was propelled by the long-standing demands of secondary and post-secondary students for free, good quality education as a social right, their protests were part of a broader mobilization of workers, pensioners, fisherfolk, and others who wanted substantial changes to the country's political and economic model. Under the banner of '*Recuperar la educacion publica*' (Let's recover public education), students had staged massive national demonstrations and strikes which paralyzed the country for two months in 2011, one year into Piñera's first term in office. According to polls taken at the time, the support for student actions was widespread, around 70 percent.[7] When Bachelet returned to power in 2014, private university enrolments made up around 70 percent, the highest in Latin America, and Chilean university students paid the fourth highest fees in the world. In the end, Bachelet's *Nueva Mayoría* delivered partial changes that did not deviate from the market logic regulating higher education. The education reforms had planned to subsidize education fees through a tax reform that in the end did not materialize, forcing the kind of compromise Chileans had seen since 1990. Thus, instead of free education for all, only 60 percent of the most 'vulnerable' students would qualify for free tuition, with its implementation over a two-year period.

Despite undeniable social achievements, among them the passing of an abortion law which returned abortion to its legal status in place from 1931 to 1989, and the approval of a civil union law that applies to homosexual and heterosexual couples, Bachelet's government failed to deliver on the ambitious agenda to make Chile a more just society. Instead, the promised tax reform on which the radical reform to education was based, did not happen, and the attempted labour reform was ultimately watered down. Thus, as with education, those changes that were achieved were partial and inadequate. To these shortcomings must be added the inability of successive governments to offer answers to the escalating environmental and social costs of extractivist economic activities and to the legitimate demands of Chile's indigenous peoples. Emblematic of the latter is the failure of *Concertación* governments to negotiate a solution to conflicts between the Mapuche, the state and the private sector over territorial claims, natural resources, and collective rights in the southern region of the Araucania. The Mapuche, Chile's largest indigenous group, whose sovereignty was recognized through key treaties with the Spanish Crown, where defeated in 1883 by the Chilean state, when it engaged in a bloody military war of annexation and usurped 95 percent of Mapuche lands. Today, an estimated one and a half million hectares of ancestral Mapuche land is in the hands of the forestry industry and under cultivation of environmentally unsustainable species that have been directly linked to the water crisis and pollution in the area. Rather than seeking a political solution, successive centre-left and centre-right governments have defined the conflict in security terms, invoking the *Ley Antiterrorista*, the anti-terrorism law passed in 1984 by the dictatorship, and imposing military force on the region.

Furthermore, the demand for water as a social good, with human consumption as a priority, was not addressed, nor was the demand to abrogate the so-called *Ley Longeira*, or fishing law, passed during Piñera's first term in office (2010–2014), which gave fishing rights in perpetuity to seven powerful families. The pension reform demanded by large sectors of Chileans under the banner of '*No Mas AFPs*' or No More AFPs (the acronym for *Adminstradoras de Fondos de Pensiones* or Pension Fund Administrating Agencies) was also not tackled.

The project of constitutional reform which promised, among other things, to guarantee the public right to social goods like health, education, and pensions, and to recognize the constitutional status of indigenous peoples, was presented to parliament five days before Bachelet left her post in March 2018. The proposed constitutional process contemplated the drafting of a new charter based on citizen consultations, which was preceded by a period of constitutional civic education. The constitutional project was dismissed as last minute, poorly conceived and 'absurd' by sectors of the incoming government of Piñera, and was simply set aside. In the end, Bachelet's ambitious plan had floundered on the shoals of a constitutional, economic, and party-political system designed to perpetuate Chile's neoliberal capitalism and market rationality of governance, and an unwillingness among some in her own governing coalition to press for significant reforms and greater wealth distribution.

The plan offered by Piñera's incoming second government (2018–2022), '*Construyamos Tiempos Mejores para Chile*' (Let's Build Better Times for Chile) promised a better future for all Chileans, with a focus on 'citizen security' and, once again, an agenda promoting the private sector as the motor of growth, employment and wellbeing. It called for a return to a 'culture of dialogue and agreements', that is, a clear rejection of the specter of adversarial politics and a more insistent return to the form guaranteed by the prevailing constitution of 1980. This political framework had enabled the centre-left coalition and right-wing governments to entrench neoliberalism, reforming and ameliorating it, but without threatening capitalist interests or its fundamental market rationality for society at large. As critics agree, and as I elaborate in the subsequent section, the Constitution instituted a political form that would preserve existing institutional and economic structures. Jaime Guzman, the most powerful and influential civilian figure in Pinochet's government and a key architect of that constitution, expressed it clearly at the time: 'The Constitution must attempt, should adversaries reach government, to constrain them to act in ways not too different from those one would choose'.[8]

Hence, as a result of promises unkept by the entire range of political parties since 1990, Chileans have increasingly moved into ever-wider and unprecedented scales of contentious politics, all of which can be seen as harbingers of the explosion of social rebellion in October 2019. An expanding literature has by now well-documented the high degree of mobilization and extent of demands of the population. More recently, studies have begun to widen the scope of analysis beyond urban movements, most especially the student movement which has garnered much scholarly attention. They have revealed a vast number of movements and mobilizations engaged in environmental and regional struggles that demand fundamental changes, many of which have remained understudied. Thus, along with organized mobilizations by teachers, health workers, and other local and national public sector workers, and the iconic ones of high school and university students, must be added those by labour in key areas such as fishing, mining, and port-work, and increasingly more extensive ones by pensioners. Outside urban centres, complex and diverse territorially based environmental mobilizations have become massive and more visible ever since they emerged in the early 1990s. These include movements fighting against hydroelectric, mining, and other environmentally damaging projects, as well as ever more widespread ones demanding that water be recognized as a human right, and the calling for an end to highly contaminated industrial areas deemed officially to be inevitable 'zones of sacrifice' as the necessary price of development. Organized women have a strong presence in these territorially-based environmental movements, often acting as its visible leaders and spokespersons.[9]

Institutionalizing a neoliberal governing rationality: the Constitution of 1980

Present-day Chile's capitalist development project began with the imposition by military force, from 1975 to 1981, of a radical experiment based on a neoliberal utopian vision. The project, which aimed to restructure social relations, drastically reduce the role of the state, and disarticulate civil society, became widely known as an early and emblematic case of neoliberal restructuring. Its main elements included initial stabilization policies, privatization of economic activities, the shrinking of state regulatory and social functions, and the opening up of the economy to international trade and financial flows. These initial policies were followed by a so-called 'second generation' of reforms, completed between 1979 and 1981, through the privatization, either total or partial, of health, education, and social security/pensions; the deregulation of labour relations and the disarticulation of collective actions; and reforms to the judicial system and to the administrative bureaucracy (i.e. decentralization). Collectively, these radical structural reforms were known as the 'seven modernizations' and were defended by their architects as a 'silent revolution' or a 'true libertarian revolution'.[10]

The post-1990 period ushered in a period of 'pragmatic' politics, and changes *en la medida de lo posible* (in so far as possible), in the words of incoming president, Christian Democrat Patricio Aylwin. Chile once again became a trailblazer, this time in the pursuit of an ambitious development project through a strategy that sought to combine 'growth with equity and political democracy' (Leiva, 2008). The question remains, however, a model of exactly what? For its architects, including key figures who had collaborated in the model's formulation at the Economic Commission for Latin America and the Caribbean (ECLAC), the strategy was an instance of post-neoliberalism. According to them, for the past 30 years, Chile has set aside an ostensibly narrow, drastic agenda of economic and institutional reforms in favour of a more humane, 'progressive' model of development.[11] However, this claim is misleading because a closer examination reveals that 'economic freedom' and the sanctity of the 'free market' remain the unquestioned principles of the model. Indeed, as a political rationality shaping institutional modernizations and bureaucratic practice, these principles have reconfigured state-society relations, and helped (re)define citizenship and participation as expressions of individual market freedom.

The source of this entrenching of the ethos of the market, now in the form of democratic freedoms, lies in the Constitution of 1980, a charter that has been amended multiple times but never changed in its fundaments. Despite modifications and undeniable improvements in some areas (particularly social rights), the Constitution continues to be the critical means by which the primacy of private property rights, a labour code that upholds the flexibilization of labour, and the commodification of public goods all remain essentially unchallenged. Indeed, as some of us have argued for some time, the return to electoral democracy and progressive politics in Chile did not mark the end of neoliberalism; rather, it led to its transformation into a mature, entrenched form. In other words, neoliberalism as an entrenched form is best understood as a 'form of regulation' – or as an 'adaptive rationale for ongoing projects of state and societal restructuring' (Peck et al., 2018, p. 2). Chile's 'progressive' or 'new left' political forces, in government uninterrupted from 1990 to 2010, are the primary architects of neoliberalism in its present mature form.[12] Thus the Constitution of 1980 needs particular attention if we are to understand both the continuities that characterize Chile's 40-year-old neoliberal modernization project, and the present crisis of representation and legitimacy that has resulted in demands for a new Constitution.

The Constitution of 1980 was designed to entrench the structural reforms implemented by Pinochet's government between 1975 and 1979. As correctly anticipated by its architects, this Constitution has not only insulated Chile's predatory capitalist decision-making from democratic demands, it has also created the conditions for its unprecedented expansion. The transformation of party politics has also created the possibilities for widespread political corruption. Influence peddling, exorbitant salaries and bonuses, and price collusions affecting all levels of the state bureaucracy, politicians of all stripes, the military, the police and powerful corporations, are among the well-publicized cases of corruption and impunity that have contributed to the delegitimization of politics in Chile (Leiva, 2021, pp. 173–207; and Matamala, 2015a, 2015b). Furthermore, the protection of private property rights against public goods and public interest rights, along with restrictive labour legislation and the neutralization of collective action and other limitations designed to depoliticize unions, have all led to the radical opening of the Chilean economy to global markets through a diversification of commodity exports, from copper (Chile's traditional export), to agricultural exports, timber and wood products, and fish products.[13] Thus, the 'success' of Chile's capitalist development strategy has been premised on the radical transformation of labour reforms of the Pinochet period, enshrined in the Constitution of 1980. The *Plan Laboral* (Labour Plan) in place since 1979, which despite reforms remains fundamentally unchanged, has rendered labour vulnerable to exploitation in the name of preserving the freedoms of labour 'flexibility'.[14] It destroyed the gains made by the labour movement throughout the twentieth century–defended at that time by progressive and leftist parties alike–and paved the way for the precarization and cheapening of labour that persists until today.[15] Women are a key ingredient of Chile's economic strategy, and the agro-export sector offers a stark example.[16] It has been radically transformed through the use of technology and reliance on labour intensive production under exploitative conditions. These changes, in turn, have fundamentally transformed the rural sector, with profound effects on gender relations, the organization of rural livelihoods, and women's well-being. Certainly, women's key role in the formula of success in the technologically sophisticated agro-export sector is undeniable; they are recruited for the most poorly paid, precarious, and seasonal jobs.[17]

However, as critically, the Constitution of 1980 also aimed to set the legal parameters of government action in the eventual return to electoral democracy. In the words of Jaime Guzmán, the *eminence gris* of the *political project* of the dictatorship, the goal was to guarantee that Chile would be a 'protected democracy'. As Fernando Atria rightly insists, the clear political intent of the charter was 'to neutralize the political agency of the people' (Atria, 2013, p. 44). Indeed, the restructuring project initiated by the coup in 1973 was always a political project that aimed to insulate market forces from democratic politics, and one 'that found its normative justification in its claim to enhance the form of freedom that only a competitive market could provide' (Whyte, 2019, p. 171). Thus, the Constitution of 1980 created both the cultural and the politico-institutional infrastructure for Chile's marketized-regulatory form. After 30 years of formally democratic rule, this charter continues to guarantee the primacy of the market and the protection of private property rights as the foundation of all other rights. As importantly, and deaspite some important subsequent amendments, among the critical elements that continue to be embedded in the Constitution are those that insulate economic decision-making from politics.

For the past 30 years, successive centre-left and centre-right governments have continued to affirm the role of the private sector and to entrench the rationale of the market in state action, affecting both the organization and purpose of the state bureaucracy as well as the design and delivery of public policy. Rather than *universality*, it is the principle of *subsidiarity*, in the form of the 'efficient' targeting of spending, that guided the drastic reduction of social spending during the dictatorship and that has been preserved and enhanced as a rationale of social spending and social assistance.[18] Moreover, as mentioned above, the intensified commercialization of goods once considered fundamental non-marketable public social resources, such as water, transportation, and basic infrastructure, has continued apace. Indeed, as studies show, private health, education, and social security have not only thrived as private enterprises since 1990 but have also become lucrative investment opportunities for Chilean and international capital.[19] Thus, Chile's 'progressive' model of development, linking growth to democracy and equity, is not hitched to the principle of universality and a guaranteed right to health, education, and social security/pensions as entitlements of citizenship, but rather as rights specifically to targeted social spending and as guaranteed *access* to these goods as commodities in the market. However, this promise of equal access can only be exercised by those who can afford it and, increasingly for vast sectors of the middle class, it means incurring personal debt.[20] For those who simply cannot afford private health plans and hospitals, private schools, or adequately self-financed social security in the form of private old age pension plans, there are inadequate, targeted subsidies, a chronically underfunded public health and education system, and pensions that fall overwhelmingly below the poverty line.[21] Thus, the ultimate goal of the Constitution of 1980 was successfully achieved: to preserve a new order imposed through state violence by locking into place binding political rules that guaranteed the protection of economic liberty as well as a significantly reduced representative function of political parties.

The government of Socialist Ricardo Lagos (2000–2006), in particular, successfully entrenched a new form of the subsidiary state as an 'enabling' state by expanding the competitive businesses of health, education, and pension procurement, and building on existing restrictive labour relations and market freedoms to further open the Chilean economy to global competition. These modernizations have been deepened by successive, democratically elected centre-left and centre-right governments for the past 30 years. The consequences for democratic politics in Chile have been long lasting and have culminated in a devaluing of the party system and the present crisis of political legitimacy.[22] It can therefore be argued that the 'progressive' coalitions that have ruled Chile for most of the past 30 years have not simply 'administered' a neoliberal model inherited from the dictatorship, as some would have it, but that they have actively built on it.

The costs for women of Chile's brave new world: a crisis of care and social reproduction

The massive feminist mobilizations of 2018 and 2019 have largely remained invisible in attempts to explain the social rebellion of October 2019. By March 2019, the demand for a *'Fin a la Precarización de la Vida'* (End to the Precarization of Life) had become a critical rallying cry of the commemoration of the annual March 8th Women's Day demonstrations. Moreover, the march of 2019 became the largest social mobilization in Chile's history until the social rebellion in October of that year.[23] This historic march of women was unparalleled in its diversity and its capacity to bring together tens of thousands of women, young and old, university students, pensioners and activists engaged in a range of urban, rural, and environmental social justice struggles. The demands of demonstrators were telling: they ranged from a call to put an end to precarious life conditions for women and for society more broadly, to demands for a life free from sexism and violence, for sexual and reproductive rights, to calls for an end to exploitative and precarious employment, both urban and rural. Also present were calls for the recognition of water as a human right and for the right to live in communities free from environmental contamination, and, in the case of Mapuche indigenous feminists, for the right to recognition and territorial sovereignty. In other words, unlike earlier feminist marches, the one in March of 2019 made visible the different conditions and challenges faced by women in the country, and by the communities in which they live, and succeeded in unifying their demands under the banner *'Fin a la Precarización de la Vida'* (End to the Precarization of Life). These multiple grievances and demands, coalescing under the broad theme of precarious life, suddenly made visible by the sheer number of women marching together, would reemerge six months later in October 2019 when, to the surprise of so many mainstream observers and scholars, women and men would irrupt onto the scene with a loud, *'Basta Ya!'* This unprecedented feminist mobilization would only be surpassed in size by the march of March 9, 2020, when an estimated 2 million women mobilized throughout Chile demanding an end to state terrorism.

What explains these ever louder and more diversified expressions of women's and feminist discontent? As Daniela López, director of Fundación Nodo XX notes, 'the feminist movement had announced for two years this social crisis' that resulted from the marketization and precarization of everyday life, health, housing, old age, education, and water. She adds that 'If you do not have the means to pay, you cannot access the market for public services'.[24] More was to come, however; the social and economic crisis triggered by the government's mismanagement of the health crisis associated with the COVID-19 pandemic of 2020 has revealed with stark brutality the limits of a 30-year model of development of 'growth with equity' premised on the precarization of labour, privatization of social goods, and fiscal austerity. Studies of the COVID-19 pandemic in Latin America and of government policies to address the health, social and economic crises associated with it, highlight the meager response of Chile's government and 'stingy' economic recovery plan (Blofield & Filgueira, 2020; Castiglione, 2020).

The health crisis and the government's response to it have had an inordinately severe impact on women. An estimated one million women lost their employment as a result of the impact of the lockdowns imposed by the government, and nearly half a million seem to have left the labour force permanently (INE, 2021). Although women in all areas of employment have been affected, the highest job losses have affected those employed in paid domestic services and in retail jobs. According to the Instituto Nacional de Estadísticas, INE, Chile's National Institute of Statistics, these are two of the most precarious sectors of the economy, where the overwhelming majority of women are employed (INE, 2021). Since 1990, women have been called upon to be empowered workers and rational consumers–also, increasingly, responsible debt holders–while at the same time they are expected to be the social support for reproductive and caring work.[25] This 'naturalized' expectation, and by now culturally ingrained self-expectation, is extended to women's participation in both private and public sector work and contributes to the exploitation and self-exploitation of female workers. Until 2019, women made up 37 percent of the private sector labour force and, as mentioned above, their labour participation was concentrated in the most precarious and poorly paid sectors of the economy. Moreover, they constituted 60 percent of all public employees, making the neoliberalized social state the employer with the greatest percentage of women.[26]

Thus, the paid and unpaid labour of women has been the secret ingredient in the successful consolidation of a model of development and institutional reconfiguration premised on 'growth with equity'. The national employment statistics are damning; three out of four women with remunerated employment earn less than 550,000 pesos net per month (USD660), and 50 percent of employed women receive 343,234 pesos (USD412) or less; only 9.1 percent receive over 1 million pesos (USD1,193).[27] In addition, the overall income gap between male and female employment is 14 percent (Barriga et al., 2020, p. 7). The responsibility for the procurement of care activities associated with social reproduction also continues to fall heavily on women. Regardless of their age, women are overwhelmingly responsible for the provision of unpaid care to families and continue to be the invisibilized force supporting their communities.[28] Of the estimated one and a half million Chilean-born and immigrant workers who toil in labour intensive, seasonal agricultural activities, the majority are women. In fact, as recent studies show, 90 percent of stable jobs with contracts in the agro-industry are held by men, while the majority of seasonal and informal jobs are held by women.[29] Moreover, this pattern of precarious, poorly paid women's employment is repeated in other areas of private and public sector employment, especially in undervalued, feminized areas.[30]

Particularly dramatic is the situation faced by women employed as domestics, who constitute over 90 percent of those employed in this service sector. For example, of an estimated 360,000 who are affiliated with the *Sindicato de Trabajadoras de Casa Particular* (Union of Private Home Workers), 53 percent are informal workers, and many of them are heads of household. Precarious female employment has also spread to the public service, where the vast majority of professionally trained women, including teachers, social workers, and those in health-related areas are among the most poorly paid and precarious public workers.[31] As I have argued elsewhere, this is the modality of female employment on which the rise of an enabling, decentralized 'caring' state has been built for the past 30 years (Schild, 2013, 2015b, 2019).

However, women are not only the poorest workers, they are also the poorest pensioners, and many are forced to work well past the retirement age of 60 years, on average to age 67, to compensate for what are commonly referred to as *pensiones de hambre*, or hunger pensions. Since 1979 Chile has pioneered a system of mandatory private savings that, until recent reforms, operated exclusively as an individual savings account without contributions from employers or the state.[32] Chile's privatized pension plan was introduced in 1979 as one of the 'seven modernizations' spearheaded by José Piñera, designed primarily as a means to generate a pool of capital for investments but also, as revealed in Piñera's book *El cascabel al gato: la batalla por la reforma previsional*, as a deliberate political move to significantly 'reduce the political power of the state over the economy' (Matamala, 2016).[33] A recent study based on Chile's official monthly economic activities index (the IMACEI or *Indices Mensuales de Actividad Económica Interna*) revealed that for 2019 only one third (34 percent) of the money collected in obligatory fees – by law, workers must pay 10 percent of their income into the pension – was destined by AFPs to pay out pensions, while the remaining two thirds (66 percent) of the funds saved by individual contributors were transferred in perpetuity to the administrating companies and the financial system (CENDA, 2020). As critics point out, although the AFP system was created during the dictatorship, it matured during the 1990s, when 'doing business, whether legal or illegal with pension funds, was our daily bread'.[34] Thus, it is estimated that since 1980, when the pension scheme was created, the funds paid out to pensioners (in today's money) have amounted to 35 billion US dollars. At the same time, the funds diverted as commissions and investment funds amount to 70 billion US dollars. The CENDA study concludes by stating that 'this is the principal way in which a handful of big business pockets the money of contributions, at the cost of leaving pensioners in penury, two thirds of whom are women' (CENDA, 2020, p. 3).

According to the latest figures, in 2019 the privatized pension system paid out 980,000 old age pensions, making this the first generation of Chileans who have invested fully under the system of individual accounts with AFPs. The outcomes are, in the words of one study, 'disastrous': by December of 2019, 50 percent of the total of 984,000 retirees received a pension amounting to less than 202,000 pesos – 145,000 pesos if the state subsidy, or *Aporte Previsional Solidario (APS)*, is not taken into account (Gálvez & Kremerman, 2020, p. 5). The case is not better for those who contributed for 30–35 years, who received less than 301,000 pesos. Particularly concerning is the situation of women. A full 50 percent of women retirees received a pension lower than 149,000 pesos (or, 138,000 if the state subsidy is discounted). Even those who contributed to a pension throughout 30–35 years of uninterrupted working life, managed to collect a pension of only 287,000 pesos. The conclusion of this study is that 'practically 80 percent of the pensions paid fall below the minimum wage, and only 12.5 percent managed to obtain a total pension greater than 472,000 pesos' (Gálvez & Kremerman, 2020; Sáez, 2020). Once again, these figures paint an even more dire picture of the situation of women pensioners. These are the crude figures behind the reality of precarization of life for a majority of Chilean women, whose life in old age is characterized by financial insecurity and an increasing reliance on personal debt to make ends meet.[35] It is what has fueled their calls for 'dignity', and an end to 'hunger pensions' and to precarious life.

The longstanding burdens of care placed on women and the record of promises unmet reached a critical point by 2019. Calls for a new 'social contract' were the loudest demands emanating from the spontaneous, self-organized *cabildos* (town halls) and *asambleas ciudadanas* (citizen assemblies) that sprung up in ever increasing numbers in middle- and working-class neighbourhoods of cities and towns throughout the country after October 2019.

Since March 2020, as the health crisis associated with the COVID-19 pandemic further intensified the country's social and political crisis, Chileans have continued to demand an end to privatized social goods and the precarization of life. What is distinctive, though not surprising, is the presence of women, especially older leaders, in the work of generating social spaces at the local level in working class and poor neighbourhoods throughout the country. They often include their own distinctive traditions of popular organizing, including soup kitchens and other street activities. This participation of women would become dramatically evident in the months to come, as the government's inept and insufficient response to the COVID-19-related health crisis spiralled into a social and economic one. Women once again stepped up to organize soup kitchens to help feed their neighbours, and to identify and reach out to help the elderly in their community cope with hunger and despair. In the words of Roxana Pey of the University of Chile:

Women workers, pensioners, the 2.15 million heads of households, women in informal and precarious work, all of them are managing the control of this pandemic, they are the ones who provide care, who organize soup kitchens, who act in solidarity, and the ones who are bearing the brunt of the crisis. Gender violence and sexual violence have increased. The worsened economic conditions have affected women to such a point that they do not manage to satisfy their basic needs. (Pey, 2020)

Conclusion

I have argued that the post-1990 modality of capitalist accumulation in Chile, and the institutional framework buttressing it, even in its neo-developmentalist garb, is best understood not as a superseding of neoliberalism but as an entrenched neoliberalization, now in the form of an adaptive governing rationality that has not only reshaped the economy but also social and political life. A careful, historically contextualized and gender sensitive examination of the institutional underpinnings of the political economy of this well entrenched project of 'progressive' government challenges broad claims about its status as the most successful and stable Pink Tide government in the Latin American region. It reveals instead, some essential continuities with the neoliberal modernization imposed by Pinochet's civilian–military dictatorship.

For 30 years the country's centre-left and centre-right government coalitions pursued a programme of 'growth with equity' that included increases in social spending and an explicit commitment to address poverty and advance an agenda of women's rights and gender equity. For many, the changes and innovations ushered in by Chile's 'pragmatic' left, furthered during the two terms of centre-right governments under Sebastián Piñera, were grounds for optimism. The achievements of the Chilean strategy of 'growth with equity' and political democracy have been defended by its chief architects (a 'new breed of pragmatic leftists', according to *The Wall Street Journal* at the time) as the conclusive overcoming of Chile's neoliberalism. Yet, as a transnational political-economic project, it has primarily served to justify and legitimize efforts to re-establish the conditions for capital accumulation and to install market values as the *sine qua non* of modernity. It has allowed for the removal of barriers to capital accumulation, and has encouraged the expansion and deepening of markets, thus actively enabling the restoration to power of dominant economic groups. Perhaps former presidential candidate for the right-wing party UDI, Pablo Longeira, best characterized the fruits of the pursuit of 'growth with equity' and political democracy when he asserted in 2013 that:

> The last twenty-five years have been the most successful period for the right. There is no other generation of the political right that can show a more notable victory in the battle of ideas. Chile has reached its privileged place because our political and economic philosophy was implemented.[36]

The cultural, political and social processes of restructuring associated with entrenched neoliberalism, I have argued, are profoundly gendered, both in their configuration and in their effects. Moreover, the subjection of individuals and widespread social domains to the model of the market has had serious implications for the social relations of reproduction. Indeed, the erosion of the conditions of care which are fundamental for the reproduction of society and human beings, with particularly harsh consequences for the overwhelming majority of Chile's women, is something they many Chileans no longer willing to tolerate. The social and economic reality has brought millions of them to the breaking point, and has brought women in unprecedented numbers to the forefront of demands for fundamental changes in the organization and governance of society. Their massive participation in the demonstrations of 2018 and 2019, as well as the social rebellion of October 2019, highlights the continuing relevance of Karl Polanyi's warning about the costs of subjecting societies and individuals to market rule.

Now that Chile's majority has spoken, and a citizens-only Convention to draft a new constitution – with gender parity – has engaged in widespread consultations, some of the key priorities for constituents are becoming clear. Among the central concerns that have been singled out are: greater regulation of the economy and an environmentally sustainable economic model; meaningful political decentralization and regional representation; the reconfiguration of the social state into one that recognizes the substantive contribution of paid and unpaid care; and guarantees of access to essential public goods such as health, education and social security as fundamental rights of citizenship. An unprecedented and widely acknowledged innovation is the mandate of the Convention to deliberate jointly on a sustainable economic development model, the rights of nature, and the recognition of natural common goods as fundamental rights. The possibility of enshrining some of these key institutional changes, along with the protection of labour rights, and the recognition of indigenous peoples and their legitimate demands, in a new legal framework would indicate that the balance of power is tilting away from unencumbered market rule in the direction of greater protection in what Polanyi described as the complex and dynamic political terrain of capitalist societies.

The election on December 21, 2021 of Gabriel Boric as Chile's next president has signalled the possibility of enshrining a new constitution containing some of the proposals under debate. President-elect Boric has announced that his will be a government of regions that will facilitate the approval of the new constitution and endorse the fundamental changes required to advance on an environmentally and socially sustainable economy. Elected with 56 percent of the vote, and the overwhelming support of women, especially those 30 and under, Boric and his incoming left-coalition Frente Amplio – a coalition of new left parties, with a strong presence of women and feminists, that have been part of social movements pushing for change for the past 15 years – have promised to strengthen the Ministry of Women and Gender Equality and to make it a key player in the configuration and implementation of public policy. Moreover, in terms of concrete policy areas, three have been identified as critical for advancing on a gender sensitive sustainable economic recovery: a national childcare programme; official recognition of unpaid care work; and co-responsibility for activities that have historically been undervalued, invisiblized, and feminized in the economy. The pledge to make feminist demands politically central, along with the commitment to reconfigure the social state, with greater autonomy and resources for regions, are some of the government's planks to initiate a programme of necessary structural changes. The incoming government of Boric promises a renewed turn to the left in Chilean politics, and an economic recovery programme focused on stimulating investments, expanding formal employment, especially for women and the young, and respecting the environment. Many questions remain to be answered about how far the new constitution will set the terms for deeper structural changes. Will this new constitution open up the possibility for the fundamental transformations most Chileans desire, or will it constitute yet another trap to preserve the structural conditions of Chilean capitalism? Will the transformations help rebuild public goods like health, education and pensions, which are now private goods? Will they once again grant public status to water, making it a basic human right? Provide living wages? And bring an end 'zones of sacrifice', areas with high concentrations of industrial pollution that have been accepted until now as the inevitable price of development and modernity? Ultimately, changing the constitution will be an initial, if necessary, moment of a longer struggle, albeit one whose specific outcome remains uncertain for the moment. The extent to which Chile's renewed left turn offers an innovative path forward for the Latin American region will depend on this outcome.

Notes

1. Ordinary Chileans who were interviewed by the media as they watched subsequent mobilizations unfold on their way to and from work – when it was still possible to move across the city of Santiago – expressed it succinctly: '*Se veia venir*' (We saw it coming). Indeed, surveys conducted during the early days of the demonstrations showed an approval rate of over 80 percent.
2. In this article, I rely on my previous research as well as participant observation conducted in Viña del Mar and Santiago during the months of October to December 2019.
3. On November 4, 2019, *the Instituto Nacional de Derechos Humanos de Chile*, INDH (National Institute of Human Rights of Chile) reported 4,364 detainees, of these 670 women, 3,060 men, and most alarming, 479 children and adolescents, both male and female. In 2020, 4,681 human rights violations by police and military personnel had been registered by the *Ministerio Publico* (Public Ministry), though most of these cases languish in the courts. A shocking legacy of wanton police brutality was the high number (460) of catastrophic eye injuries registered during the months of demonstrations, according to INDH. On October 16, 2020, Sergio Micco, Director of the INDH, concluded that these incidents resulted in the most serious, systematic violations of human rights since the return to democracy in 1990 (INDH, 2020a).
4. The feminist critique of political economy that theorizes the links between social reproduction and capitalism is longstanding. For an overview of its present renewal see, Ferguson (2020); Bhattacharya (2017).
5. To date my long-standing research in Chile has focused on the gendered configuration and effects of transformations in statecraft, specifically on the neoliberalisation of political subjects and the social state (Schild, 2000, 2007, 2013). My overall methodological strategy is based on grounded, contextualized exploration of the making of active social policy as a key dimension of the progressive agenda of centre-left, or *Concertación*, governments and centre-right governments.
6. For this purpose, I rely extensively on recent official statistical surveys and give primacy to studies from Chile, many of which have remained overlooked or untranslated to date. All translations are mine.
7. These demands were part of earlier mobilizations, the so-called *revolución de los pinguinos* (the Penguin Revolution), which had captured the world's attention. Spearheaded by high school students in 2006 whose school uniform had given them the name of 'penguins', nationwide demonstrations had demanded an end to the Ley Organica Constitucional de Enseñanza (the Constitutional Educational Law), or LOCE. Introduced in 1989 by the outgoing dictatorship, the law guaranteed the perpetuation of a system of privatized secondary and post-secondary education, and although modified in 2009 during Bachelet's first term in office, the fundamental market driven criteria remained untouched.
8. Quoted in Atria (2013, p. 41). Key limiting requirements included: the proscription of 'Marxist' parties; the law guaranteeing that one third of senators would be designated; the introduction of a binomial electoral system designed to limit the role of parties and political representation; the granting of unprecedented presidential powers; and the creation of an independent Constitutional Tribunal that would oversee legal reforms. Most significantly, the Constitution enshrined the requirement of super majorities – 2/3 or 5/6 approval – for amending any of the charter's clauses or its organic laws. The binomial electoral system would only be abolished in 2015 during Bachelet's second government. Several of these were removed in piecemeal fashion over the past 30 years, but the requirements on presidential powers, the Constitutional Tribunal, and super majorities all remain.
9. For example, the National Association of Rural and Indigenous Women (ANAMURI) has been a pioneer in environmental organizations waging struggles for an end to 'zones of sacrifice'. Women have also been at the forefront of local and regional organizations struggling for water as a basic human right, such as Patagonia Sin Represas, Alerta Isla Riesco, Defendamos Chiloé, Alto Maipo, Movimiento Defensa por el Acceso al Agua, la Tierra y Protección del Medio Ambiente (Modatima), Defensa Caimanes, and Asamblea de Freirina.
10. The literature on the configuration of Chile's early and paradigmatic neoliberal project is extensive. See, for example, Letelier (1976), Valdés (1995), and especially the more recent and comprehensive study by Huneeus (2000).
11. See, for example, Lagos (2016). For a critical review, see, Leiva (2008, especially Chapters 4 and 9), and Garretón (2012).

12. A recent literature on neoliberalism offers a complex account of the configuration of the Chilean variant and its role in transnational intellectual circuits, including the neglected story of James Buchanan and the Mont Pelerin Society. See, for example, MacLean (2017); Whyte (2019); Plehwe et al. (2020).
13. In 2019, China was the main market for Chilean exports, 31.1 percent, with the U.S. a distant second, with 14.1 percent of exports. Although copper continues to dominate Chilean exports, with 45 percent of total exports, so-called non-traditional commodities like timber, wood pulp, seasonal fruits and nuts and wine, fresh, chilled and frozen fish and salmon, are among the country's top ten exports. Figures from, Trading Economics (2020).
14. The Plan stipulates four fundamental pillars: collective action exclusively at the enterprise level; strikes that do not paralyze production; parallel labour organizations ostensibly fostering competition; and finally, the depoliticization of unions. This means that in Chile there is no effective right to strike, and that in a highly 'flexibilized' labour context, the struggle for decent work and living wages is ongoing. The attempted labour reform of Bachelet's second term (2014–2018) did not include the issue of quality of employment, and maintained untouched the stipulation that strikes occur at the level of the enterprise only. In other words, the fundamentals of the Pinochet era Plan Laboral remained unchanged. As of 2015, the rates of unionization remained low, at half of what they were in 1973, or 14.2 percent. 53 percent of unions had 40 members or less, and only 8.4 percent of unions were covered by collective agreements (Narbona, 2015).
15. The most important sectors of Chile's export-based economy, i.e., mining, agriculture, forestry, and fishing are owned and controlled by large conglomerates. These are the sectors that depend on unregulated and poorly paid workers to get their products to export markets. In particular, agriculture, hospitality, domestic service, retail and fishing concentrate the highest numbers of minimum or below minimum wage work. See the chart based on the national survey, CASEN, in Durán and Kremerman (2020, p. 10).
16. With the reversal of the land reform during the dictatorship, changes in land property rights, and the extension of land property rights to foreign entities, an estimated 60 percent of land was removed from small peasant and collective production. A further 50 percent of small producers was forced to sell lands for lack of technical assistance (FAO, 1998, pp. 206–207). These changes led to a radical transformation of Chile's rural sector. It should be noted that this process also involved a loss of Mapuche land to private owners and large forest cultivation. For a comprehensive analysis of these transformations, see Gómez and Echeñique (1988); Valdés and Araujo (1999); Kay (2006, 2015); Bellisario (2007).
17. More recently, women jostle with other vulnerable categories, principally undocumented migrants and indigenous peoples, for positions at the lowest rungs of seasonal, poorly paid, and often dangerous work. See Valdés (1987, 2020). As the long-standing research by Ximena Valdés makes clear, these rural transformations have also created new political opportunities for rural and indigenous women. The emblematic National Rural and Indigenous Women's Association, ANAMURI, for example, which was created in 1998 to struggle for rural women's labour rights and protections, is a key protagonist in present national and regional demands for a socially and environmentally sustainable development model. See, Cid Aguayo and Latta (2015).
18. For a recent, comprehensive review of policies in the area of poverty reduction since 1990 and their cultural political effects, see Ramos Zincke (2016). As I have shown, this policy area has been gendered in its configuration and effects (Schild, 2002, 2007). Furthermore, my research has argued that the transformation of female clients into workers and consumers has been a deliberate state policy since 1990. See, Schild (2013, 2015a).
19. The private health system, for example, has experienced a boom in great part because it has been a direct beneficiary of the amendments and expansions introduced by *Concertación* governments that aimed to guarantee health access for certain types of illnesses, e.g. Plan AUGE now GES, Plan de Garantías Explícitas en Salud (Plan of Explicit Guarantees in Health). See, Goyenechea and Sinclaire (2013).
20. According to figures from Chile's Central Bank in 2019, the level of household debt in relation to income reached a historic record of 74.5 percent. For the latest figures linking low wages to debt, see Durán and Kremerman (2020). Studies have persistently shown that Chileans identify overwhelmingly as 'middle class', although this seems to be more fantasy than reality, given that large sectors of society must subsidize their lives through heavy debt loads. See, for example, Pérez-Roa (2019); Espinoza and Barozet (2008); PNUD (2017).

21. For up-to-date figures, see Gálvez and Kremerman (2020). In the case of health, 'freedom of choice' is more easily accessed by those who are low risk, young, healthy, and with high incomes, i.e., approximately 17–18 percent of the population. The rest, that is, 'women and those who are poorer, older, and sicker' are covered by *Fondo Nacional de Salud, FONASA* FONASA. In 2015, the average premium of the private ISAPRE health plans was equivalent to 45 percent of the minimum wage (Crispi et al., 2020). For an analysis of privatized health in Chile, see Goyenechea and Sinclaire (2013).
22. For a recent analysis of the present political crisis see, for example, Huneeus (2018).
23. The trend toward increasingly massive and diverse feminist mobilizations began in 2015 with Chile's *Me Too* movement and demands for free abortion, and in 2016 with student mobilizations against sexual harassment and violence. These were followed by the historic march of May 16, 2018 – known as the *Mayo Feminista*, in reference to the student rebellions of May 1968 – calling for an end to sexual violence in universities and for a dismantling of its sexist structures (Segovia, 2020).
24. Daniela López, Director of *Fundación Nodo XX* quoted in Segovia (2020).
25. According to official statistics, women's participation in the labour force increased from 35 percent in 1990–1953 percent in early 2020, to fall once again to 41.3 percent in the trimester May to July 2021 (INE, 2021). Furthermore, the majority of women work in paid domestic services and in retail, either in small businesses or markets, two of the sectors most affected by lengthy lockdowns. Furthermore, according to the most recent national survey, CASEN 2017, an estimated 42 percent of all households in Chile are headed by women, a figure that reaches 53 percent among the poorest households. This suggests that figures for formal employment do not capture those informal activities that women, including today many immigrant women, are compelled to engage in to make ends meet. For a timely and informative overview of the impact on Chile's women of the pandemic and government policy, see *Mujeres en tiempos de esperanza, crisis y pandemia*, edited by Bórquez Polloni and published by the Library of Chile's National Congress (Biblioteca del Congreso Nacional de Chile), 2021.
26. Women's work in the public sector is also concentrated in highly feminized areas: for example, 74.1 percent work in health provision, and 72.2 percent in teaching (Barriga et al., 2020). Combining public workers and career functionaries, Chile's public sector is the smallest in Latin America, and represents approximately 7 percent of Chile's total labour force. Here too, women in the public sector are the most precarious and poorly paid workers (de la Puente 2011, p. 14). See, also, Yañez & Rojas, 2017.
27. Chile does not have a minimum hourly wage. The minimum or basic monthly wage for full time work as of January 2021, is 326,500 pesos (USD390). The working hours are among the longest in the world, or 45 h spread over five or six days. Studies based on Chile's official statistics show that many workers work in excess of the statutory maximum, that this monthly wage only covers 69 percent of what a family of three needs to be above the poverty line, and that a significant number of workers do not earn the minimum (Durán & Kremerman, 2020; Kremerman & Sáez, 2021).
28. Official statistics suggest that on average women provide over 41 h per week of unremunerated domestic and care activities. For men, the average figure is slightly over 19 h (Barriga et al., 2020, p. 7).
29. Valdés et al. (forthcoming 2020, p. 54; 2015). Migrant workers, predominantly from Peru, Bolivia and Haiti who have proper status in the country, earn on average 276,000 pesos (USD330), while those without papers earn on average 184,000 pesos (USD220) (Valdés et al., forthcoming 2020, p. 54).
30. According to the comprehensive analysis of national employment statistics found in the document, 'No es Amor, es trabajo no remunerado', of the 1,079,208 jobs created in the past 10 years which are performed by women, 60 per cent correspond to precarious employment: 30.3 percent are subcontracted jobs, and 29.7 percent are forms of self-employment. Self-employment includes home based textile production. Chile was the first country to sign a free trade agreement with China and during the period 2005–2016 saw a major restructuring of the textile industry, a highly feminized, long-standing sector of industrial production (See, Fundación Sol 2017).
31. See, Durán et al. (2016).
32. Only since the Bachelet reforms of 2008 did the business sector make a contribution of 1.53 percent through a disability and survivors' insurance, the *Seguro de Invalidez y Sobreviviencia (SIS)*. The reforms also created a 'solidarity pillar', or subsidized benefit for pensioners falling below the poverty line. This addition has not made much difference, forcing many seniors to continue working well past retirement age to supplement their miserly pensions. The increasingly militant and massive No+AFP movement must be seen in relation to the failure of *Concertación* governments to change a pension

scheme that condemns millions to a life of poverty in old age. For the most recent, comprehensive overview of pensions, see Gálvez and Kremerman (2020).
33. Well before the present debacle of the AFPs, official figures from the regulatory agency *Superintendencia de Pensiones* revealed a history of illegal investments by AFPs, as well as the names of political figures from the centre-left and centre-right who, after leaving office, have joined the boards of directors of AFPs. As Daniel Matamala points out, the political donations made by corporations to electoral campaigns also come from funds collected by the AFPs. See Matamala (2016) and Weibel Barahona (2017).
34. From Sergio Jara Román, *Piñera y los leones de Sanhattan* (2018), Chapter 3, published in Jara Román (2020).
35. An estimated 80 percent of Chilean adults have significant personal debt, and 5 million people of a population of 18 million have defaulted on their debt (Pérez-Roa and Gómez, 2020; Banco Central, 2018). Studies show that personal debt is a strategy widely used by middle-class and popular sector households to increase the monthly household, and that women play a fundamental role (Pérez-Roa & Troncoso Pérez, 2019).
36. Quoted in Goyenechea and Sinclaire (2013, p. 35).

Acknowledgements

I thank Charmain Levy, Manuel Larrabure, Aparna Sundar, Ted Schrecker, and Malcolm Blincow, as well as the three anonymous reviewers, for their substantial comments and suggestions. From October to December 2019, I was Visiting International Researcher at the School of Psychology of the Universidad Católica de Valparaíso, Chile, with funding from the National Commission of Scientific and Technological Research (Comisión Nacional de Investigación Científica y Tecnológica, CONYCIT), Ministry of Education, Government of Chile. I am grateful for the support and intellectual stimulation of my colleagues Maria Isabel Reyes and Luisa Castaldi during what turned out to be a singular moment in Chile's history.

Disclosure statement

No potential conflict of interest was reported by the authors.

References

Atria, F. (2013). *La Constitución tramposa*. LOM.
Banco Central de Chile. (2018). *Encuesta financiera de hogares. Principales Resultados 2017*.
Barriga, F., Durán, G., Sáez B. and Sato A. (2020). No es amor, es trabajo no pagado. Un análisis del trabajo de las mujeres en el Chile actual. *Documento de Trabajo*, Marzo. Santiago: Fundación Sol.
Bellisario, A. (2007). The Chilean agrarian transformation: Agrarian reform and capitalist 'Partial' counter-agrarian reform, 1964?1980. *Journal of Agrarian Change*, 7(1), 1–34. https://doi.org/10.1111/j.1471-0366.2007.00138.x
Bhattacharya, T. (2017). *Social reproduction theory: Remapping class, recentering oppression*. Pluto Press.
Blofield, M., & Filgueira, F. (2020). *COVID-19 and Latin America: Social impact, policies and a fiscal case for an emergency social protection floor*. CIPPEC.
Bórquez Polloni, B. (2021). *Mujeres en tiempos de esperanza, crisis y pandemia*. Ediciones Biblioteca del Congreso Nacional de Chile.

Borzutzky, S., & Perry, S. (2020). It is not about the 30 pesos. It is about the 30 years! Chile's elitist democracy, social movements and the October 18th protests. *The Latinamericanist, 65*(2), 207–232. https://doi.org/10.1353/tla.2021.0016

Brenner, N., Peck, J., & Theodore, N. (2010). Variegated neoliberalization: Geographies, modalities, pathways. *Global Networks, 10*(2), 182–222. https://doi.org/10.1111/j.1471-0374.2009.00277.x

Brown, W. (2015). *Undoing the demos. Neoliberalism's stealth revolution.* Zone Books.

Castiglione, R. (2020). La política chilena en tiempos de pandemia. *Nueva Sociedad, 287,* 68–79. https://nuso.org/articulo/la-politica-chilena-en-tiempos-de-pandemia/

CENDA. (2020, January). Chile: Indices Mensuales de Actividad Económica Interna. *Resúmen Ejecutivo.* https://www.cendachile.cl/series-cenda/%C3%ADndices-mensuales-de-actividad-econ%C3%B3mica-interna

Cid Aguayo, B., & Latta, A. (2015). Agro-ecology and food sovereignty movements in Chile: Sociospatial practices for alternative peasant futures. *Annals of the Association of American Geographers, 105*(2), 397–406. https://doi.org/10.1080/00045608.2014.985626

Crispi, F., Cherla, A., Vivaldi, E. A., & Mossialos, E. (2020). Rebuilding the broken health contract in Chile. *The Lancet, 395*(10233), 1342–1342. https://doi.org/10.1016/S0140-6736(20)30228-2

de la Puente, R. (2011). Empleo público y derechos laborales. In J. Insignia, A. Fürher (Eds.), Reforma del Estado y relaciones laborales en el Chile de hoy (pp.12-22). Friedrich Ebert-Stiftung.

Durán, G., Gálvez, R., & Narbona, K. (2016). Salarios en el sector público. El mito en torno a los funcionarios públicos en Chile. *Ideas para el Buen Vivir, 9.* (pp.1-10) Santiago: Fundación Sol https://fundacionsol.cl/blog/estudios-2/post/salarios-en-el-sector-publico-6142.

Durán, G., & Kremerman, M. (2020). Los verdaderos sueldos de Chile. *Documentos de Trabajo del Area de Salarios y Desigualdad.* Santiago: Fundación Sol.

Espinoza, V., & Barozet, E. (2008). De qué hablamos cuando decimos "clase media"? Perspectivas sobre el caso chileno. *En Foco* 142. Expansiva UDP/Instituto de Politicas Publicas.

Ferguson, S. (2020). *Women and work: Feminism, labour, and social reproduction.* Pluto Press.

Food and Agriculture Organization. (1998). *The State of Food and Agriculture.* FAO Agricultural Series No. 31. The Food and Agriculture Organization of the United Nations.

Gálvez, R., & Kremerman, K. (2020). Pensiones bajo el mínimo. Los montos de las pensiones que paga el sistema de capitalización individual en Chile. *Documento de Trabajo 2020,* Santiago: Fundación Sol.

Garretón, M. A. (2012). *Neoliberalismo corregido y progresismo limitado. Los gobiernos de la Concertación en Chile, 1990-2010.* Editorial Arcis-CLACSO.

Gómez, S., & Echeñique, J. (1988). *La agricultura chilena. Las dos caras de la modernización.* FLACSO.

Goyenechea, M., & Sinclaire, D. (2013). La privatización de la salud en Chile. *Políticas Publicas, 6*(1), 35–51. http://www.revistas.usach.cl/ojs/index.php/politicas/article/view/1196/1120

Heiss, C. (2021, May). Chile: La Constitución que viene. *Nueva Sociedad.* https://nuso.org/articulo/chile-la-constitucion-que-viene/

Huneeus, C. (2000). *El régimen de Pinochet.* Editorial Sudamericana.

Huneeus, C. (2018). La democracia semisoberana y la representación política tecnocrática. In C. Huneeus, & O. Avendaño (Eds.), *El sistema político en Chile.* (pp.19-56) LOM.

Instituto Nacional de Derechos Humanos (INDH). (2020a). INDH entrega un balance a un año de la crisis social. https://www.indh.cl/indh-entrega-balance-a-un-ano-de-la-crisis-social/.

Instituto Nacional de Estadísticas (INE). (2021, March 8). *Boletín Estadístico. Género y empleo. Impacto de la crisis del COVID-19.* https://www.ine.cl/docs/default-source/genero/documentos-de-an%C3%A1lisis/documentos/g%C3%A9nero-y-empleo-impacto-de-la-crisis-econ%C3%B3mica-por-covid19.pdf

Jara Román, S. (2020, July 9). La era de las AFP: Así nació y operó la estrecha relación entre Sanhattan y los fondos de pensiones. *El Desconcierto.* https://www.eldesconcierto.cl/reportajes/2020/07/09/la-era-de-las-afp-asi-nacio-y-opero-la-estrecha-relacion-entre-sanhattan-y-los-fondos-de-pensiones.html.

Kay, C. (2006). Rural poverty and development strategies in Latin America. *Journal of Agrarian Change, 6*(4), 455–508. https://doi.org/10.1111/j.1471-0366.2006.00132.x

Kay, C. (2015). The agrarian question and the neoliberal rural transformation of Latin America. *European Review of Latin American and Caribbean Studies, 100,* 78–83. http://doi.org/10.18352/erlacs.10123

Kremerman, M., & Sáez, B. (2021). *Reajuste del salario mínimo. Propuesta de reajuste del salario mínimo (2021-2023) con criterios de suficiencia para una reactivación no precaria.* Fundación Sol.

Lagos, R. (2016). *En vez del pesimismo: Una mirada estratégica de Chile al 2040*. Penguin Random House.
Leiva, F. I. (2008). *Latin American neostructuralism: The contradictions of post-neoliberal development*. University of Minnesota Press.
Leiva, F. I. (2021). *The left hand of neoliberalism and the left in Chile*. SUNY Press.
Letelier, O. (1976/2016). The Chicago boys in Chile: economic freedom's awful toll. *The Nation*, September 21.
MacLean, N. (2017). *Democracy in chains. The deep history of the radical right's Stealth plan for America*. Scribe Publications.
Matamala, D. (2015a). *Poderoso caballero. El peso del dinero en la política chilena*. Catalonia/UDP Escuela de Periodismo.
Matamala, D. (2015b). La lista completa. La verdad sobre las 1,123 empresas que financian la política en Chile. *CIPER.CL*. Retrieved April 23, 2015, from https://www.ciperchile.cl/2015/04/23/la-lista-completa-la-verdad-sobre-las-1-123-empresas-que-financian-la-politica-en-chile/
Matamala, D. (2016). *AFP: el poder impotente*. CIPER Chile. https://ciperchile.cl/2016/07/26/afp-el-poder-impotente/
Narbona, K. (2015). Para una historia del tiempo presente. Lo que cambió el Plan Laboral de la Dictadura. *Ideas Para el Buen Vivir*, 6. (pp.3-13). Santiago: Fundación Sol. http://www.researchgate.net/publication/299404372
Palma, G. (2009). The revenge of the market on the rentiers.: Why neo-liberal reports of the end of history turned out to be premature. *Cambridge Journal of Economics*, 33(4), 829–869. https://doi.org/10.1093/cje/bep037
Panitch, L., & Gindin, S. (2012). *The making of global capitalism: The political economy of American empire*. Verso.
Peck, J., Brenner, N., & Theodore, N. (2018). Actually existing neoliberalism. In D. Cahill, M. Cooper, M. Konings & D. Primrose (Eds.), *The sage handbook of neoliberalism* (pp. 2–14). SAGE Publications.
Peck, J., & Theodore, N. (2019). Still neoliberalism? *South Atlantic Quarterly*, 118(2), 245–265. https://doi.org/10.1215/00382876-7381122
Pérez-Roa, L. (2019). Consumo, endeudamiento y economía doméstica: una historia en tres tiempos para entender el estallido social. In K. Araujo (Ed.), *Hilos tensados. Para leer el octubre chileno* (pp. 83–105). Editorial USACH.
Pérez-Roa, L., & Gómez, C. M. (2020). Endeudamiento desigual en Chile: Cuánto debemos, en qué lo gastamos, y cómo está parado cada uno para la crisis. *CIPER Chile*. https://www.ciperchile.cl/2020/07/02/endeudamiento-desigual-en-chile-cuanto-debemos-en-que-lo-gastamos-y-como-esta-parado-cada-uno-para-la-crisis/
Pérez-Roa, L., & Troncoso Pérez, L. (2019). Deudas, mujeres y programas sociales en sociedades financiarizadas: Resituando la "vida económica" en la intervención social. *Revistas Rumbo TS*, 19, 11–25. https://revistafacso.ucentral.cl/index.php/rumbos/article/view/326
Pey, R. (2020). Las AFPs maltratan a las mujeres. *Radio Universidad de Chile*, July 20. http://radio.uchile.cl/2020/07/20/593063/
Plehwe, D., Slobodian, Q. S., & Mirowski, P. (Eds.). (2020). *Nine lives of neoliberalism*. Verso.
PNUD. (2017). *Orígenes, cambios y desafíos de la brecha social en Chile*. Programa de las Naciones Unidas para el Desarrollo, Junio.
Ramos Zincke, C. (2016). *La producción de la pobreza como objeto de gobierno*. Ediciones Universidad Alberto Hurtado.
Sáez, B. (2020, July 8). Pensiones: al servicio del capital, sin el aporte del capital. *El Desconcierto.cl*. http://www.eldesconcierto.cl/2020/07/08/pensiones-al-servicio-del-capital-sin-el-aporte-del-capital/
Schild, V. (2000). Neo-liberalism's new gendered market citizens: The 'civilizing' dimension of social programmes in Chile. *Citizenship Studies*, 4(3), 275–305. https://doi.org/10.1080/713658800
Schild, V. (2002). Engendering the new social citizenship in Chile: NGOs and social provisioning under neo-liberalism. In S. Razavi, & M. Molyneux (Eds.), *Gender justice, development and rights. Substantiating rights in a disabling environment* (pp. 170–203). Oxford University Press.
Schild, V. (2007). 'Empowering consumer citizens or governing poor female subjects? The institutionalization of "self-development" in the Chilean social policy field. *Journal of Consumer Culture*, 7(2), 179–203. https://doi.org/10.1177/1469540507077672

Schild, V. (2013). Care and punishment in Latin America: The gendered neoliberalization of the Chilean state. In M. Goodale, & N. Postero (Eds.), *Neoliberalism, interrupted. Social change and contested governance in contemporary Latin America* (pp. 195–224). Stanford University Press.

Schild, V. (2015a). Feminism and neoliberalism in Latin America. *New Left Review, 96*, 59–74. https://newleftreview-org.prox1.lib.uwo.ca/issues/ii96/articles/veronica-schild-feminism-and-neoliberalism-in-latin-america.pdf

Schild, V. (2015b). Geschlecth und Staat in Lateinamerika: Die zwei Gesichter neoliberale Regulation. In H.-J. Burchardt, & S. Peters (Eds.), *Der Staat in Globaler Perspektive. Zur Renaissance der Entwicklungstaaten* (pp. 195–218). Campus Verlag.

Schild, V. (2019). Feminism, the environment and capitalism: On the necessary ecological dimension of a Latin American critical feminism. *Journal of International Women's Studies, 20*(6), 23–43. https://vc.bridgew.edu/jiws/vol20/iss6/3

Segovia, M. (2020, March 6). El movimiento feminista. La resistencia al sistema político que precipitó la Revuelta de Octubre y que pone en jaque al gobierno. *El Mostrador.cl.* https://www.elmostrador.cl/noticias/pais/2020/03/06/el-movimiento-feminista-el-eje-central-de-resistencia-al-sistema-politico-que-precipito-la-revuelta-de-octubre-y-que-pone-en-jaque-al-gobierno/

Trading Economics. (2020). https://tradingeconomics.com/chile/exports.

Valdés, J. G. (1995). *Pinochet's economists: The Chicago school in Chile.* Cambridge University Press.

Valdés, S. X. (1987). Los procesos de incorporación y exclusión de las mujeres del mercado de trabajo agrícola. In X. Valdés, V. Riquelme, J. Medel, L.Rebolledo, V. Oxman, V. Quevedo, M. Mack (Eds.), *Sinópsis de una realidad ocultada (las trabajadoras del campo)* (pp. 23–50). CEM.

Valdés, S. X., & Araujo, K. (1999). *Vida privada. Modernización agraria y modernidad.* CEDEM.

Valdés, S. X. (2020). Urdiendo resistencias, tejiendo rebeldías: las temporeras de la fruta en Chile. In L. Rodríguez Lezica, J. Kropovickas, A. Migliaro, J. Cardeillac, M. Carámbula (Eds.), *Asalariadas rurales en América Latina: Abordajes teórico-metodológicos y estudios empíricos sobre procesos de organización y resistencia* (pp. 46-73). Universidad Academia de Humanismo Cristiano.

Valdés, S. X., Rebolledo, L., Pavez, J., & Hernández, G. (2015). *Trabajos y familias bajo el neoliberalismo. Las faenas de hombres y mujeres en la fruticultura, la salmonicultura y la minería.* LOM.

Weibel Barahona, M. (2017, January 5). AFP-Gate: Empresas hicieron inversiones ilegales por US$120 millones con fondos de cotizantes. *El Desconcierto.cl.* https://www.eldesconcierto.cl/2017/01/05/afp-gate-empresas-hicieron-inversiones-ilegales-por-us-120-millones-con-fondos-de-cotizantes/

Whyte, J. (2019). *The morals of the market. Human rights and the rise of neoliberalism.* Verso.

Yañez, S., & Rojas, I. (Eds.). (2017). *Empleo público en Chile. Trabajo decente en el estado? Apuntes para un debate.* FLACSO.

Roundtable: the Latin American state, Pink Tide, and future challenges

Manuel Larrabure, Charmain Levy, Maxwell A. Cameron, Joe Foweraker, Lena Lavinas and Susan Jane Spronk

ABSTRACT
In May 2020, the guest editors of this special number organized a roundtable discussion centred on six themes and covered a broad range of topics pertaining to Latin American development, politics and economics. The context of 'pink tides' and 'right turns' are a backdrop that represent both the consequences and the lead up to what comes next. At the centre of the analysis are the core dynamics of the political systems we intend to explore. The perspectives of the roundtable represent a theoretical and methodological spectrum ranging from neoWeberianinstitutionalism closely associated with the work of O'Donnell, and comparative studies of democratization, to critical-world systems analysis, associated with Marxian historical materialism, typically found within the development studies and political economy disciplines. Although the authors may draw more from one end of the spectrum than from the other, throughout their research careers, they have considered all of them in their intellectual reflections.

In May 2020, the guest editors of this special number organized a roundtable discussion with Susan Spronk, Lena Lavinas, Joe Foweraker and Max Cameron. The discussion centred on six predetermined themes and covered a broad range of topics pertaining to Latin American development, politics and economics, with a particular focus on the pink tide, its decline and the rise of the new right. The context of 'pink tides' and 'right turns' are a backdrop that represent both the consequences and the lead up to what comes next. At the centre of the analysis are the core dynamics of the political systems we intend to explore. The perspectives of the roundtable represent a theoretical and methodological spectrum ranging from neoWeberian-institutionalism, closely associated with the work of O'Donnell and comparative studies of democratization, to critical-world systems analysis, associated with Marxian historical materialism, typically found within the development studies and political economy disciplines. Although the authors may draw more from one end of the spectrum than from the other, throughout their research careers, they have considered all of them in their intellectual reflections.

Particularities of the Latin American state

An important part of studying Latin American political and social institutions is identifying specific and endogenous attributes that set Latin American democracies apart from those in North America and Europe. From the perspective of mainstream Western social science, Latin America, like other regions outside of Europe and North America, was always considered the 'exception' understood in terms of its deviation in comparison to the West. From the division between democracy and authoritarianism at the heart of political science to modernization theory in development studies to the Kuznets curve in environmental science, just to name a few examples, Latin America is in the process of becoming. In other words, from the perspective of mainstream social science, Latin America is permanently 'developing', working its way to becoming a full democracy, consequently adopting the principales of Western democracy, integrating into the global economy and therefore following the predominant regime of accumulation.[1] As Foweraker notes, the region's long history of constitutionalism notwithstanding, as a 'developing' region, the Latin American state is from this perspective said to be deeply 'patrimonial', meaning that it tends to represent various private rather than public interests. While this patrimonialism is characteristic to Latin America, it is also present in Western democracies to different degrees, although it is no longer as profoundly engrained as presently in Latin American democracies. Despite recent attempts to break with this oligarchic and patrimonial profile by instituting multinational states (Ecuador and Bolivia), Latin American states are still subject to delegative rule, corruption and clientelism, an expression of remaining chronically low capacities.

As Foweraker put it: 'the problem with Latin American democracies is the relatively low capacity of states. Suboptimal states lead to suboptimal democracies'. In addition, 'democratic procedures are not sufficient to reform the state and the state is not sufficient to allow democracy to work effectively.' If suboptimal is what historically defines Latin American states, then what are they supposedly developing towards? For Cameron (2019), the work of Argentine political scientist Guillermo O'Donnell is a basic point of reference. O'Donnell (1999) argued that the expansion of capitalism and the growth of the modern bureaucratic state in Europe was accompanied by the establishment of bourgeois subjective rights in civil and commercial law. This was followed by the juridification of society and culminated in the *Rechsstaat* – the legal regulation of executive and administrative authority. All of this preceded the extension of the suffrage to adult males, and the development of welfare states in the twentieth century. This sequence contrasts markedly with the historical development of Latin America. Political rights were extended before civil rights and the construction of a legal state. As mentioned above, the Latin American state is often described as 'neopatrimonial,' meaning that the boundaries between public and private are porous, various forms of corruption and encroachment occur, and basic civil liberties are unevenly protected. Consequently, welfare provisions tend to be provided through clientelistic mechanisms. The Latin American historical sequence has profound implications for the functioning of democracy. The ineffectiveness of the rule of law – which O'Donnell found reflected in flaws in existing law, uneven application of the law, improper relations between vulnerable citizens and the bureaucracy, lack of access to due process and sheer lawlessness – resulted in 'low-intensity citizenship' that vitiated democratic regimes. Violations of liberal rights and freedoms are endemic in Latin America, creating such 'monsters' as polyarchies without the rule of law or horizontal accountability.

In order to understand the Latin American state and democracy, we also need to ask questions about the class formations. At times, scholars in development studies put the cart before the horse asking questions about the institutional formation rather than the issues and the factors that explain those institutions, such as the basic relationships of production, distribution and consumption (that is, the 'economic base'). As Spronk puts it: 'the question about the Latin American state seems to be begging for an ideal type, which simply doesn't exist'. From the political economy perspective, the often-discussed features of the Latin American state, the nonconsolidated character of democracy, propensity towards populism, and marked economic instability, are part of a broader pattern of peripheral development directly related to the insertion of former colonies into global markets. In other words, the 'illiberal' characteristics of Latin American states are part of a much broader pattern that peripheral economies very commonly face. Hence, as Spronk notes:

> Of course, we can draw distinctions from North America and Europe. I think one of the unfortunate things about the way the question is cast is that it leads to theorizing that puts the lens in the wrong place to begin with ... If I were to write this question, I would write it differently. I understand the North America and Europe framing (because we are North American scholars, we speak English together), but we also need to understand Latin America vis-a-vis sub Saharan Africa and East Asia. I think that would make it a better question.

If we are to follow this path, then the work of Peter Evans (1989) becomes an important part of this discussion. Under Evans' framework, using the spectrum between developmental state all the way towards a predatory state, most Latin American states fall somewhere between the two extremes. Nevertheless, the historical and therefore changing character of Latin American states needs to be recognized, particularly when taking into consideration the changes in recent decades. As Lavinas highlights:

> I think that during the 2000s we saw some fabulous novelties in Latin American countries like Ecuador and Bolivia have created plurinational states, based in the recognition of the rights to indigenous peoples and the rights of nature. This is a revolution that must be celebrated, if we consider that Latin America has yet to bury its colonial past. The role of the State was turned upside down. It was radically democratised. So, I think that there were really structural shifts in the way of shaping the state and integrating new representations of citizenry and the nation – now in the plural - that were completely illegitimate, or even out of reach, prior to the 2000s because of the strong colonial legacy.

These differences in theoretical and methodological starting points are rooted in the framing question that births the foundational argument. The first of these has to do with unit of analysis. Those who lean towards the institutionalist approach use the individual nation state, or at most the region, as the unit of analysis in which it is recognized that Latin America's developmental path is forged in a world in which Europe and the US have already emerged as the dominant centre of the global economy. Importantly, this also became the methodological assumption of Latin American scholars, notably the CEPAL school of thought that for all of its criticism of mainstream developing theory, nevertheless agreed that the region was indeed underdeveloped and that individual Latin American nation states could take specific steps to catch up to the west. As Fernando Fajnzylber (1988), Chilean economist and a prominent figure within CEPAL in the early 1980s shows, this also became the assumption of Latin American elites that closely followed the North American prescription for development.

In contrast to the state-centric perspective, in the critical political economy perspective, as Lavinas emphasizes, Latin American states are embedded in a global hierarchy that has placed the Latin American region, along with other 'developing regions', at the bottom. In other words, the unit of analysis is a global system and the international division of labour. Given this, progressive projects in Latin America are conditioned by region's insertion into the historical development of global capitalism, one in which Latin America has largely served as a provider of cheap raw materials and labour. Highlighting the continuing importance of the Prebisch thesis of declining terms of trade, the decline in value of raw materials in comparison to manufactured goods, Lavinas highlights:

> We have been lagging behind because we missed the two last industrial revolutions, and now more than ever we must import high and middle-tech inputs and products. For this, we need reserves that are obtained from our commodity exports.

For Lavinas, this insight is what ultimately explains the failures of the Workers Party (PT) in Brazil, whose progressive project relied upon the historic natural resources boom experienced by Latin America in the first decade of the 2000s. The upsurge in revenues during this period allowed the party to increase consumption of imported goods among lower and middle-class sectors, but simultaneously cemented the country's historic place in the global hierarchy as a natural resource provider to the north, only this time under the logic of financialization. Hence, the PT's pro-poor programs actually further exposed popular sectors of the country to the logic of the market, in effect, tying domestic development to powerful foreign financial groups (pension and private equity funds, mining corporations) that ultimately depend on a process of primitive accumulation (Foweraker, 1981). As she puts it:

> The land continues to be expropriated from small peasants and Indigenous communities. This process continues to be extremely violent. The difference is that big financial corporations are not directly involved in the first steps of the process of primitive accumulation. They come later, just to buy the land that has already been 'cleaned up' and put into the market. My point is that the profile of the oligarchies, linked to the exploitation of land and extractivism, has changed under financialized capitalism. Therefore, it would be opportune to update our understanding and featuring of the content and reach of these new oligarchies and their links to national states. Of course, landowners continue to be there, but this group is now much wider, encompassing big national farmers, foreign and national institutional funds, tech companies, etc.

This approach is therefore rooted in tracing the dynamic interaction between local and global actors, particularly the relationship between economic and political elites and the popular classes. This argument goes back to Mandel's analysis: traditionally the Latin American ruling class existed in the form of an oligarchy (landowners and comprador bourgeoisie), in alliance with global capital. The economic interests of this oligarchy influence their political choices in how far to push democratization and social and political inclusion and representation (Mandel, 1971).

Lessons learned from the Pink Tide

Given that Latin American politics is traditionally dominated by elite interests (in the media, judiciaries, legislatures, regional organizations, etc.), it is important to understand how far can a Leftist or even progressive socioeconomic agenda be taken. As indicated in the previous section, all of these governments took power within political constraints that were both structural (constitutional, systemic) and contextual (composition of legislatures, strengths and weaknesses of allies and adversaries). All participants recognize the constraints of the political economy, the international division of labour and the traditional path dependency of Latin America. This section delves into the different ways Pink Tide governments succeeded or failed to overcome the political limits imposed by political systems and elite interests and the lessons we learned in different countries about what is possible and what is still impossible when in government.

The answers given by the roundtable reveal different methodological perspectives, in addition to the unit of analysis (i.e. state-centric vs. global systems), between political science and political economy, namely the approach to conceptualize contemporary democracies. From a comparative democratic theory perspective, contemporary Latin American societies are comprised of oligarchies that intermingle with democracy. These two aspects of society condition each other, sometimes supporting and sometimes undermining one another (Foweraker, 2018). Hence, on the one hand, Foweraker notes that democratic regimes tend to protect property rights, which is something that supports oligarchic rule. On the other hand, 'oligarchies by definition exclude', denying political participation of wide sectors of the population. Furthermore, Cameron notes (see Cameron, 2021 for further discussion), oligarchies exploit 'negative power':

> … the power that rests on the purposeful destruction of those forms of infrastructural power that might enable collective action, threatening property, market competition, and corporate power. Negative power is the opposite of the kind of power that mobilizes the society's resources for collective purposes. It is the power to dissolve, to obstruct, to discourage, to exclude, to undo and not do things. This is a power that primarily operates through the micro level effects of competition, but it also comes in the form of direct interventions in politics.

In the specific case of Latin America, the relationship between democracy and oligarchic rule is profoundly conditioned by extreme inequality. This means that progressive governments in the region face tremendous barriers to implementing changes that significantly threaten oligarchic rule. Hence, as Foweraker notes, upon the election of Lula in 2002, George Soros was confident enough to (correctly) predict that the electoral victory of the Workers' Party would have very little impact on the basic parameters of elite rule in the country. After all, Foweraker continues, 'What makes civil oligarchy so powerful is that they don't have to occupy executive positions or the state bureaucracy. They have lobbying, campaign financing, media and capital flight at their disposal'. Given the barriers to progressive change in the region, Foweraker reaches rather discerning conclusions:

> So how do we overcome the political limits imposed by those elite interests? We do not overcome them. It seems to me that we negotiate, and we demand more democracy and we ask for more rights. There is a vibrant history in Latin America of popular organizations, popular demands for greater representation, greater fairness, more rights, and more protections or more immunities and so on and so forth. So, all those activities are absolutely not unimportant. They are a vital part of the whole process, but we have to take them within this broader context of what I would call Polity (Foweraker, 1995). So, what we are doing here is we are pushing all the time at limits. We are pushing the boundaries, but we are never going to overcome those political limits.

Furthermore, as Cameron highlights, in Latin America, attempts at progressive change have overwhelmingly taken a populist character, and indeed 'populist power can reproduce oligarchic modes of rule ... in fact, these two things often tend to reinforce each other.' Both Cameron and Foweraker point to the case of *chavismo* in Venezuela as a classic case of populism gone wrong. Referring to Venezuela, Foweraker observes that 'new oligarchies may be more predatory than old ... so we have change but is not necessarily the change that we really want.' What is there to be done from this perspective then? For Foweraker, the answer can be found in conservative political philosophers, democratic theorists who:

> Many, like Schumpeter, take this question seriously. In the sense that oligarchies have to be educated over time in order to become benign or at least republican-minded.

To this, Cameron adds, from a social democratic perspective, the need to strengthen the power of organized labour as well as the state's capacity to provide welfare and other public goods. In short, democratization in the region has often involved the syncretic fusion of oligarchy and democracy, whether by formal pact or tenuous equilibrium of forces, softening the exclusionary impulses of oligarchy and providing access to basic public services to the popular sectors.

The critical political economy perspective centres on the particular capitalist form that the democratic state expresses. For this school of thought, in contrast, democracies and civil oligarchies don't merely coexist. They form a unity, along with working-class and popular sectors, under the concept of the capitalist state. According to this view, as masterfully outlined by Guillermo O'Donnell in his classic work *Bureaucratic Authoritarianism*, the capitalist state provides the coercive force to guarantee capitalist relations of production, 'articulating and buffering the relationships among classes and … providing elements necessary to their 'normal,' and unchallenged reproduction' (1999, p. 2). The capitalist state, therefore, protects not specific fractions of the bourgeoisie, but the capitalist class as a whole, guaranteeing their position as the dominant class vis-à-vis the dominated classes, a responsibility that at times includes placing constraints on elements and impulses of the bourgeoisie that could undermine their long-term reproduction (pp. 2–3). It is this role taken by the capitalist state that explains both the persistence of the profound inequalities that are evident in Latin America today, as well as the challenges to the domination of capital that popular sectors can at times force upon the state. In other words, from this perspective, the form of elite rule is not a product of the benevolence or education of a ruling class, but rather of the effective mobilization of popular sectors.

Furthermore, elite domination cannot be taken as a given, and it is indeed possible to overcome. From this point of view, the question becomes not how to educate elites but rather how to challenge their oligarchic rule (Foweraker, 2018). As Spronk highlights, the well-known Miliband versus Poulantzas debate is instructive in this regard. Miliband's strategic outlook consisted in populating the state apparatus with committed leftists, who would then use the avenues of the democratic state to progressively push through reforms that would eventually add up to a new society (Miliband, 1983). Miliband's pluralist viewpoint was that the state was a largely neutral institution that could be pushed one way or the other depending on who controls it. In contrast, Poulantzas argued that that the capitalist state existed to ensure the domination of capital in society. Hence, for Poulantzas (1978), the capitalist state ultimately needed to be transformed by an alliance of workers and popular sectors and a political left. In other words, for Poulantzas, electing left-wing politicians to the office was not sufficient. What was needed was rather a strategic class struggle in economic, social and political spheres. Indeed, this was precisely what the social movements that supported the MAS in Bolivia and *chavismo* in Venezuela embarked upon with mixed results.

Although certain scholars (Brewer-Carías, 2010; Corrales & Penfold-Becerra, 2011; Mayorga, 2017; Weyland, 2013) tend to focus exclusively on the authoritarian features of these cases and furthermore argue that this outcome was inevitable, it is important to point out that Morales in Bolivia and Chavez in Venezuela challenged the traditional elite rule as well as the foundations of Eurocentric liberal notions of development and democracy. From this perspective the fact that both of these cases of historical ruptures ultimately reached their limits in recent years (particularly the case of Venezuela), demonstrates not the impossibility of social change and the necessity for more conservative strategies, but rather that these hegemonic struggles buckled under insurmountable odds that reflect their adversaries strengths and their own weaknesses. Furthermore, as the cases of Brazil and Chile demonstrate, even when pursuing a conciliatory path to progress, the outcome is *also* authoritarianism in the form of oligarchy based backlash and societal polarization. The case of Chile is particularly notable in this regard, as successive centre-left governments followed the liberal recipe to the letter. The result was a hollowed-out democracy, political decline and ultimately, as we saw in October 2020, a state of emergency imposed on the country by the government of Sebastian Piñera, a 30-year trajectory that Larrabure (2019) calls Chile's democratic road to authoritarianism.

Buen Vivir and another possible world

During the early 2000s among the growing momentum of social movements resisting neoliberal policies and economics and the new innovations in democratic practices (such as participatory budgeting), there was a certain hope that the sum of these collective initiatives would result in governments with the power to break with neoliberalism and implement structures and policies in favour of the traditionally marginalized populations. Another world did indeed seem possible to many through democratic elections and playing by the rules of the political game. In time, many Pink Tide governments learned that being the government did not translate into being in power as some decided to cut deals with their adversaries and others were under siege from domestic or foreign antagonists. This section explores how Latin American liberal democratic regimes and their institutions advance popular struggles (feminist, labour, LGBTQ, peasant, student) and in which ways do they limit them. It also highlights which compatible or desirable strategies available today to the Left to achieve its goals.

A more nuanced spectrum from institutionalist to Marxian, class-based analysis of the state took form in how our panelists answered this question. From the institutional perspective, Foweraker asks how one could speak of liberal democracies in Latin America: 'Liberal democratic regimes? I do not think we have seen many of those in Latin America'. From this perspective, once again, the state in Latin America lacks basic competencies:

> But the whole question of public authority, in fact the whole question of the state. The state has become extraordinarily fragmented in most countries, and its very presence has been contested in ways that it has never been contested before. (Foweraker)

In particular, Foweraker emphasizes the growth of 'gray areas' in which illegality of various kinds can thrive as part of the state, corruption, drug trafficking, etc. This reality, he continues, has tremendous implications for social movements, negatively conditioning their capacity to engage in public administration. Hence, although social movements continue to grow in Latin America, their capacity to actually produce progressive social change remains limited:

> Clearly it [social change] is going to come gradually. But it cannot be a frontal attack. I do know that because every successful democracy in the world, sooner or later, has to accommodate its oligarchies. (Foweraker, 1993)

Cameron's institutionalism, which – informed by O'Donnell – does not restrict itself to the formal institutions of democracy, but also includes the state and broader social forces and organizations, offers a less pessimistic stance. For him, liberalism can be seen as 'both a condition of possibility and a limitation on democracy'. Hence, on the one hand, the liberal democratic institutions in Latin America have been used by the left to expand citizenship rights, while on the other hand, the same institutions have been used by neoliberals to uphold the status quo in the name of the liberal principle of individual autonomy. As opposed to a neoliberal view, Cameron emphasizes, 'we need to think about autonomy also in terms of the collective empowerment' (Cameron,

2019). From this perspective, he highlights the achievements of Bolivia under Morales, particularly the notion of *Buen Vivir*:

> *Buen Vivir* offers a horizon of the future, not a blueprint or a model. It poses the challenge of how to flourish in a context of pluralism, to fuse horizons – to use German philosopher Hans-Georg Gadamer's phrase – across diverse cultures, allowing us to think about what it means to live in harmony with nature and in a more cooperative spirit with other social beings (and not just humans). *Buen Vivir* poses a fundamental challenge to liberalism, and capitalism. It complicates the way that private property is off the table for discussion in liberal capitalist societies. It is not about extracting resources, metals, and fossil fuels to feed an ultimately unsustainable materialistic understanding of the good life, but rather how we can live in harmony with one another and harmony with the natural world in a way that allows us to live better lives, and to fulfill our human potential.

Cameron concludes by adding that the horizon of *Buen Vivir* and the values that it implies cannot be achieved through the market, as neoliberals demand, but through the state and civil society. Indeed, for him, 'the idea of a Left unconcerned with the state as a programmatic dead-end.'

The question of how liberal democratic regimes can advance popular or progressive struggles is approached in a completely different way by political economists. Indeed, for Lavinas, the question needs to be reversed: 'to what extent have feminist, LGBT, anti-racist and indigenous movements contributed to take the Left to power in Latin America?' To this question, she adds a second: 'why did the Left brake with its own commitments? Bohn and Levy (2019) point out how the PT's alliances with Evangelicals, present in most political parties,[2] in order to achieve governability led them to renege on their promises to their feminist base, which in turn ceased to openly criticize its government allies. Lavinas highlights an example from Brazil:

> When feminists claimed for more progressive regulations regarding women's reproductive rights in Brazil, Dilma sent us a message: 'I can't give you what you ask for because I need to compound a majority, so please stop claiming for abortion rights and for reproductive rights: these issues are not in the agenda ... '

Picking up on this point, Spronk highlights that, for the Left, electoral strategy should be seen as temporary and contingent. In other words, the left must have 'one foot in [and] one foot out' of the state. For her, the left must give up what she sees as autonomist fantasies based on a profound misreading of the Zapatistas who 'were clearly negotiating with the state!'. Therefore, what is needed when discussing the topic of *Buen Vivir* is to

> ... distinguish between the project, which is a project that comes from below and tries to articulate some of the long-term demands of Indigenous people in places like Bolivia, versus what it becomes when Evo and Àlvaro (the former President and vice-President) put it in a pamphlet ... (Spronk)

In other words, the suggestion is to focus on processes from above and from below, and how they interact in ways that are both complementary and divergent.

Pink Tide alliances with traditional elites

Several Pink Tide governments opted for alliances with traditional political and economic elites as a way of creating political stability and achieving some progressive and pro-poor socioeconomic policies. In many cases, these alliances came back to drive the Left from power. The most explicit is the case of Brazil when PT President Rousseff's vice-president fully endorsed her impeachment and subsequently became president. Given that hindsight is 20/20, what lessons can we learn from these alliances? Are they inevitable in Latin American democracies?

The roundtable answered this question with much more unanimity than previously. Since the return to democratic regimes, the absence of legislative majorities in many Latin American countries has meant that government coalitions are assembled and managed by the ruling party to sustain governability. As Foweraker asserts, this kind of coalitional activity – building alliances with people outside your own party – is at the heart of legislative politics in Latin American democracy (Foweraker, 1998). Using the case of Brazil, for example, it has typically been extremely difficult to form any kind of governing alliance without some kind of understanding with the PMDB. Cameron goes further, asserting that in Latin America it is simply not possible to construct a winning electoral alliance exclusively with the popular sectors (workers, peasants, the middle sectors). In every case that the Left comes to power in a parliamentary democracy, it does so by means of making class compromises and class alliances.[3] Foweraker notes: ' … it is not a question of choosing or not choosing. It is a question of what you choose and when you choose, what tactics you use and how broad do you extend.'

The inevitability of coalitional strategies in the region then produces a number of political tensions about the quality of democracy. Foweraker highlights:

> Juan Pablo Luna and David Altman showed how representation is lost when governability is achieved, and all that then followed – the parties becoming detached from the grassroots, personality becoming more important …

The result of this, Foweraker continues, is that 'governability is privileged over representation', as governments have to engage in deal-making that inevitably invites corruption. Lavinas adds that for the Left in particular this has also meant succumbing to the formation of broad ideological alliances. For Cameron, the reality of coalition-building and its impacts raises a broader question about democracy itself:

> So, what is democratic about voting in any political regime in which we elect leaders and delegate authority to them to govern on our behalf? An electoral democracy is only democratic to the degree that those who we elect actually represent us. However, what if the mechanisms of representation are broken? For example, we may have weak or ephemeral political parties, political parties that are invented for the purposes of running for election and then have no meaningful life outside of that, that are disbanded after elections are over, and have no meaningful organization, nor roots into society. If that is the way governance is managed, it really is not democratic at all. It may be something more like what Foweraker in his 2018 book called 'polity' – a kind of mix of democratic and oligarchical elements.

In other words, when democratic procedures and institutions cannot be trusted to guarantee adequate representation, representative democracy becomes more oligarchical than democratic (Cameron, 2021).

Another by-product of the necessity of coalitions and alliances in the region is that the middle classes can often play a decisive role. This creates particular problems for the Left. Cameron asserts:

> The challenge for the Left is whether to challenge the interests of the middle classes, which is extraordinarily risky, or to accommodate them. And what the Left has often tended to do is to try to leave the entrepreneurial elite alone, allow it to continue to make profits, but try to build its political power outside of those elites.

This provides important insights about the decline of the pink tide in the region, which attempted to both increase the living conditions of popular sectors and maintain (or expand) the power of upper-middle classes and economic elites. However, Sousa argues that it was the expansion of the middle class (through the inclusion of working-class sectors) that prompted a severe backlash from the upper middle classes who feared losing their social and political capital and traditional privileges (Souza, 2010). In other words, it seems that the strategy of attempting to placate elite and upper middle classes backfired. Furthermore, as Lavinas emphasizes using the case of Brazil, the strategy of lifting millions out of poverty and into the middle class via market incorporation, that is, increased consumption via financialization, rather than stable labour relations, helped these new middle classes to assimilate a middle-class ideology of security and prosperity that insertion into financial circuits could not provide, helping in part to explain the growth of evangelicalism in the country. Once again, it seems the PT's dual strategy ultimately failed.

Given the failures of the Pink Tide, one might ask what could have been done differently? Spronk emphasizes a focus on the empowerment or disempowerment of popular classes:

> We are always dealing with the combination of what in the traditional old terms be called the objective conditions and the subjective conditions, and there are choices to be made within those confines. The best these governments could have done – it happened unevenly – was not to destroy the popular sectors and not to take over their organizations and build parallel organizations. But that is what they did, most clearly in both Ecuador and Bolivia. The governments in office literally, set up parallel organizations, sometimes with the same names. They gave these organizations vehicles, offices, and jobs within the State. (See Spronk & Leon, 2018)

However, cooptation is only part of the story. In some cases, the popular sectors were themselves fragmented (Fernandes, 2019) and lost popular appeal and support of the larger population. This fragmentation reflects a broader political ambiguity within popular sectors and social movements, that between building a new radical left politics, on the one hand, or retreating to the classic populist left of decades past (Larrabure, 2019). Ultimately, this fragmentation and ambiguity within the popular sectors contributed to loss of influence on Leftist parties and governments as the latter concentrated their efforts in giving into influential middle classes and their demands. This coupled with an economic crisis that limited government welfare spending and corruption investigations put Left government on the defensive leading to their increased compromise to elites who in turn took advantage of the Left's vulnerable position.

Neo-developmentism

There is a consensus that Pink Tide macro-economic policy was based on extractivism and relied on the export of primary commodities (Pickup, 2019, 24). Within this model, the state was the driver of the economy and the implementation of redistributionist policies to reduce poverty and increase social welfare. We asked our participants, what lessons can be learned from the neo-development/neo-structuralist state model pursued by Pink Tide governments? In addition, despite the dependence on the extractivist and primary commodities export model, certain government integrated an environmentalist tone to their political discourse. We attempt to understand to what extent the greening[4] of the Left took place in Latin America.

Soon after the pink tide swept through the region, scholars began to theorize the possibility that a new development model was emerging, one that was more socially just and addressed the pressing issue of climate change. Somewhat of a consensus was reached on the concept of neo-structuralism or neo-developmentalism (Webber, 2010; Bresser-Perreira, 2010). Unlike neoliberalism, this new model invested in equity and poverty reduction, nevertheless it continued to feature alliances with transnational capital that undermined the political and economic power of organized labour (Leiva, 2008). As Lavinas points out, 'Center Left governments in Latin America partly implemented developmentalist strategies, but they complied with neoliberalism, and thus with neoliberal values.' Specifically, the PT in Brazil, Lavinas continues, deepened deregulation mechanisms relating to finance and capital flows, while granting tax cuts for big companies and defunding social provisions, like the healthcare system. Lavinas asserts that the PT ultimately 'vowed to reduce the public pillar' by fostering financialization'.

Further mechanisms supporting neoliberal continuities were the approach to poverty reduction. Lavinas highlights the example of Latin American social protection systems. On the one hand, several national governments adopted pro-poor programs, named CCTs – conditional cash transfers. Unfortunately, the provision of public services that was essential to improve peoples' wellbeing did not follow the pace of the expansion of CCTs. CCTs therefore ended up supporting the market logic, as popular sectors used the cash for consumption of affordable consumer goods from abroad, ultimately paid for by the natural resource export boom. Indeed, Latin America's neo-developmentalist model became heavily dependent on resource extraction, particularly in order to meet demand from China, why many began to refer to this model as neo-extractivism (Rosales, 2013; Svampa, 2015; Veltmeyer, 2016).

The case of Ecuador is perhaps emblematic of the contradictions of neo-extractivism and the difficulties it poses for a green agenda and the limits to the monetarization of green policies. The Correa government asked the global community to financially contribute to a campaign to help conserve the Yasuní National Park, a site of tremendous cultural and biological diversity, as well as oil. However, by 2013, Correa's campaign failed and the government decided to exploit this resource with the argument that the international community did not fulfil its obligation and that it needed the revenue for the country's economic development. This case highlights how internal pressures (middle classes, comprador class, coalitions, etc.) and external forces (multilateral rules and systems, bilateral negotiations, global commodity markets, etc.), came together to prevent change in the direction of sustainability. It also shows how a voluntaristic model of social change a la Cardoso et al. is simply not viable.

For Lavinas, once again the problems faced by the Left in the region can be traced to the region's particular insertion into the global market, and the left's failure to think outside of the neoliberal box:

> … during the 2000s, all Latin American countries except Mexico, continued to de-industrialize. The problem lies not only on the decline of the global demand of commodities during the 2010s, due to the slowdown of the Chinese economy, but also because Latin American States did not successfully implement national policies oriented towards paving the way to innovative waves of industrialization in order to overcome our industrial backwardness. Latin America countries have missed the two last technological revolutions, the most recent, the digital one. Several factors may explain this bad performance, including historical ones. However, Latin American countries continued to adopt macroeconomic policies oriented towards preserving interest rates in order to curtail high inflation and attract capital inflows. It goes without saying that austerity measures prevented the productive sector to take out loans and make investments in the long run. Volatility and economic instability also make it difficult to boost productive investment. The main characteristics of the economic development in Latin America during the 2000 thus have nothing to do with the drive of developmentalist strategies. This is very important, because the idea of developmentalism is to move up in the value chain. It did not happen.

Neoliberal continuities and financialization tied to extraction, in turn greatly narrows the scope governments have for action on climate change. Hence, although there was a significant debate (see Cameron & Hershberg, 2010) about how different left governments did or did not meet expectations of economic and political justice, all of the Pink Tide, from the centrist Chile, under the governments of la Concertación and Nueva Mayoría, to Chavismo in Venezuela, can be said to have massively underperformed in the area of environmental sustainability. The reality is that the region and indeed the whole world is currently facing multiple simultaneous challenges and a multiplicity of intersecting crises, and as a result, a strong green agenda has not been articulated. As Cameron states:

> We have not only a crisis of neoliberal globalization, the virtual collapse of the coherence of global liberal institutions, the inability to manage the externalities of globalization, the massive inequalities created by neoliberalism within countries, although not globally, and these crises intersect with an ecological crisis arising from climate change and the destruction of natural ecosystems.

Consequently, Left parties need the courage and conviction to address this issue and push for a greener economy. As Cameron asserts:

> societies that have not made social and green investments are going to suffer massively in the context of the kinds of crises that we are facing. Therefore, the agenda for the Left becomes, increasingly, about how we build resilient societies. How do we build up our capacity for education, healthcare, so that we can deal with pandemics and other kinds of global challenges? The place of government in this is crucial. How do we get leaders who listen to evidence, are able to bring evidence and knowledge and expertise to bear, whether it is in the area of public health or other areas, on the construction of a politics that is able to mobilize entire societies in order to protect collective security? The agenda for the Left is to reframe debates that have centered on competition, on winner and losers, to an agenda based on collective resilience.

Current and future political scenarios

In this final section, our participants analyse the 'post pink-tide' phase (2014–present) of politics and development. We asked them if and how useful are comparisons to the 1970s concerning economic recession and authoritarian practices and rhetoric. We also asked them to consider the present 2020 context of the public health crisis and deepening economic depression taking place in Latin America and across the world an opportunity for the Left to regain power and push its agenda forward.

Looking at the rise of authoritarianism in the region today suggests a possible comparison to the authoritarian regimes of the 1970s. Indeed, it is not surprising to learn that Guillermo O'Donnell's *Bureaucratic Authoritarianism* was very recently re-printed by the University of California. Nevertheless, as Heraclitus noted in Greek antiquity, one can never step into the same river twice, and indeed much has changed in the region since the 1970s wave of 'bureaucratic coups' that O'Donnell focused on. Foweraker in particular is somewhat skeptical about drawing comparisons, and points to insecurity as a key factor:

> The state was an intrusive presence in Latin America in the 1970s and was considered the problem not the solution to anything. As Weffort (1992) said, civil society had to be invented in order to produce something that could test/contest the state. So that was the only way in which the 1970s mirrors what goes on today, because at least in pockets of the population – what was shocking was that it was also in middle-class pockets - there was massive insecurity. This insecurity and the gravity of the economic recession ahead might lead to authoritarian policies surfacing again.

In contrast, Spronk sees this as part of a recurring pattern of accumulation and crisis linked to the internal contradictions of capitalism:

> The financial crisis of 2007–2008 is not over and this is an organic crisis of capitalism. We have seen the absolute collapse of the world economy and the tsunami of austerity is upon us; while the governments

of advanced capitalist countries are dumping liquidity into the world markets, the debt crisis in developing countries will intensify in coming years.

Lavinas follows up by reminding us that according to CEPAL, the recession may last for 5 years. We still lack the good economic and social policies for correctly addressing these multiple crises. We are guaranteeing the reproduction of capital, that is big capital, not small enterprises, who are not really benefiting from these relief measures.

The magnitude of the economic, health, political and climate crisis has opened new debates about the transformative potential of the current moment (Gills, 2020). This is precisely what is emphasized by Cameron:

> This is a very awkward moment for any neoliberal who believes that markets provide the solution for everything. We are really in a transformative moment, I believe, in terms of our understanding of citizenship, in terms of our understanding of what we owe to one another, and how we can work together to make sacrifices in order to attain desirable collective goals.

However, the potential for transformation will have to grasp with important realities. As Lavinas emphasizes:

> As COVID-19 spreads into Latin America, growing at an especially alarming rate in Brazil, one of the things that this is going to expose is when anywhere between 50–80 percent of your workforce is in the formal economy, when you have not provided welfare mechanisms to protect people in times of hardship and crisis, then the response to this pandemic is going to look very different. In Latin America, the urbanization pattern, which is a mark of deep social exclusion, makes it almost impossible for low income and poor families to respect social distancing, confinement and stay-at-home orders. They end up infringing the law and held responsible for the deterioration of the infection rates. At the macro-economical level, the dismantling of the commons is undoubtedly one of the most pervasive and appalling outcomes of the neoliberal era (not only the state, the public sphere is also the collective). I think the first thing that I hope we will rescue from all this is to rebuild the public sphere.

Echoing Lavinas emphasis on the public sphere, Cameron adds:

> The pandemic has surely reinforced Marshall McLuhan's claim that we live in a global village. There are global public goods that have to be providing collectively in a democratic and decentralized way, but with far more not less coordination. That is, perhaps, a vision of what a different kind of future could involve.

In other words, the trajectory of Latin American political and economic development is at a profound crossroads with many more obstacles than clear paths forward. Whether this is a profoundly different moment with few parallels with previous eras in the region's history, or whether we can expect long-standing dynamics of authoritarianism and political violence to resurface as a 'solution' to the current crisis will certainly be a key question for researchers of the region going forward.

Concluding thoughts

In light of the discussion above, we now take the opportunity to provide two key questions that could guide future research on the region. The first and most general is whether the traditional division of the world between European and North American developed democracies, on the one hand, and the underdeveloped, authoritarian South, on the other, should be decisively abandoned. This is of course not a new concern. At the core of traditional dependency theory is precisely the assertion that Europe and North America are developed because the global south is underdeveloped, and that ultimately the two empirical realities are inextricably linked. However, as

Grosfoguel (2000) has powerfully argued, Latin American developmentalism of the postwar period (much of which was inspired by dependency theory) believed that 'catching up' to Europe and North America was nevertheless both possible and desirable, something that for the author reflects a nagging 'denial of coevalness', that is, the refusal to accept the reality that Latin America co-evolved with Europe and North America on the same temporal line. In other words, if we are to truly give up on the Eurocentric and neocolonial division between global south and north, this means giving up on the illusion of catch-up (Foweraker & Landman, 2004). Indeed, this is consistent with the recent experience of the pink tide and the neo-structuralist model pursued by these left governments, which as Lavinas has made amply clear, completely failed at 'moving up the value chain', the traditional concern of developmentalism. Furthermore, the persistent pathologizing of Latin America completely misses uncomfortable realities of the supposedly more developed North (Foweraker, 2021). As Spronk puts it:

> In terms of research on the developmental states, I have always asked: why is the US not considered to be this kind of state? Well, pharmaceutical companies in the US spend more money pedaling their drugs for Viagra, than they do on development of vaccines.

This leads us to a second question, namely that if we are to abandon the idea of 'catching up' and accept that Latin American will never be able to economically compete with the North or consolidate the ideal type Weberian state, then what does development actually mean for the region? Perhaps the most likely answer to this question might be framed under what could be called 'managed underdevelopment'. This path would limit itself to preventing the worst possible outcomes of the current crisis, leaning on notions of resilience and adaptation, evident today in mainstream debates on climate change and its differential impact on the global south (Andersen et al., 2017; Araos et al., 2017). A second and certainly less likely option would be to reach the same conclusion that more radical dependency theorists of the 1960s and 70s came to. Namely that any notion of Latin American democracy and development requires a complete rejection of the material and intellectual apparatus of capitalist centres (Frank, 1967), and that authentic paths to development ultimately have to come from within and take into account the needs and wellbeing of the majority of the population. This in turn requires new forms of democratic representation through which a new relationship between humans and nature can be articulated and then operationalized at both micro- and macro-political and economic levels. The task is certainly gargantuan, but the region's rich history of popular education, social movements and bold political thinking, the essential ingredients for any alternative path of development, remains very much alive and well.

Notes

1. As shown by Bértola and Ocampo (2013) regarding the Economic Development of Latin American, the income gap between LA and the Expanded West has widened on a regular basis (p. 4) throughout the twentieth century.
2. Evangelicals have laid out a very wise strategy. They are present in most parties at the Parliament (there are 36!). This makes them much stronger because their demands are not an issue raised by a few parties, but rather flagships incorporated by a wide range of political parties, from the left to the right.
3. I think Venezuela went farther than any other country in terms of challenging the power of the entrepreneurial elite, but that is probably because Venezuela had an extraordinarily weak private sector, by virtue of just being an oil economy.
4. We define the greening as the set of theories that advocate a socially just and ecologically sustainable economy and society breaking with unlimited economic growth and consumption inherent in

capitalism. They go beyond the monetization of Green policies and practices within capitalism and aim at an anti-capitalist adoption of policies for de-growth.

Acknowledgements

The authors would like to thank our research assistant Monika Imeri for transcribing the roundtable session. This article was made possible thanks to an SSHRC Insight Grant.

Disclosure statement

No potential conflict of interest was reported by the author(s).

Funding

This work was supported by Social Sciences and Humanities Research Council of Canada [grant number 777967].

ORCID

Maxwell A. Cameron http://orcid.org/0000-0003-4873-9851

References

Andersen, L. E., Verner, D., & Wiebelt, M. (2017). Gender and climate change in Latin America: An analysis of vulnerability, adaptation and resilience based on household surveys. *Journal of International Development, 29*(7), 857–876. https://doi.org/10.1002/jid.3259

Araos, M., Ford, J., Berrang-Ford, L., Biesbroek, R., & Moser, S. (2017). Climate change adaptation planning for global south megacities: The case of Dhaka. *Journal of Environmental Policy & Planning, 19*(6), 682–696. https://doi.org/10.1080/1523908X.2016.1264873

Bértola, L., & Ocampo, J. A. (2013). *The Economic Development of Latin America since Independence.* Oxford: Oxford University Press.

Bohn, S., & Levy, C. (2019). The Brazilian women's movement and the state under the PT national governments. *European Review of Latin American and Caribbean Studies,* (108), 245–266.

Bresser-Pereira, L. C. (2010). *Globalization and Competition.* New York: Cambridge University Press.

Brewer-Carías, A. R. (2010). *Dismantling democracy in Venezuela: The Chávez authoritarian experiment.* Cambridge University Press.

Cameron, M. A. (2019). Liberalism and its competitors in Latin America: Oligarchy, populism, and the left. In M. Balán, & F. Montambeault (Eds.), *Legacies of the left turn in Latin America: The promise of inclusive citizenship* (pp. 44–68). Notre Dame University Press.

Cameron, M. A. (2021, January 11). The return of oligarchy? Threats to representative democracy in Latin America. *Third World Quarterly.* https://doi.org/10.1080/01436597.2020.1865794

Cameron, M. A., & Hershberg, E. (Eds.) (2010). *Latin America's left turns: Politics, policies, and trajectories of change.* Lynn Rienner Publishers.

Corrales, J., & Penfold-Becerra, M. (2011). *Dragon in the Tropics: Hugo Chavez and the Political Economy of Revolution in Venezuela.* Washington, DC: Brookings Institution Press.

Evans, P. B. (1989, December). Predatory, developmental, and other apparatuses: A comparative political economy perspective on the third world state. *Sociological Forum, 4,* 561–587.

Fajnzylber, F. (1988). Competitividad internacional: evolución y lecciones. *Revista de la CEPAL*, N° 36, LC/G. 1537-P.

Fernandes, S. (2019). *Sintomas Mórbidos: a encruzilhada da esquerda brasileira*. Autonomia Literaria.

Foweraker, J. (1981). *The struggle for land: A political economy of the pioneer frontier in Brazil, from 1930 to the present*. Cambridge University Press. (paperback edition 2002).

Foweraker, J. (1993). *Popular mobilization in Mexico: The teacher's movement, 1977-1987*. Cambridge University Press. (paperback edition 2002).

Foweraker, J. (1995). *Theorizing social movements*. Pluto Press.

Foweraker, J. (1998). Institutional design, party systems and governability – differentiating the presidential regimes of Latin America. *British Journal of Political Science*, 28(4), 651–676. https://doi.org/10.1017/S0007123498000295

Foweraker, J. (2018). *Polity: Demystifying democracy in Latin America and beyond*. Lynne Rienner Publishers.

Foweraker, J. (2021). *Oligarchy in the Americas: Comparing oligarchic rule in Latin America and the United States*. Palgrave Macmillan.

Foweraker, J., & Landman, T. (2004). Economic development and democracy revisited: Why dependency theory is not yet dead. *Democratization*, 11(1), 1–20. https://doi.org/10.1080/13510340412331294112

Frank, A. G. (1967). The Thesis of Capitalist Underdevelopment. In André Gunder Frank (Ed.), *Capitalism and Underdevelopment in Latin America: Historical Studies in Chile and Brazil* (pp. 3-28). London: Monthly Review Press.

Gills, B. (2020). Deep restoration: From the great implosion to the great awakening. *Globalizations*, 17(4), 577–579. https://doi.org/10.1080/14747731.2020.1748364

Grosfoguel, R. (2000). Developmentalism, modernity, and dependency theory in Latin America. *Nepantla: Views from South*, 1(2), 347–374. https://muse.jhu.edu/article/23893/

Larrabure, M. (2019). Chile's democratic road to authoritarianism. *European Review of Latin American and Caribbean Studies/Revista Europea de Estudios Latinoamericanos y del Caribe*, (108), 221–243. https://doi.org/10.32992/erlacs.10481

Leiva, F. I. (2008). *Latin American neostructuralism: The contradictions of post-neoliberal development*. University of Minnesota Press.

Mandel, E. (1971). Imperialism and National Bourgeoisie in Latin America. *International*, 1(5), 6–12.

Mayorga, R. A. (2017). Populismo autoritario y transición regresiva: la dictadura plebiscitaria en la región andina. *Revista Latinoamericana de Política Comparada 12*, 39–69.

Miliband, R. (1983). Socialist advance in Britain. *The Socialist Register*, 103–120.

O'Donnell, G. (1999). *Counterpoints: Selected essays on authoritarianism and democratization*. University of Notre Dame Press.

Pickup, M. (2019). The political economy of the new left. *Latin American Perspectives*, 46(1), 23–45.

Poulantzas, N. (1978). *State, Power, Socialism*. London: New Left Books.

Rosales, A. (2013). Going underground: The political economy of the 'left turn' in South America. *Third World Quarterly*, 34(8), 1443–1457. https://doi.org/10.1080/01436597.2013.831538

Souza, J. (2010). *Os batalhadores brasileiros: Nova classe média ou nova classe trabalhadora?* UFMG. (Coleção Humanitas).

Spronk, S., & Leon, J. (2018). Socialism without workers? Trade unions and the new left in Bolivia and Ecuador. In F. Rossi, & E. Silva (Eds.), *Second wave of incorporation* (pp. 129–156). University of Pittsburgh Press.

Svampa, M. (2015). Commodities consensus: Neoextractivism and enclosue of the commons in Latin America. *The South Atlantic Quarterly*, 114(1), 65–82. https://doi.org/10.1215/00382876-2831290

Veltmeyer, H. (2016). Extractive capital, the state and the resistance in Latin America. *Sociology and Anthropology*, 4(8), 774–784. https://doi.org/10.13189/sa.2016.040812

Webber, J. R. (2010). Carlos Mesa, Evo Morales, and a divided Bolivia (2003—2005). *Latin American Perspectives*, 37(3), 51–70.

Weffort, F. (1992). *Qual democracia?* CIA. EDITORA DAS LETRAS.

Weyland, K. (2013). Latin America's authoritarian drift: The threat from the populist left. *Journal of Democracy*, 24(3), 18–32.

Index

Page numbers in **bold** refer to tables and those in *italic* refer to figures.

agrarian extractivism 27
agricultural sector, importance of 27
agro-ecological agriculture 26–7
Aguayo, G. 40
ALCESTE (Contextual Lexical Analysis of a Set of Text Segments) 60
Andrade, Pablo 30
Andrés Manuel López Obrador (AMLO) 2
anti-canal campesino movement 84–6
authoritarianism 8, 86–7

Bachelet, Michelle 96
'bag of words' approach 44
Bolivarian Revolution 26
Bolivia 26–8
Bolsonaro, Jair: campaign platform 60; concept of populism 60–4; diverse discursive areas 59–60; and the people 64–9, *68*; visual presentation 63
Braga, R. 5
Brazilian Schools without Party 48
Brenner, Neil 94
broadened embedded autonomy 20–3
Bureaucratic Authoritarianism 118, 124

Cameron, M. A. 113, 114, 117, 123, 125
Carneiro, F. 6, 11
Car Wash scandal 5
cash transfer programmes 4
Catholic and Protestant churches 75
Catholic opinion leaders 38
Centre for Justice and Human Rights of the Atlantic Coast of Nicaragua (CEJUDHCAN) 82
Chamorro, Violeta 75
Chávez, Hugo 24
Chiasson-LeBel, T. 2
Chile: Constitution of 1980 98–100; crisis of care and social reproduction 101–4; growth with equity 95–8
Citizens' Power Councils (CPCs) 7
clientelism 8
comparative institutional approach 20
concept of populism 60–4

Confederation of Indigenous Nationalities of Ecuador (CONAIE) 7
Constituent Convention 93
Constitution of 1980 98–100
Correa government 29
correlation coefficient calculation 44
corruption of customs 66
corruption of the soul 66
creole activism 84
crude and thuggish populist 59
Cuadra, E. 80
cultural Marxism 42

defensive authoritarian rentierism 24
democracy breakdowns 42
dependent development 20
Descending Hierarchical Analysis (DHA) algorithm 60
Dilma's administration 7

Eaton, K. 40
Economic Commission for Latin America and the Caribbean (ECLAC) 21, 98
Ecuador 28–30
#EducaciónNoSexista (non-sexist education) 10
elites 9
embedded autonomy 12
endogenous socialist development 25
Evangelical and Pentecostal politicians 9
evangelical pastors 38
Evans, P. B. 22, 24, 115
'experimental' phase, neoliberal restructuring 95
extractivism 2

Fajnzylber, Fernando 115
far-right populist 59
feminazis 42
food sovereignty 26–7
Foweraker, J. 113, 114, 117
FSLN-COSEP consensus model 79

Gabriel, Carlos 82
Gaudichaud, F. 4, 7–8

graphing RWI: correlation graph 46, *47*; Márquez, Nicolás (@NickyMarquez1, Argentina) 48–50, *49*; Rosas, Christian (@xtian_rosas, Perú) 51–2, *52*; Winter, Sara (@_SaraWinter, Brazil) 50–1, *51*
'growth with equity,' post-1990 period 95

Haddad, Fernando 64
Hawley, G. 43
Heller, P. 22

Import Substitution Industrialization (ISI) 5, 21
indigenous-afro-descendant alliances 81–4
indigenous movements 10
influencers, activists and politicians **45–6**
inside-out hegemony 6
intersectionality 37
Iramuteq, computer program 60, 69

Lagos, Ricardo 95–6, 100
Laje, A. 40
Larrabure, M. 2, 76, 119
Latin American political and social institutions 114–16
Lava-Jato Operation 9
Lavinas, Lena 113
left-leaning governments 19
Leiva, F. I. 76
López, Daniela 101
Lulism 5
Luna, J. P. 40

Maduro government 2
Mapuche indigenous feminists 101
Márquez, N. 40
massive human rights violations 42
media manipulation 8
Michel Temer's government (2016–2018) 67
Military Dictatorship (1964–1985) 66
mixed-methods approach 38
moral corruption 66
Morales government 6–7
Movimiento al Socialismo (MAS) party 26

national-level politics 23
neo-collectivism 27
neocorporativist strategy 6
neo-developmentalism 2, 20–3
neo-developmentism 122–4
neo-extractivism 20
neo-structuralism 2, 76, 77–81, 86–7
neoWeberian-institutionalism 113
New Ministry of Foreign Affairs' (Novo Itamaraty) 65
Nicholls, Esteban 30
NRC Word-Emotion Association Lexicon 44

O'Donnell, Guillermo 114, 124
Oliveira, F. 6
Ortega administration 7, 76–7, 82

participative democratic institutions 10
Partido Progressista (PP) 64
Partido Social Liberal (PSL) 67
'patron-client' relationships 78
Peck, Jamie 94
penguin revolution 12
Petras, J. 7
Petróleos de Venezuela (PDVSA), state oil company 24–5
Piñera, Sebastián 93
Pink Tide governments 2–5, 116–17, 120–2
Pink Tide model 19
poder moderador 67
Polanyi, Karl 94
popular power 25
populist 59; conservative 59
post/anti-capitalist aspirations 26–7
post-neoliberal development project 93–4
'post pink-tide' phase (2014–present) 124
Poulantzas, N. 118
Prebisch, Raúl 20
primitive accumulation process 116
protagonistic and participatory democracy 25

#RepealtheTransgenderLaw 48
resource nationalism 20
right-wing intersectionality (RWI) 12; features of 38; gender ideology and freedom 41–3; graphing (*see* graphing RWI); intersectional perspective 39; Latin American right 40–1; Marxism and feminism 39; separability/inseparability 39; tweeting 43; us-*versus*-them kind of politics 39
right-wing movements 8
right-wing populist 59
Rosas, C. 40
Rovira Kaltwasser, C. 40

Sandinista Front of National Liberation (FSLN): anti-canal campesino movement 84–6; cupulism 76; development discourse and strategy 76; and indigenous-afro-descendant alliances 81–4; neostructuralism 77–81; neostructuralism and authoritarianism 86–7; Nicaraguan population 76–7
Sandinista Revolution 77
'second generation' of reforms 98
sexualized communism 42
Shils, Edward 63
Shivakumar, S. 14
Similarity Analysis algorithm 60
Singer, A. 5
social democratic strategy 5
social movements 6
socio-economic disparities 11
Spronk, S. 113, 115, 118
state-society relations 23
state terrorism 42
Superior Council of Private Enterprises (COSEP) 79
Svampa, M. 3

Theodor, Nik 94
'thin-centered' ideology 63
tightrope model 6

unions and guerilla groups 5

Veltmeyer, H. 7
Venezuela 23–6
Vivir, Buen 119–20

Washington consensus 3
Western Civilization 38
Worker's Party (PT) government 12, 23, 65, 116

YATAMA, Miskitu-led political organization 81–2

zero-base budget 64

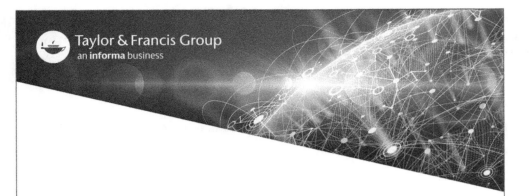